ALSO BY BETTE HAGMAN
AND PUBLISHED BY HENRY HOLT

The Gluten-free Gourmet (1990)

More from the Gluten-free Gourmet (1993)

BETTE HAGMAN

The Gluten-free Gourmet Cooks Fast and Healthy

Wheat Free with Less Fuss and Fat

AN OWL BOOK

HENRY HOLT AND COMPANY   NEW YORK

Henry Holt and Company, Inc.
Publishers since 1866
115 West 18th Street
New York, New York 10011

Henry Holt® is a registered
trademark of Henry Holt and Company, Inc.

Published in Canada by Fitzhenry & Whiteside Ltd.,
195 Allstate Parkway, Markham, Ontario L3R 4T8.

Library of Congress Cataloging-in-Publication Data
Hagman, Bette.
The gluten-free gourmet cooks fast and healthy: wheat free
with less fuss and fat / Bette Hagman.
p.   cm.
Includes bibliographical references and index.
1. Gluten-free diet—Recipes.   2. Wheat-free diet—Recipes.
I. Title.
RM237.86.H338   1996   95-24964
641.5'63—dc20   CIP

ISBN 0-8050-3981-3

Henry Holt books are available for special promotions
and premiums. For details contact:
Director, Special Markets.

First published in hardcover in 1996 by
Henry Holt and Company, Inc.

First Owl Book Edition—1997

Designed by Kate Nichols

Printed in the United States of America
All first editions are printed on acid-free paper.∞

1   3   5   7   9   10   8   6   4   2

To my daughter Karol,

for her love and support through all the years,

especially in the dark time

before my diagnosis

Contents

Foreword

For many individuals, reading a cookbook is a pastime. For people with celiac disease and other severe food intolerances, cookbook browsing represents much more than a mere pastime. It is a matter of survival.

There are two journeys that every celiac undertakes. The first is the often arduous time before the individual becomes diagnosed. This can often take many years—in one case I have seen, fully forty-five years of continuous symptoms prior to diagnosis.

The clinical syndrome of malabsorption and wasting that characterizes the "coeliac affliction" (celiac disease) had its first modern description in 1888 by Samuel Gee. There are, however, several much older descriptions of a similar syndrome dating back as far as two thousand years ago. Many physicians, unfortunately, base their concept of celiac disease on these classic descriptions. Recent research from Europe and my clinical impression from seeing a large number of patients suggest that celiac disease often causes problems that do not resemble the classical concept. Celiac disease may present in many diverse ways, including chronic fatigue, bone pain, short stature, anemia, dental problems, infertility, and many other symptoms far removed from the small intestine. In these patients the more common complaints of diarrhea, weight loss, gas, and bloating are often absent. In many of these people, the diagnosis of celiac disease is greatly delayed and in some, I suspect, may never be reached.

Because of the adherence of physicians to the classic syndrome of celiac disease that is commonly taught in medical school, many misconceptions abound. These include the idea that celiac patients cannot be obese or tall, or that they must have diarrhea. There is also the misconception that celiac disease is a disease of childhood, when in my experience and that of others, it is predominantly diagnosed in adulthood. It has been thought by many to be limited to certain races, particularly to individuals of northern European extraction. However, as modern diagnostic methods and awareness of the disease spread, so too have the ethnic groups and countries in which celiac disease is now diagnosed.

Celiac disease can run in families. Indeed, the majority of patients I see with celiac disease will have at least one other affected family member. Of course, the relative may not have the same symptoms as the original case. Celiac disease may be seen more frequently in other conditions, including insulin-dependent diabetes mellitus, lupus, and other so-called autoimmune diseases (*autoimmune* implying the individual's immune system is attacking part of the body).

All too often, the diagnosis is reached because of the patient's suggestion, or indeed insistence, on consideration of celiac disease as a potential cause of his or her symptoms. There have been several significant advances in our understanding of celiac disease and its diagnosis. The more widespread use of blood tests for diagnosis and screening has made it easier to screen for celiac disease. However, while these blood tests have been improving in diagnostic accuracy, they still have not yet been accepted as a substitute for small intestine biopsy.

The second journey for the celiac is the journey to recovery. When patients are informed of the diagnosis and that gluten is the cause of their symptoms, most respond with a degree of shock and undergo a grieving process for their previous food lifestyle. I take a different approach and encourage patients to see their diagnosis as empowering them to achieve and maintain their own health. Unlike most other significant conditions affecting the digestive system, which often require potent and sometimes dangerous medication, the treatment for celiac disease is very much in the hands of the patient.

The individual with gluten sensitivity is launched on an odyssey—the adaptation to a gluten-free lifestyle. Some will be overwhelmed by the restrictions and not see beyond what they cannot eat. Hopefully, most will explore the culinary potential of a gluten-free diet. Bette Hagman's books are three vital guidebooks for the traveler. They provide a vast array of information that will turn what seems a restrictive diet into a culinary adventure. Many of you will surprise yourselves at your newfound abilities in the kitchen. With Bette's help and a positive outlook, which is not always easy to have in the early stages of recovery from celiac disease, the gluten-free lifestyle can lead to a life of good health and culinary enjoyment for patients with celiac disease.

Joseph A. Murray, M.D.
Coordinator, Celiac Disease Clinic
University of Iowa

Preface

*I*t's hard to realize that it's been over twenty years since I started exchanging recipes with five of my writing students who were also gluten intolerant or allergic to wheat. I never dreamed this would be the beginning of my writing a series of cookbooks. After all, I was the worst cook of the group. It was pride that forced me to the stove to keep up with the others, and my doctor's orders of sticking to a strict gluten-free diet that made me search for more interesting recipes.

This was before the introduction of xanthan gum and the first recipe for yeast-rising rice bread developed in the University of Washington diet kitchens, but I still remember my cravings for breads, cakes, and cookies, most of which had to be filled by the ubiquitous puffed rice cakes. If anything would force one to seek tastier fare—even to the extent of learning to cook—the thought of a permanent diet of rice cakes surely would.

When I finished my second cookbook, *More from the Gluten-free Gourmet,* I thought I had given my readers all I could learn about cooking, living, and traveling gluten free. I realized the recipes were rich, fattening, and sometimes hard to prepare, but they tasted so good a celiac shouldn't be tempted to stray from the diet.

To my dismay, readers begged for more changes. "Your recipes are turning me into a whale. Can't you cut the calories?" "I only have time to cook some of your recipes on weekends. Why don't you give us some quick and easy ones?" "Help! I am allergic to rice. Aren't there any recipes for bread or cake that don't start with rice flour?"

Finally, my doctor issued a challenge directly to me: "Your cholesterol is far too high. You've got to lower it."

That did it! Three egg yolks in every loaf of bread had to go. Cheese in every casserole must be cut. Extra eggs in cakes should be eliminated somehow. I learned to make a low-calorie yogurt cheese for my cheesecakes—which I refused to give up. In my books, I'd blithely told my readers to follow the directions for "lightening" food given in magazine and newspaper articles. When I tried to take my own advice, I found only part of it worked. Yes, butter could be replaced by vegetable oil to cut cholesterol, but there were still too many calories for the woman who didn't want to turn into a whale. And, to my dismay, replacing fat with applesauce often turned our cakes into puddings. Rice flour just isn't as amenable as wheat flour when it comes to lightening. This led to a lot of cooked messes sliding down my ever-hungry garbage disposal. In fact, there was one cake that tasted great but simply wouldn't firm up until, thanks to a persistent tester, we made nine sets of changes in the formula.

As for the requests for "quick and easy"—I could understand that cry. For the first ten years of my diet, I, too, had worked away from home with no time to prepare a leisurely casserole from scratch and little time for shopping for unusual ingredients. I was already working out ways to cook in less time, using shortcuts of prepared mixes and bases. You'll find many of them in this book.

But the biggest plea was still to be answered. Aren't there any other basic flours for us but rice? I found indeed there are when, a couple of years ago at a conference in Canada, I was introduced to "new" flours made from beans. Of course the use of beans and lentils in cooking is not new, but bean flours that actually could be used in baking were a marvelous discovery for me. They taste great, are higher in fiber, and will give us all a change of diet, since I have worked out formulas to use these new flours without any rice flours.

I found a Canadian bean flour made from cranberry or Romano beans very good for making cakes or bread and worked with it along with a second bean flour available in California, a mix of garbanzo and broad beans. This California flour is lighter tasting, and if the eater isn't told, he or she seldom guesses that the cake, pie crust, bread, or pasta contains bean flour.

The addition of variety to our diet from the many recipes using bean flour will not only be excitingly different but will help those who want to rotate their grains. A warning, though! The sudden addition of huge quantities of legumes into the diet might cause some gastric distress and flatulence. Thus, introduce bean flour (as you would any new food) with care and in small quantities in the beginning. If you enjoy it as much as I do, it will not be long before you are using it as often as the rice flour for your basics: bread, cake, and pasta.

This has been an exciting book to write, but a difficult one. I was working with a lot of new formulas requiring much testing and, to my dismay, much discarding. Could I satisfy my readers with tasty food they could serve to the whole family, as I do, and also serve with pride to guests? Would the ones who demanded "quick and easy" be satisfied with some of the twenty-minute meals, the many shortcut mixes, and the whole new chapter of stir-fries? Would those who couldn't tolerate rice accept the bean flour substitutes?

I leave it to you readers to see if I succeeded. I hope you can use these recipes, as you've used the others, for the whole family and for guests, serving them with pride and no apologies for eating "gluten free."

B.H.

Acknowledgments

This cookbook is not my work alone. I could never have conceived or completed it without the contributions of many people. I owe a great debt to the following:

Elaine Hartsook, R.D., Ph.D., Executive Director of the Gluten Intolerance Group of North America; Joseph Murray, M.D., Coordinator of the Celiac Disease Clinic of the University of Iowa Hospital and Clinics; and Donald Kasarda of the U.S.D.A. Research Service for their generous help with medical research and information. Michael Marsh, D.Sc., D.M., F.R.C.P., Reader in Medicine, Salford, England, for his written contribution. A special thanks to Dr. Murray, who did the medical review of the text and carefully wrote his corrections in my "voice."

Hope Sandler, R.D., of the Seattle Culinary School, for her tips on "cutting the fat" and Beth Hillson of the Gluten Free Pantry for her generous tips on cooking and the donation of some of her family recipes.

The food editors of newspapers and magazines, especially the *Seattle Times,* the *Seattle Post-Intelligencer,* the *Sacramento Bee, Bon Appetit, Best Recipes, Fast and Healthy, Better Homes and Gardens,* and *Woman's Day* for the latest ideas in healthy eating and faster food preparation.

My testers, to whom I owe the success of many recipes; they not only fed them to their families but they often made practical changes to improve the taste or shorten the preparation time: Doris Beck, Betty Boughton, Martha Christiansen, Donna Jo Doepkin, Mary Gunn, Regina Hines,

Eileen Kiera, Julie Kron, Kathy Muller, Pan Murray, Regina Nykoliuk, Tom Pickles, Genevieve Potts, Gayle Randle, Sherry Reshoft, Kathy Samuel, Virginia Schmuck, Allan and Paula Smith, and Louise Streuli.

Toni Richardson, who generously gave me the formula for her machine-made pasta to use in this book. And to my many readers who sent in recipes for me to try or suggestions for improving an old one.

Kay Spicer, who introduced me to bean flour through her book *Full of Beans,* and encouraged my experimentation.

The many companies that contributed supplies and equipment for the testing: Authentic Foods, Creative Technology Corp., Dietary Specialties, Ener-G-Foods, Grain Process Enterprises, Ltd., Red Star Yeast, Salton/Maxim Housewares, Inc., Toastmaster, Inc., Welbilt Appliance, Inc., and the West Bend Company.

Finally, to a wonderful editor, Beth Crossman, for her unfailing faith in my work and patient prodding when I procrastinated over the difficult chapters.

The Gluten-free Gourmet
Cooks Fast and Healthy

Eating Your Way to Good Health

The Gluten-free Diet and More

When we are dining out, my husband often tries to help me convince a doubting waitress that I really do want my chicken or fish grilled without breading or flour, my vegetables unsauced, my potatoes without gravy, a salad undressed (no croutons, please), and skip the dessert menu. He'll add, "She's on a strict diet."

"Oh, honey, I know what that's like. I tried one last month—two milkshakes a day and some solid food at night. Boring, isn't it?"

I don't explain that my diet as a celiac is for life, that a gluten-free regimen is a way of eating my way to remission and not a fad idea. As a celiac I know I must avoid gluten in wheat, rye, barley, and oats, but if I'm bored it's my own fault, for there are lots of great dishes to be made and lots of choices within the diet. Of course, if by chance we get a waiter who is interested, or a chef who comes out to query in person, I'm willing to explain the disease briefly and the healthy result of staying gluten free.

Over the years I've discovered that more and more people working in food service jobs are learning about us (celiacs) and our restrictive diet. Many take great pride in preparing plates that look (and taste) as good as anything on the menu. And now we have more recipes, more suppliers, and the wonderful home bread machines to make living gluten free easier and healthier. It may be a diet for life, but I certainly have a much better life than I lived before my diagnosis.

Some celiacs won't need to read beyond this as long as they realize that eating gluten free is not for a month or a year but for the rest of life—or until medicine has come up with another answer. But who needs that? Think of the time when no one recognized that gluten was the toxic factor causing the distress from eating and the only known safe diet was one of bananas and rice. We've come a long way, haven't we?

Other Allergies and Intolerances

Although in this book I've eliminated wheat, rye, barley, and oats from all recipes, I recognize that millions of people are allergic just to wheat. This may be a lifelong reaction or it may be temporary and eventually the sufferer will be able to allow wheat back into the diet. Still, for the wheat allergic, baking will be as difficult as for the celiac, since wheat flour is the basis for most of our breads, pastries, and even our pastas. Those allergic only to wheat will have a few more cereals to choose from the grocery shelf and can add oats to their crisp toppings and cookies.

But I have learned through my readers that those who suffer from wheat allergy also often (like celiacs) have other foods they must avoid.

Many celiacs, especially when first diagnosed, have an intolerance to lactose and have to avoid all dairy products. Medical experts suggest that the damage to the villi (minute fingerlike projections lining the small intestine) in the beginning may cause the celiac to lose the ability to digest lactose. As the healing progresses, most can gradually add dairy items back into the diet, starting with hard, aged cheeses like Cheddar. By the end of the first year they may be having no noticeable problems with lactose. Others, like myself, find that even after twenty years, dairy products are not well tolerated. Some may be able to use products like Dairy Ease or drink Lactaid milk; others find this little help. One consolation: there are many liquids on the market to use in place of dairy products. You'll find them in the dairy case of your grocery store or in the baby food section, and in health food stores. *Warning:* These have become such a popular substitute for the general public that celiacs should check to be sure some form of gluten has not been added to enhance the flavor. For those who use no dairy products, proteins can be added to your diet in the form of soy, nuts, and beans; for calcium you should consider taking a daily supplement (see pages 20–21).

There are other foods that cause some celiacs to feel many of the same symptoms they had before diagnosis. Soy, eggs, citrus fruits, chocolate, and MSG are just a few of the common offenders. Others include shellfish, nuts, legumes, apples, and yeast. I discovered I cannot tolerate cucumbers and watermelon. You may have some allergies that are just as weird. I've had letters from readers listing everything from corn and beans to rice. Yes, rice, the staple of the gluten-free diet.

Although these offenders do not damage the villi as gluten does, they do cause distress, and they should be ferreted out so that eating becomes fun again. To do this, list all the foods eaten for several days before the reaction occurred. Repeat the possible offenders one at a time and watch for reactions. Some of these may be allergies, which will gradually disappear as your healing progresses; others may continue.

If you don't have any reaction when suspect foods are reintroduced, it is possible you are getting gluten in some form you don't suspect. Was your chicken or turkey injected with hydrolyzed vegetable protein? Has wheat from baking for others in your kitchen drifted into your gluten-free flours? Did you scoop up your brown rice flour from a health food bin with a contaminated scoop? Has the formula changed in some product you've been using? One celiac friend found that a vitamin supplement she'd taken for years now contained gluten. It took months for her to discover this was the culprit. I was upset recently to find that my favorite chicken soup base had changed hands, the new company adding wheat to the formula. Thank goodness I automatically read the ingredient list before buying. A thorough reading of all ingredient lists should become an automatic must for celiacs.

It does seem at times that sticking to the diet in today's gluten-filled world is like walking blindfolded through a quagmire; but I can assure anyone that it becomes easier as one progresses in eating gluten free. It also becomes a habit. For example, in our house, there is never any gluten flour to spread dust around. If anyone wants wheat-based bread, cake, or cookies, they are brought in already baked. Many celiacs, to avoid any cross contamination from crumbs, have separate toasters and jam and peanut butter jars.

Is Your Cholesterol Count Rising?

In my pre-diagnosis days when I felt as weak as a wet noodle, I weighed 81 pounds, ate full meals—and snacked between meals—and always felt hungry. I never realized there would come a time when I would have to watch calories in order to preserve a semblance of a waistline. That time arrived with a shock a few years ago, and I had to cut my portions and any between-meal snacking.

And I used to think smugly that high cholesterol was one problem I wouldn't have. Wrong again! This past year I was forced to join the cholesterol counters, but instead of feeling sorry for myself, I remember a doctor at my first national celiac convention explaining that a high cholesterol count indicated that food was now being assimilated into the body system. With the malabsorption of celiac disease, the fats pass as fatty stools (steatorhea). Good. I'll hold that positive thought while I eliminate some of the extra cholesterol from my diet, as I've done in many of the recipes in this book.

The whole population seems to have an obsessive interest in fats, calories, and cholesterol these days, which is fortunate because it's easy enough to count them in prepared products with the new labeling laws. But problems arise in the foods we make at home that contain fat and cholesterol. To help you make changes in your eating, if this is one of your problems, I've compiled the chart opposite. By making ingredient substitutions, you can make significant changes in your baking, in casseroles, and in sauces. Compare the numbers between regular, low-fat, and nonfat in some dairy products. Watch especially the cholesterol values. *Warning:* Some of the low-fat products may contain gluten, so always read labels if you are making changes.

On cartons and cans of these products, the figures given are often for one serving, which may range from a tablespoon of cream for your coffee to ½ cup of cottage cheese for a salad. To make accurate comparisons to use for cooking and baking, I've given the figures for ½ cup of each food. Remember, different brands may have slightly different counts, so if you are counting calories and fat, read the labels on your preferred products.

As you can see in the table, you can cut the cholesterol in baking by using margarine instead of butter, but you will still have fat. This is what adds the flavor and often improves the texture. You can reduce fat in many recipes by using apple, pear, or prune puree for up to half of the fat. But with our flours, it is difficult to substitute for more than half the fat unless you are willing to toss out a lot of failures.

½ CUP:	CALORIES	FAT	CHOLESTEROL
Regular milk	80	4 g	17½ mg
Low-fat milk (2%)	65	1½ g	10 mg
Nonfat milk	45	0 g	2½ mg
Half-and-half	160	12 g	60 mg
Whipping cream	416	45 g	160 mg
Nondairy creamer	160	12 g	0 mg
Nondairy whipped topping	100	6 g	0 mg
Regular sour cream	208	22 g	100 mg
Light sour cream	120	8 g	40 mg
Nonfat sour cream	80	0 g	20 mg
IMO sour cream substitute	200	20 g	0 mg
Regular yogurt	95	4 g	15 mg
Low-fat yogurt	72	2 g	10 mg
Nonfat yogurt	65	½ g	5 mg
Evaporated milk	169	10 g	20 mg
Evaporated skim milk	100	0 g	0 mg
Sweetened condensed milk	520	12 g	40 mg
Low-fat sweetened condensed milk	480	6 g	20 mg
Ricotta cheese	200	12 g	120 mg
Light ricotta cheese	120	4 g	50 mg
Cream cheese	400	40 g	210 mg
Light cream cheese	280	16 g	160 mg
Fat-free cream cheese	200	0 g	19 mg
Yogurt cheese	190	8 g	20 mg
Butter	800	88 g	240 mg
Margarine	720	80 g	0 mg

Another way of cutting cholesterol is by using liquid egg substitutes—¼ cup for each large egg. These are made from real egg but most of the cholesterol is removed and some of the fat. The ones that contain some fat are more successful in baking. I used Second Nature in all my testing, because it contains less than half the fat of regular eggs and none of the cholesterol. I found Egg Beaters are the best-tasting nonfat liquid egg substitute for eating if you want to really cut all fat. You may prefer another brand. *Warning:* Some egg substitutes contain gluten! You can also use just the egg whites in some baking, but you may have to add up to 1 tablespoon of oil for each egg yolk to make up the fat.

I've discovered that by using a powder called Egg Replacer (which contains no egg product) found in health food stores and obtainable from Ener-G-Foods, I can cut the number of eggs in my baking and still have a light texture.

Other Fat Busters

Chicken and turkey: Always skin your chicken; the most fat is in the skin. Leave the bones in for flavor. Use breasts of chicken whenever possible, for the white meat contains less fat and cholesterol than the dark meat. If you want the flavor of the fat from a chicken or turkey breast, roast it on a rack with the skin on and then remove it before serving. Don't baste. Use ground turkey breast as an alternative to beef. If you still want the flavor of beef, mix them half and half.

Beef: When browning ground beef for spaghetti sauce or fillings in enchiladas, cook the meat and then pour on about 1 cup of hot water. Pour off immediately. This will remove much of the fat. When cooking meats, fish, or poultry consider baking, broiling, or grilling instead of frying or roasting. Baste, if necessary, with lemon juice or broth rather than melted butter or oil. Trim the fat from meats as much as possible.

When sautéing try using juice or chicken or vegetable broth rather than oil, but be sure to keep a layer of moisture between the food and pan.

As it dries out, add more liquid. Use nonstick pans for all frying and sautéing.

Toppings and Dressings: Top baked potatoes with nonfat yogurt blended with a dash of mustard instead of butter or sour cream; sprinkle on chives for color and flavor rather than bacon bits. Use Molly McButter for flavoring potatoes, vegetables, popcorn, and other foods where you would miss the butter flavor: always sprinkle on after cooking. Some people enjoy olive oil (a healthier fat) with their baked potatoes, and chicken broth can replace butter and milk in mashed potatoes.

In salads that call for mayonnaise, use some nonfat yogurt to thin your light mayonnaise. Seasoned vinegar is great for adding flavor in both cooking and salads. You can substitute other liquids for the oil in salad dressings; try vegetable broth or juice.

Baking:

1. When baking cakes, bread, or cookies, spray the pans with vegetable spray rather than greasing them or, to avoid all fats, use parchment paper.
2. Reduce the amount of nuts in recipes and keep the flavor by toasting the nuts.
3. Use Yogurt Cream Cheese (page 369) in place of cream cheese in dips and baking.
4. Substitute cocoa powder (unsweetened) for baking chocolate, using 3 tablespoons of powder plus 1 tablespoon added liquid for each ounce of chocolate called for in recipes. This will save about 110 calories and 14 grams of fat.

Warning: When planning an exchange of low-fat or nonfat yogurt, sour cream, or margarine in baking, read the labels carefully. Some do not work well. Usually they are labeled "Not Suitable for Baking."

Cookies are the one bakery product that doesn't take well to cutting the fat. To avoid disappointment, use recipes that have already been perfected rather than just cutting a favorite recipe.

Other Helpful Hints

Remember we taste with our eyes as well as our mouths, so textures are important. Salsas and chutneys are a good way of jazzing up low-fat foods in both taste and looks. Rotate your grains (corn, rice, beans) when on a low-fat diet for more taste variety.

No matter what other problems you have, if you are a celiac, never sacrifice eating gluten free to another diet. This is your yellow brick road to health, and any deviations that include gluten (as in some low-fat condiments) will only increase your problems.

I've discovered through writing this book that we can have great gluten-free, fat-reduced, and cholesterol-lowered meals without sacrificing any flavor, texture, or looks. I still enjoy casseroles, stews, and cakes within my diet, and I always feed family and guests the same foods I can enjoy. Most never realize they are eating "diet" food, and I still receive praise for my cooking.

REFERENCES

Frazier, Claude A., M.D. *Coping with Food Allergy.* New York: Quadrangle/The New York Times Book Co., 1974.

Katahn, Martin, Ph.D., and Terry Katahn. *The Rotation Diet Cookbook.* New York: W.W. Norton and Co., 1987.

Kidder, Beth. *The Milk-Free Kitchen.* New York: Henry Holt and Co., 1991.

Rockwell, Sally. *Sally Rockwell's Allergy Recipes.* Seattle: Nutrition Survival Press, 1984.

Sandler, Hope, R.D. "Cutting the Fats," Seattle Culinary School class, February 1995.

Wedman, Betty, R.D., Ph.D. "Food Allergies, Food Sensitivities, Food Intolerances." Paper delivered to the Gluten Intolerance Group of Florida, 1994.

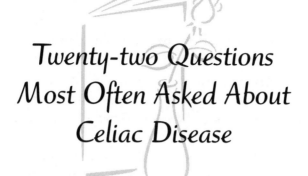

Twenty-two Questions
Most Often Asked About
Celiac Disease

When I was diagnosed, I had never heard about celiac disease. I now realize most people still haven't, but at the time I thought I was stupid and was much too embarrassed to ask the doctor to try to explain his diagnosis. I grabbed the diet list he gave me and was most grateful he had finally put a name to my suffering and hadn't just sent me on to more psychiatrists, who had already instilled in me a feeling of complete stupidity. I later learned that a lot of other celiacs had this same experience before some enlightened doctor ferreted out the real problem.

My stops on the way home included the public library, where I discovered that it was termed a "rare" disease, and the local health food store, which had one cookbook written by the wife of a celiac in England. Her beginning pages contained an excellent description of the disease written in everyday language. This was the beginning of my search for enlightenment. It will probably never end, for the medical world and celiac support groups are continually discovering answers to questions we all have about this condition.

1. What is celiac disease and how long have doctors known about it?

Celiac disease, or gluten-sensitive enteropathy, is an autoimmune reaction causing damage to the small intestine, usually leading to malnutrition and its consequences. This is induced in certain genetically dis-

9

posed people by eating gluten found in wheat, rye, barley, and oats. The damage can be healed and the patient will stay in remission on a gluten-free diet, but the sensitivity is permanent. This means that "gluten-free" is the diet not only for immediate health, but for life.

Physicians have been aware of the evidence of a "wasting" disease caused by malnutrition since the second century, but it wasn't until about a century ago that it was suggested the patient could be cured by diet. Doctors still didn't know what to exclude from the diet. Some were as strict as limiting patients to rice and bananas, which relieved the symptoms but certainly must have been boring.

After World War II, a doctor in the Netherlands recognized that his celiac patients had had remission from their symptoms during the years they could have no grains. When wheat was reintroduced into their diets, the celiac symptoms recurred. From this came the discovery that it was the gluten factor in wheat, rye, barley, and oats that caused the damage to the gut. When this factor is removed from the diet, the patient is quickly relieved of the symptoms and, in time, the damage to the villi heals.

Another group of gluten-sensitive patients have symptoms of an itching, burning rash with small blisters that appear mainly on elbows, forearms, knees, and back but can appear other places, such as buttocks and even in the hair. These patients may need medication to relieve the rash, but it is now well confirmed that almost all of them will show some degree of damage to the villi if biopsied. The medical term for this evidence of the disease is called dermatitis herpetiformis (DH).

2. I was diagnosed with non-tropical sprue. Now doctors say I have celiac disease. Was the original diagnosis wrong?

No. That is what my own doctor called it twenty years ago.

For a long time "celiac disease" was the term for the childhood diagnosis of the disease. In fact, because children often have no symptoms as adolescents, doctors formerly considered them cured. Now they are aware that the disease is still there and damage is still being done when they eat gluten. When symptoms recurred or when an adult appeared with the same symptoms, doctors called it "non-tropical sprue" but the treatment was the same—a gluten-free diet. Other terms have been "celiac sprue" and the more tongue-twisting "gluten-sensitive enteropathy."

Now, in most cases, we speak of it as celiac disease and call ourselves celiacs.

3. Why me?

Some of the answers to this question are still being sought. But one of the answers might be that you were already programmed with genes that would respond to some trigger factor that activates the disease.

If you search the medical background of your parents and grandparents you might turn up a relative who had the symptoms but was never diagnosed. Did a grandparent, aunt or uncle, or one of your own parents have constant trouble with "gastritis," diarrhea, or wasting sickness, or did some child in the family die early of what was once called "summer complaint," a watery diarrhea leading to dehydration and often death?

In children, some doctors feel that too early an introduction to gluten might be a trigger factor and now encourage a longer period of breast-feeding and a much later introduction to gluten-containing grains. For adults, the trigger factors might be as diverse as a shock to the system such as death in the family, surgery, pregnancy, childbirth, or possibly an adenovirus (which often causes respiratory or eye infections) that was not recognized at the time.

4. Will my children be celiacs?

At this time the doctors making a study of the disease feel that the possibility of first-degree relatives actually being celiacs is about 10 percent. This figure was reached through serum screening of a large group of first-degree relatives and later biopsying those with positive antigliadin and antiendomysial antibody tests. They encourage anyone who has doubts about a close relative to have them take the noninvasive blood tests. These are specialized tests familiar to doctors who specialize in the disease, but other doctors may not be aware of them. They have to be requested and are not automatically given as standard blood tests. Your doctor will send the blood samples to special labs equipped to do the testing.

5. Is the blood test for celiac disease accurate?

At this time, blood tests are considered valuable screening tools, but they are not the final gold stardard for diagnosing celiac disease. That standard still remains the small intestinal biopsy.

But now that doctors have the tests, serum screening can help them find possible celiacs. They can also test a known celiac with recurring symptoms to discover if he is getting gluten without realizing it, or if the doctor should look for other causes for the distress.

For screening purposes to discover new celiacs, a combined test for IgG and IgA antigliadin antibodies and antiendomysial antibodies is used. With these three, the rate of finding those who should be further tested by biopsy of the small intestine is very high. Some rare patients will have celiac disease and be truly negative on all three tests. The test should become negative with the institution of a gluten-free diet; therefore for screening purposes it is important that the individual not go on a gluten-free diet beforehand. Sometimes a rare condition called selective IgA deficiency renders the blood tests faulty. Thus if a person still feels he or she may have celiac disease and the tests come back negative, it may be one of the rare exceptions and a more complete examination by biopsy should be requested.

6. What are the symptoms of celiac disease?

The classic textbook symptoms of the disease in childhood are anemia, failure to grow, behavioral disorders, anorexia (loss of appetite), and, as the child progresses in the illness, chronic diarrhea (sometimes with fatty, foul-smelling stools that may float) or, in some cases, severe constipation, some vomiting, and noticeable abdominal distention and/or pain. Not all children present with all or even most of these, and often the diagnosis is delayed because these can be symptoms of other diseases. Dental enamel defects are common in celiac children, but the cause may not be recognized.

In adults, the diagnosis often becomes more difficult, although there may be plenty of signs that something is terribly wrong with the body. For the adult, too, this is often a "wasting illness" with anemia, weight loss, diarrhea, constant fatigue, abdominal distention from bloating, and bone pain. In others there may be no significant weight loss or diarrhea. Some may present with constipation, or only physical and mental fatigue or infertility. One woman wrote me saying she had no symptoms other than "feeling like a slug." The gluten-free diet turned her into a vital, energetic woman, happy to be working and losing weight.

7. What happens when celiac disease is misdiagnosed or not discovered?

For children and adults alike the effect of misdiagnosis is often traumatic. There may be permanent stunted growth, developmental delay, chronic ill health (often leading to the inability to hold a job), skeletal disorders, dental problems, possible infertility, increased health costs, and a much higher risk of malignancy. This is often in the form of lymphoma in the upper gastrointestinal tract, and the diagnosis of celiac disease is sometimes made only when the lymphoma is discovered.

8. Why does it often take so long to diagnose? I'm angry at all the doctors who told me, "It's all in your head. Quit feeling sorry for yourself."

Now we're getting to the real problem of celiac disease. Because it is considered a rare disease, most doctors spent little time studying it in medical school. This was even more true a couple of decades ago. Only now are our American doctors being trained to recognize the disease earlier, with special celiac clinics for both adults and children in several medical schools.

This is a serious disease, very damaging to the body, but since it's not always in itself fatal, celiac disease hasn't received the amount of public recognition in the United States that we could wish for. Nor does it have commercial possibilities for any drug company, so funding for research is low. By forming organizations, celiacs have done a lot to alert others to the disease and to help them live well on the restrictive diet.

It is possible that children may have found, when able to choose their own food, that refusing gluten-containing items such as bread, cake, and pasta, and choosing instead rice and potatoes made them feel better. I know that was true with me, and although I was the "sickly" child in the family, I managed to pick and choose foods that didn't cause distress, for we lived on a farm with a lot of fresh fruit, vegetables, and meat. When I had to eat only what was served in the Commons at college (always toast for breakfast and often pasta for lunch), all my early symptoms recurred, and I found myself spending days in bed, close to the bathroom in my dorm or in the infirmary.

I've heard this story over and over from adults who had years of misdiagnosis and were told—as I was—to seek the answer from psychiatrists.

Celiacs themselves, by spreading the word about celiac disease through their own organizations, through distributing pamphlets about the disease, and by being willing to speak of their problems can help to make it as well known as cystic fibrosis and other "rare" diseases.

9. How do I explain celiac disease to relatives and friends?

Start with the positive. Most of them know how sick you've been. Say, "I'm so lucky. The doctors found out what's wrong, and I don't need surgery, nor even medication. All I need is to avoid eating gluten."

Then get serious. "But I'm going to need your understanding. *Can't eat* means *not ever, not even a little taste, not even to be nice just because you made it.*"

A lot of hostesses are afraid of attempting to cook for any diet—and ours is certainly awesome—so offer suggestions about easy and simple meals if they want to have you to dinner: plain meats, plain potatoes (no gravy, you'll just use butter, thanks), and plain vegetables. Offer to bring your own bread and, for dessert, suggest fruits or a meringue stuffed with fresh fruit. Don't take a chance on their buying gluten-free ice cream. It takes experience to learn to read labels and recognize that gluten can lurk in hydrolyzed vegetable protein (HVP) or hydrolyzed plant protein (HPP), natural flavorings, or modified food starch.

Emphasize to well-meaning friends that they shouldn't take offense if you don't take a serving of some dish, and you shouldn't be embarrassed to tell them why: you'll get sick!

10. Are there other diseases or conditions frequently associated with celiac disease?

Celiac disease causes our body to respond inappropriately to gluten, so that the immune system turns against our own tissues. There are several other autoimmune diseases in which the immune system attacks parts of our own bodies, and there is evidence that they can occur together. Most celiacs, however, will not necessarily have another disorder. Sometimes in researching his or her medical history, a celiac will find one or more of these diseases in the family background.

The diseases most frequently associated with celiac disease are diabetes mellitus (insulin dependent), thyroid disease, Sjögren's syndrome, systemic lupus erythematosus (SLE), and rheumatoid arthritis. Others that are mentioned are Addison's disease and Down syndrome.

11. What are osteoporosis and pancreatic insufficiency, and what connection do these have to celiac disease?

Osteoporosis is a thinning of the bones, causing them to become brittle and easily fractured. Bone density decreases naturally with age, but in patients who have celiac disease, leading to malnutrition, there may be very severe early bone-mass loss. Doctors now recommend that all celiac patients be tested for bone-mass loss and, if necessary, put on a regimen of extra calcium. This is especially important for those who are lactose intolerant and unable to get their calcium from dairy products. Weight-bearing exercises such as walking or stair climbing will help, along with the supplement, to decrease the possibility of suffering from brittle bones or osteoporosis.

Celiacs who fail to respond to the gluten-free diet either at the beginning of the diet or later in their life may have impaired pancreatic function, in which too few enzymes are released for complete digestion of their food, thus causing diarrhea, abdominal swelling, and pain, with resulting malabsorption of nutrients. When pancreatic enzymes are added to the diet with each meal, the symptoms disappear.

This may happen to celiacs who were slow to be diagnosed or had a long history of illness before their diagnosis. The enzyme treatment is a long-term treatment, which the doctor usually checks annually.

12. Can any doctor diagnose celiac disease?

Unfortunately, the only sure diagnosis is still secured with an endoscopy and biopsy of the small intestine, and these are usually performed by gastroenterologists.

A general physician should, in patients where celiac disease is suspected, or in patients whose abdominal symptoms don't respond to other treatment, send a patient to this specialist. Again, unfortunately, it can be a long time before some physicians recognize the need. This may not be all the doctor's fault, because many patients (and I know I was one) mention only a few of the symptoms at a time. Perhaps the physician's overall view is clouded by the patient's complaining about just one thing. For example, because I was so very tired before diagnosis, I had continual backaches and tried to get the doctor to rid me of them. I never mentioned the fact that I had frequent bowel movements, thus leading to malnutrition and fatigue (I had lived with this so long, I thought it normal). If I had been aware, as I now am, that listing all the things that seem to be wrong and presenting them all to the doctor would help in finding the cause, I might have shortened the time it took for my own diagnosis.

13. How is the biopsy for celiac disease performed?

Speaking as one who has been through it, I am happy to say there has been a wonderful improvement in this surgical procedure in the last thirty years. Most patients are quite unaware of any discomfort and often are sedated to such a point that they are not even conscious of the examination. This is usually done on an outpatient basis.

The biopsy tissue is obtained through a fiber endoscope tube, which the patient swallows. The pieces of tissue are taken from the small intestine in several places in order to be sure to get a good test. This takes a very short time, and the patient usually goes home in an hour or so. Preparation for the examination is simple. Usually the doctor will order that the patient have nothing to eat or drink after midnight the day before the test.

14. I've heard that rectal challenge is a way of diagnosing celiac disease. What does this mean?

Although most damage in celiac disease is done to the upper bowel, because that is where the greatest concentration of diet-derived gluten is concentrated, the medical profession has discovered that other parts of the bowel can become inflamed when exposed to gluten.

In a rectal challenge, gluten as a saline preparation is directly introduced into the rectum, and only four hours later a biopsy is taken. There are usually no symptoms of having any gluten except, perhaps, in the case of DH patients, who might experience temporary skin itching for a day. The patient will not have to endure X-ray exposure, as is needed for the intestinal biopsy in placing the tube, and it can be done on very young children. According to testing done in England for over ten years, the rectal response to gluten in celiacs is specific, thus separating those with celiac disease from the non-celiacs.

At this time, the rectal challenge is not yet accepted as a first diagnostic test in celiac disease, but the medical field looks to it optimistically as a possible tool in working with celiacs. Eventually it could be used to replace the "gluten challenge," in which a patient is forced to go back on a gluten diet (and become ill again) in order to verify that the original diagnosis was correct.

The future of this diagnostic tool in the United States is unpredictable at present, but it does show progress in the knowledge and testing of celiac disease.

[Information for this section was provided by letter from Michael N. Marsh, D.Sc., D.M., F.R.C.P., Reader in Medicine, Hope Hospital, Salford, England.]

15. What happens if I go on a gluten-free diet and get free of symptoms before I have a biopsy?

You are on the horns of a dilemma here. If it has been only a couple of days, the villi would still show signs of damage, and the doctor could get an accurate diagnosis. If it has been several months, the biopsy might show enough healing that the doctor wouldn't know if you were truly a celiac. At this point you might have to return to a gluten-filled diet to bring back the diagnostic lesions in the gut and the flattened villi to be certain that you are intolerant to gluten. This might not be a pleasant prospect, which is why most people are urged to get to a doctor as soon as possible if they test themselves and find that eliminating wheat, rye, barley, and oats makes them feel better immediately.

Formerly one of the tests of whether a person was a celiac was their response to a gluten-free diet, but now biopsies have become the standard for making the diagnosis. The response is considered an important confirmation that the diagnosis is correct. The diagnostic accuracy obtained by combining both biopsy and the beneficial effect of the diet greatly reduces the risks of missing a different disease or unnecessarily imposing a gluten-free diet on a patient for life.

16. I was diagnosed with dermatitis herpetiformis and given medication. Now my doctor tells me I should go on a gluten-free diet. Why?

Dermatitis herpetiformis (DH) is a form of gluten sensitivity that is usually associated with enteropathy. The doctors have long been aware that DH patients (like celiac disease patients) have a genetic predisposition and are intolerant to the glutens in wheat, rye, oats, and barley and that some trigger factor will set off the symptoms.

The difference is that the most irritating symptoms are the skin lesions, in the form of small itchy blisters. Until recently, the major focus of doctors has been on relieving the itching and preventing more sores from erupting. This was done with medications like dapsone, sulfapyridine, and sulfamethoxypyrizine, all of which can have moderate to severe side effects, depending on how much has to be taken to control the outbreaks.

It is now recognized that most DH patients who continue on a gluten-filled diet do show intestinal damage similar to but often less severe than that seen in celiac disease patients. This has led doctors to prescribe the gluten-free diet along with the medication, hoping that a complete withdrawal of the medication can eventually be effected.

Why should you stay on this gluten-free diet? Since the diet has been shown to reduce the risk of lymphoma for those with celiac disease, one would predict that the diet would also decrease the incidence of that cancer in those with DH, although no large study of this has been done. But wouldn't it be great just to lower the amount of, or completely eliminate, the medicine and avoid the side effects? There is strong hope that eventually many patients with DH may stay healed of eruptions by diet alone.

17. I don't have any symptoms if I eat a little gluten. Does that mean that I am only a little bit celiac?

Being a little bit celiac is like being a little bit pregnant. If you have been diagnosed with celiac disease, you are a celiac and should adhere strictly to the gluten-free diet to prevent any later complications of the disease which, doctors suggest, could range from pancreatic insufficiency (see page 15) or recalcitrant sprue to cancer.

You are both fortunate and unfortunate that you don't have warnings when ingesting gluten, because you can't always know whether you have eaten any of the hidden glutens without being aware. You also may be getting small symptoms such as mental or physical fatigue and don't relate that to diet. Why some celiacs are very intolerant to the slightest trace of gluten and others have few symptoms is yet to be understood. But it seems that there is a wide variation in the degree of symptomatic pain that different celiacs suffer.

18. I am on a gluten-free diet but still have some symptoms. Can the diagnosis be wrong?

It is highly unlikely if you were diagnosed through biopsy. But you certainly might still be feeling symptoms from several other sources. Are you getting any gluten in things you don't suspect? (See page 20 for hidden glutens.) Or you may be allergic or intolerant to something you are eating. It is not uncommon for celiacs to have other allergy problems that can cause the same symptoms. Milk products are the first suspect, because before healing of the gut, many celiacs find they cannot comfortably digest dairy products. This may pass in a few months to a year. Other allergies may be to eggs, soy, corn, or many other foods. These you might discover yourself by eliminating suspect foods or you may need to consult an allergist. A third problem might be one doctors often fail to mention, that the damaged gut just can't tolerate much roughage at first. In your passion to eat gluten free, you may be eating more vegetables and fruit than before and adding rice bran to your bread dough. Easing off on extra roughage may eliminate some of the problems.

If none of these seems to be the answer, by all means, return to your doctor and ferret out the reason for the distress. Rarely, continued symptoms may be due to refractory disease or some other complication. But if there was a misdiagnosis, you certainly don't want to have to restrict your diet the rest of your life.

19. What do you mean by "hidden glutens"?

In my first two books I warned you in whole chapters about the danger of gluten hiding under other names such as hydrolyzed vegetable protein, modified food starch, and dextrin, although these are not always made from wheat. "Natural flavorings" listed in ingredient lists on some labels are also suspect, as some are made from grain alcohol. For those trying to cut fats, many so-called light products use wheat or oats to reduce the calorie and fat count. Gluten might also be found in the alcohol used in flavorings such as vanilla and in distilled vinegar. It can possibly be present in veined cheeses such as blue cheese and Roquefort.

Gluten can be a problem in many medications, ranging from the filler in prescription drugs to laxatives, the fixative for false teeth, the alcohol in mouthwash, even in a headache reliever or vitamin pill. It can be present due to contamination in a variety of ways, ranging from a health food store bin where scoops have been exchanged to mills that grind several grains on the same stones to your own home, where someone baking with wheat flour might have spread the dust around the kitchen and into your flours.

Another source of gluten that is difficult to refuse is the wheat in the communion wafer. Many celiacs get a dispensation from their clergy to avoid taking the wafer. In some faiths, they can furnish their own gluten-free one. Just one wafer each communion is enough to cause continuing distress and poor healing in many celiacs.

20. Is the gluten-free diet nutritious? Should I be taking vitamin supplements?

The gluten-free diet can and should be nutritionally adequate to allow you to meet all your needs. The real problem is recognizing how much you are absorbing and retaining of the nutrients you eat. If you are very careful and aren't getting any gluten (whether through hidden glutens, contamination, or by cheating on the diet) you should be absorbing your nutrients well. But, again, it may take a long time for the damage to the gut to heal.

This might depend on the severity of your symptoms before diagnosis and how long you have suffered from malnutrition. Your doctor would be the one to make a decision on whether you need any strong supplement. He or she can screen with specific blood tests or other measures to determine any specific vitamin or mineral needs.

On the other hand, if you think you just want to be sure by taking a one-a-day type multiple vitamin and mineral supplement, these are often just enough to meet (but don't exceed) the need suggested by the U.S. Recommended Daily Allowances. *Warning:* Be sure you pick one that doesn't contain gluten or anything else to which you may be allergic. Many have a filler of lactose, some cornstarch, and some wheat. This is important, for you don't want to get poisoned by your vitamins.

I mentioned earlier the need for calcium in some form if you are lactose intolerant or have been tested and have low bone density.

21. I am planning a trip. How can I be sure of getting enough gluten-free food?

Take it with you! No, I'm not kidding. Whether you are traveling by car, camper, plane, or bus, the easiest way to be sure of having your breads, cereals, and sweets is to make them ahead of time and carry them along to accompany the fresh fruits, vegetables, and meats you can buy to cook or order in a restaurant.

I've traveled a lot and learned to carry along food that will keep for at least a month, such as Melba Toast (page 92), Parmesan Toast Points (page 204), Biscotti (pages 153 and 154), and Rice-free Graham Crackers (page 99). I pack these in flat, rectangular plastic containers in one of the suitcases on the way out and come home with the containers empty, snugly fitted inside each other, making room for my souvenirs. Other foods great for trips are Granola and Granola Bars (found in *The Gluten-free Gourmet* and *More from the Gluten-free Gourmet*) or, if you've no time to cook, there are GF Hol Grain rice crackers in grocery stores. Some suppliers listed in the back of the book can furnish vacuum-sealed individual packets of bread and cookies that travel well.

On airlines, never count on the advertised "gluten-free meal" being free of gluten. In my experience, it seldom is, so I carry a small plastic sandwich box (or two on long trips) in my carry-on luggage. In this I put some fresh bread (your last fresh bread until you get home), some wrapped cheese singles, and several cookies. Added to what you can eat from the meal tray, this should hold you until landing. You could also include some fresh or dried fruit.

Be wary of the term "gluten free" in foreign countries, for sometimes wheat starch is used in baking, which has been proved to have some contamination from the gluten protein. And always, if you are traveling abroad, find out whether you will be allowed to carry in food. I have carried a letter from my doctor for some countries and, in others, customs officials have accepted that I need the food for medical reasons. No official has, so far, confiscated my food.

22. I've been urged to join a support group. I'm not a joiner and don't like to socialize in groups. What would be the benefit in joining?

Celiac disease is called a "rare" disease in medical textbooks, so it's not surprising how many gluten-intolerant people think they are the only ones who suffer until they join a group. Then they begin to see how many of us there are and learn that others, too, have problems, such as eating out, carrying a lunch, traveling, and coping with peer pressure to "just take a taste—what will it matter?"

As you realize if you are a celiac, there is little information about the disease in papers or magazines or on radio or television. But there is a lot going on within the celiac organizations to further our knowledge of the disease and the diet. The only way to receive this information is by becoming a member of one of the groups and either attending the meetings or getting the newsletter by mail.

Perhaps the questions and answers above will help alleviate some of your concerns, but I would never have been able to provide them if I hadn't listened for over twenty years to others in my support group and at meetings and conferences held just for celiacs.

The final reason for being a member of a group is that in numbers we increase our "clout." We can garner more attention from the medical field even to the point where we now know that more celiacs are being diagnosed earlier—many before they have suffered the debilitating symptoms of previous patients. It's a first step in changing the medical description of this as a "rare" disease to an "uncommon" one and to doctors' quicker recognition of it in their patients.

For the most recent and complete medical information about celiac disease or to find a local support group, contact one of the following organizations:

American Celiac Society Dietary Support Coalition, 58 Musano Court, West Orange, NJ 07052-4103; phone (201) 325-8837.
Canadian Celiac Association, 6519-B Mississauga Rd., Mississauga, Ontario L5N 1A6, Canada; phone (905) 567-7195.
Celiac Disease Foundation, 13251 Ventura Blvd., Suite 3, Studio City, CA 91604-1838; phone (818) 990-2354, fax (818) 990-2379.
Celiac Sprue Association/United States of America (CSA/USA), P.O. Box 31700, Omaha, NE 68131-0700; phone (402) 558-0600.
Gluten Intolerance Group of North America (GIG), P.O. Box 23053, Broadway Station, Seattle, WA 98102-0353; phone (206) 325-6980.
Internet's Celiac Conference. Send E-mail to: celiac@ispace.com

FOR FURTHER READING

Hills, Hilda Cherry. *Good Food, Gluten Free* (New Canaan, Connecticut: Keats Publishing, Inc., 1976). As the wife of a celiac, Mrs. Hills wanted to do what was best for her husband's health and in so doing became interested enough to research the disease thoroughly. This book is old, in view of our rapidly expanding knowledge of the disease, and is written from the viewpoint of British research, but the first half contains a lot of still-pertinent information written in easily understood layman's terms. (The recipes are more nutritionally correct than gourmet.)

Garst, Pat Murphy. *Celiac Sprue and the Gluten Free Diet.* 1981. (Available by mail order to Celiac Sprue and the Gluten Free Diet, 15-A Ashwood Court, Frankfort, KY 40601.) Pat Garst, a celiac, helped found the Midwestern Celiac Sprue Association (later to become CSA/USA) and was its first president. She writes this well-researched book in a simple style and gives a lot of personal tips for living with the disease and caring for a child with it. (No recipes.)

Lowell, Jax. *Against the Grain* (New York: Henry Holt and Company, 1995). Jax Lowell is a celiac herself and writes from a celiac point of view about coping with the disease in daily living. This reads smoothly and easily with a positive attitude about living within the diet. She lists many resources. (The book contains a few gourmet recipes from famous chefs.)

REFERENCES

Ciclitira, P.J., Ph.D., F.R.C.P. Rayne Institute, St. Thomas' Hospital, London. "Vision for the Future." Lecture at Celiac Disease Foundation, Spring 1992.

Drinkwater, Barbara, Ph.D. "Osteoporosis." Lecture at annual meeting of the Gluten Intolerance Group of North America, Spring 1992.

Girous, Renee, R.D., L.D. "Supplemental Vitamin and Mineral Usage by Persons with Celiac Sprue." *Gluten Free News,* Spring 1994, 2–4.

Gregar, I., et al. "Enteropeptidase in Coeliac Disease and Exocrine Pancreatic Insufficiency." *Acta Univ. Palacki. Olomuc. Fac. Med.* 116, 247–252 (1987).

Hartsook, Elaine I., R.D., Ph.D. "Celiac Sprue: Clinical Aspects and Patient Realities. What Is Celiac Sprue?" Paper delivered on Celiac Experience I cruise, 1991.

———. "Dermatitis Herpetiformis." Paper delivered at the Gluten Intolerance Group of North America, 1993.

———. "Gluten-Sensitive Enteropathy: Up-Date for Health Care Professionals." Paper delivered at the Gluten Intolerance Group of North America, 1992.

Hopkins, Randy, M.D. "Keeping Your GI Tract in Shape." Lecture at Ballard Hospital Campus, Seattle Center for Digestive Diseases, Spring 1994.

Marsh, Michael N., D.Sc., D.M., F.R.C.P. "The Rectal Challenge for Diagnosing Gluten Sensitivity." Keynote address at Annual Meeting of the Gluten Intolerance Group of North America, Spring 1994.

———, ed. *Coeliac Disease.* Oxford: Blackwell Scientific Publications, 1992.

Murray, Joseph A., M.D. "Celiac Disease in the U.S.A.—Where We Are vs. Where We Need to Be." Keynote Speech at Annual meeting of the Gluten Intolerance Group of North America, March 1993.

Regan, Patrick T., and Eugene P. DiMagno. "Exocrine Pancreatic Insufficiency in Celiac Sprue: A Cause of Treatment Failure." *Gastroenterology* 78 (1980): 484–487.

Sherman, David J.C., ed. *Diseases of the Gastrointestinal Tract and Liver.* 2nd ed.

Zone, John J., M.D. "Dermatitis Herpetiformis." Lecture at Annual Meeting of the Gluten Intolerance Group of North America, Spring 1992.

The Weird World of Gluten-free Baking

Welcome to a whole new world of baking, where beans can be used as flour, ingredients are often added in reverse order, and wheat in any form is as welcome as rat poison.

If you've already tried using some of the gluten-free flours and had your cake turn into crumbs and your bread into bricks, you know how weird it feels. It's as if you've lost control of your baking. Take heart, you're not alone.

Gluten-free flours all lack the protein (or gluten) to which we are intolerant, and because gluten adds the "stretch" factor in baking, we must replace it with a substitute. Before the advent of xanthan gum we used more eggs, cottage cheese, and extra leavening to make a rice-flour cake or bread feel and taste somewhat like the real thing. But we've learned a lot since those beginning days and can now turn out fantastic baked products using several different combinations of flours.

The most recent additions are the wonderful new bean flours being introduced. I tasted my first sample a couple of years ago and have been a convert ever since. Bean flour, when mixed with other gluten-free flours, turns out breads and cakes with the springy texture of wheat flour—no more grainy rice feel.

The best of these new bean flours are a light flour made from garbanzo and broad beans, from Authentic Foods (hereafter called "light bean flour"), and a darker flour microprocessed from Romano beans, made by Grain Process Enterprises, Ltd., or Son's Milling in Canada (hereafter called "dark bean flour"). See pages 376–81 for these suppliers. Many recipes in this book call for a mix made of one of these flours with cornstarch and tapioca flour in equal proportions (see page 32). The two flours have a different taste, so sometimes I have specified a Light Bean Flour Mix and sometimes a Dark Bean Flour Mix. The mix made with light bean flour is great in fruit breads or cakes, while the mix made with dark bean flour goes well in cakes that contain chocolate and breads that have a stronger flavor, such as Dark Mock Rye (page 89). In many recipes they can be interchanged. Light bean flour can almost always replace soy flour in a recipe, and the mix made with light bean flour can replace the GF Flour Mix in many of your favorite baked products. To cut the taste of the beans in these recipes, replace the white sugar with brown or maple sugar. You will also be adding more fiber and flavor to the cake, bread, or muffins.

A word of caution: Introduce this new flour slowly into the diet, for, as this flour is made from beans, you may experience some flatulence at the beginning. As the body adjusts to the new flour, this will disappear for most people.

Rice flour is the usual basic flour for our diet, but (as with the bean flour) I seldom bake with rice flour alone. A better product results when rice flour is combined with other flours—potato starch, tapioca, or soy. A flour mixture and the addition of xanthan gum can make the food so tasty no one will ever guess it's a "diet" product.

For my test baking or when converting a recipe, I start with a combination I keep on hand called my GF Flour Mix (see page 33). Using that as the flour I add xanthan gum (1 teaspoon to 3 cups flour for a cake; 2½ teaspoons to 3 cups flour for bread; none for most cookies) and increase the leavening a bit and possibly add another egg or egg white.

Because the flours do not exchange in equal quantity with wheat flour, it is best to understand what each flour is. And because so many celiacs have other intolerances and allergies and must alter the formulas even more, I will explain the use of some of the substitutes available for our dietary needs.

THE NEW BEAN FLOURS

There have always been bean and lentil flours to be found in health food stores, but these new products described above from Authentic Foods and Grain Process Enterprises, Ltd., are specially milled to be used in baking. They have been tested for taste, smoothness, and compatibility with other baking supplies. Do not confuse them with the former ground bean products. These flours keep well in a dry cupboard and don't have to be refrigerated.

OTHER BEAN AND LENTIL FLOURS

Garbanzo and other bean and lentil flours may be combined with rice or other gluten-free flours for baking. I have included several recipes in this book. They can also be added in small quantities to meatloaf, hamburger patties, and meatballs. In most cases I now use the light bean flour for these purposes, but these other flours are readily available in health food or East Indian stores and Asian markets. These other flours should be refrigerated, for they are not specially processed to keep.

WHITE RICE FLOUR

This basic flour for gluten-free baking is milled from polished white rice. Its bland flavor doesn't distort the taste of the baked product, and it combines well with other flours to prevent the grainy texture of an all-rice cake or bread. This keeps well, so it can be bought in quantity. Order it through one of the suppliers listed on pages 376–81 or buy it in unopened boxes (to avoid contamination) from bakeries where it is used to dust baking pans. It is also available in many Asian markets.

White rice flour comes in several textures. Regular and Fine can be ordered from suppliers, while the very finest is sold in Asian markets. All the recipes in this book were tested in my kitchen with very fine flour, so if you use regular or medium grinds, you may have to add slightly more liquid.

BROWN RICE FLOUR

This flour, milled from unpolished brown rice, contains bran and is higher in nutrient value than white rice flour. Use it for breads, muffins, and cookies where a bran (or nutty) taste is desired. Because there are oils in the bran, it has a much shorter shelf life and tends to become stronger tasting as it ages. Purchase fresh flour and store it in the refrigerator or freezer for longer life.

RICE BRAN

As the name implies, this is the bran obtained from polishing brown rice. With its high content of minerals, vitamin B, vitamin E, protein, and fiber, it is a good addition to cookies, muffins, and some breads. This, too, has a short shelf life because of the oils it contains, so it is best to buy it as needed. Don't store it for long except in the freezer.

SWEET RICE FLOUR

This flour, made from a glutinous rice often called "sticky rice," is an excellent thickening agent. It is especially good for sauces that are to be refrigerated or frozen, as it inhibits separation of the liquids. I also use it by the tablespoon to add to breads in my breadmaker when the dough is too thin. I've found this in many grocery stores under the label Mochiko Sweet Rice Flour, but it can be ordered from several of the suppliers listed on pages 376–81. It can also be found in some Asian markets. Do not confuse it with plain white rice flour.

RICE POLISH

This is a soft, fluffy, cream-colored flour made from the hulls of brown rice. Like rice bran, it has a high concentration of minerals and B vitamins. And, like rice bran, it has a short shelf life. I don't use this in any recipe in this book, but it could be added to muffins, veggieburgers, and bread to add both flavor and nutrients.

POTATO STARCH FLOUR

This very fine white flour with a bland taste is combined with other flours to be used in baking and is used alone as a gluten-free thickening agent for cream soups. When using it in soups, mix with water first and use only about half the amount to replace wheat flour. This keeps well and can be bought in quantity.

POTATO FLOUR

Do not confuse this with potato starch flour. This is a heavy flour with a definite potato taste. I use very little of it. When called for in a recipe, it can often be replaced with Potato Buds or mashed potatoes.

TAPIOCA FLOUR

Sometimes called tapioca starch, cassava flour, or cassava starch, this light, white, velvety flour obtained from the cassava root imparts a bit of "chew" to baked goods and is excellent used in varying quantities with other flours for baking. I have used it in almost equal parts in recipes where a slightly chewy texture is desirable, such as French bread, and combined it with cornstarch and the new bean flours in the bean flour mixes. This keeps well and can be bought in quantity.

SOY FLOUR

A yellow flour with high protein and fat content, this has a nutty flavor and is most successful when used in combination with other flours in baked products that contain fruit, nuts, or chocolate. It is also excellent in waffles for its distinctive taste. Purchase it in small quantities as it, too, has a short shelf life. Some celiacs may be sensitive to this flour. Bean flour can be substituted in my recipes that call for soy.

CORNSTARCH

A refined starch obtained from corn, cornstarch is mainly used as a clear thickening agent for puddings, fruit sauces, and Asian cooking, but for celiacs it is also used in combination with other flours in baking. I use it as a part of the new Bean Flour Mix (page 32), but if you are allergic to corn, arrowroot may be substituted for the cornstarch.

CORN FLOUR

A flour milled from corn (maize), this can be blended with cornmeal when making corn breads and corn muffins.

CORNMEAL

This ground corn may be obtained in yellow or white meal. Combine this with other flours for baking or use it alone in Mexican dishes.

POPCORN FLOUR

This flavorful flour has a slightly finer texture than cornmeal and can be combined with other flours to make bread or muffins and used alone for coating meats for frying or baking. I use this in several recipes in the book. This keeps well on the shelf. See the list of suppliers (pages 376–81) for ordering this flour.

ARROWROOT FLOUR

This white flour obtained from the root of a West Indian plant can be exchanged measure for measure for cornstarch. If you are allergic to corn, use this in place of the cornstarch in the Bean Flour Mix.

NUT FLOURS

Chestnut, almond, and other nut flours can be used in small quantities, replacing a small portion of other flours to enhance the taste of home-made pasta, puddings, and cookies. Because they are expensive and often difficult to find, I suggested only one option in this book. Since they are high in proteins, nut flours are great additions to the diet, if you have the opportunity to experiment.

LIGHT AND DARK BEAN FLOUR MIXES

In many recipes using the new bean flours, I use this mix that I make up ahead. The proportions are simple: equal parts light or dark bean flour, cornstarch, and tapioca flour. I mix about:

3 cups bean flour
3 cups cornstarch
3 cups tapioca flour

This fills a three-pound coffee tin and may be stored in the cupboard with other flours.

A second mix may be made by adding a small amount of white or brown rice flour. (If you use brown rice flour, this mix will have to be refrigerated.)

THE FORMULA IS:	THIS CAN BE:
1 part bean flour	2 cups bean flour
1 part cornstarch	2 cups cornstarch
1 part tapioca flour	2 cups tapioca flour
½ part rice flour	1 cup rice flour

This formula is excellent in breads, for it gives them a finer texture. Use this mix in the same amount as the first bean flour mix.

GF FLOUR MIX

This is the mix called for in many recipes in this book. The formula is 2 parts white rice flour, ⅔ part potato starch flour, and ⅓ part tapioca flour. I mix this in large quantities and keep it on hand for baking.

EXAMPLE 1

6 cups white rice flour
2 cups potato starch flour
1 cup tapioca flour

EXAMPLE 2

12 cups white rice flour
4 cups potato starch flour
2 cups tapioca flour

If you prefer not to blend your own, this flour can now be ordered in boxes and in bulk from a supplier listed on pages 376–81. Ask for GF Gourmet Flour Mix.

Principles of Substitution

For general baking, use the following formula. For each cup of wheat flour in a recipe, substitute one of the following:

1 cup GF Flour Mix, suggested above
1 scant cup light or dark bean flour mix
⅞ cup rice flour (brown or white)
⅝ cup potato starch flour
1 cup soy flour plus ¼ cup potato starch flour
½ cup soy flour plus ½ cup potato starch flour
1 cup corn flour
1 scant cup fine cornmeal

Other Baking Supplies

XANTHAN GUM

This is a powder milled from the dried cell coat of a microorganism called *Xanthomonas campestris* grown under laboratory conditions. It works as a substitute for the gluten in yeast breads and other baking with gluten-free flours. It is now available in some health food stores and by order from some of the suppliers listed on pages 376–81.

GUAR GUM

A powder derived from the seed of the plant *Cyamopsis tetragonolobus,* this can be purchased in health food stores or ordered from suppliers listed on pages 376–81. Because it has a high fiber content and is sometimes used as a laxative, be aware that when used in baking it can cause distress to people whose digestive systems are sensitive.

NONFAT, NON-INSTANT DRY MILK POWDER

This is the milk powder I use in the bread recipes. It can be found in health food stores and in some specialty grocery stores. If you substitute the boxed instant variety found in regular grocery stores, double the amount of milk powder called for.

NONDAIRY POWDERED MILK SUBSTITUTES

For the lactose intolerant, substitute either Lacto-Free, Tofu White (both contain soy), or NutQuik (made from almonds) for the dairy milk powder. Another choice is one of the powdered baby formulas from a supermarket or drugstore: Isomil, ProSobee, Nursoy (all soy based), or Pregestimil (corn based).

LIQUID EGG SUBSTITUTES

These cholesterol-free liquid substitutes for whole eggs are made from the egg whites plus other ingredients, some containing fats and some not. They may be found in the dairy section and freezer cases of most grocery stores. The most egglike without fat is Egg Beaters, but the one I use most for cooking is Second Nature, which contains enough fat to substitute well in cooking. There are many others, but always read the ingredient label to be sure the one you choose doesn't contain gluten or some other ingredient to which you are allergic.

EGG REPLACER

This powdered substitute for eggs in cooking contains no egg product and is also free of dairy, corn, soy, and gluten. I use a little of this for extra leavening in many recipes. It is always optional unless this is the only leavening used in a recipe. Egg Replacer can be ordered from Ener-G-Foods or found in most health food stores. A similar product is also available in Canada.

DOUGH ENHANCERS

These powdered products are used in bread making to substitute for the vinegar that balances the pH in most waters. They also tend to make the bread stay fresh longer. Most dough enhancers contain either a milk or soy solid, lecithin, salt, citric or ascorbic acid, and a base of cornstarch or wheat flour. They are put out by many companies and can be found in baking supply stores and some health food stores. Always read the ingredient labels to find one that's gluten free and doesn't contain anything else to which you may be allergic.

Flours We Should Avoid

Wheat comes in many forms, and some of them will trick the unwary or even be touted by health food stores as gluten free. Never believe it! It's easy to recognize wheat flour and wheat starch flour, but other names for a variety of wheat are: *bulgur, kamut, durum, spelt, Einkorn, semolina,* and *triticale* (a cross between rye and wheat).

Rye is rated next to wheat in the toxic factor, so it's on our no-no list.

Barley is found as a grain in our soups or added to wheat bread. The next most common uses of barley are in beer in the form of malt and in cereals in the form of malt syrup and malt flavoring.

Oats are easy to recognize in the cereal form such as oatmeal, but one hidden form can cause trouble when it is mixed in ground meats to "lighten" them. Watch for this use especially in Canada.

Questionable Flours and Grains

Millet is a grain for which the research is not completed and information not in. Some U.S. celiac organizations recommend avoiding any of the varieties of millet, while Canadian organizations allow it.

Amaranth, teff, and *quinoa.* These exotic foreign grains are often touted by health food stores as being gluten free or low in gluten. Although most of the U.S. organizations recommend avoiding these grains because they have not been researched enough to be declared gluten free, Canadian organizations allow them in their diet list.

Buckwheat is not of the grain family but is related to rhubarb. The problem with buckwheat flour is that it is usually mixed with wheat. I have used Kasha, the buckwheat kernel, but I don't recommend purchasing any form of buckwheat flour, for fear of its being contaminated either in production or in the deliberate mixing for a more palatable texture.

Sorghum flour. This is a new flour introduced recently to the market by Jowar Foods, Inc. They call their flour Jowar. Sorghum is more closely related to corn than to wheat, so this shouldn't be toxic to celiacs. Again, no research has been done on this new flour. I am sincerely hoping that we can add this to our list of acceptable foods.

The above may leave you confused at first, but take heart—you'll soon be as familiar with these products as you once were with the mixes you pulled from the grocery shelf. It will take you a bit more time shopping (or ordering from one of the suppliers listed in the back of this book), but you'll be surprised how soon you'll be proudly serving some exciting and delicious home-baked (and gluten-free) delicacies to your family and friends.

The Fine Art
of Baking Better Bread

Every time I pull a plump, crusty, light loaf of bread from the oven or turn one out from my bread machine, I consider it a minor miracle. I realize I'm only an average cook, and bread making didn't come into my culinary repertoire until twenty years ago, but you'd think I could learn in that time. Well, the one thing I've learned is that making bread is not just baking; it is a fine art, and baking gluten-free loaves is one of the most difficult skills to master.

Evidently many of my readers have discovered the same thing. By far the greatest number of letters I receive ask for help in bread baking. I wish I could say "Easy, just . . ." but I can't, for so many elements are involved.

First, we have to realize we are combining not yeast and gluten (which gives bread that wonderfully springy texture) but yeast and xanthan gum (a poor substitute). Whether we work with a heavy-duty mixer and use the oven for baking or toss the ingredients into a bread machine, we still can't ever be certain of the outcome, because so many factors affect yeast products: the temperature of the water we use and of the air around us, the amount of water we use and the amount of water in the air, even the pH balance of the water and texture of our flours.

I've found lately that oven baking is more forgiving than programmed machine baking. I've also found that we can use a lot of shortcuts, and I have cut the time down considerably from the almost four hours of my original gluten-free recipes to about one and a half hours. Also, we can eliminate the second kneading and rising both by hand and in the machine. I revised my hand baking method after I made a mistake and put the ingredients into the bowl in reverse order—wet ingredients first, then dry—only to come out with a lighter, tenderer, springier loaf. Since that first accidental mixing, I've tested the two methods several times and come to the conclusion that this new way does make a better-textured, lighter gluten-free loaf and the results are more predictable. To shorten the time even more, I double the amount of yeast and use the rapid-rise variety, thus getting my bread ready for the oven in about 35 minutes. (See page 68 preceding the bread recipes for the exact procedure.)

The amount of liquid in a recipe is still the answer to whether the bread will be lead or light. No wonder the old recipes never gave exact amounts of flour but said: Add enough flour to make the bread suitable for kneading. That's a bit difficult to determine, because with our flours, we don't do any kneading and our dough should resemble heavy cake batter more than a dough ball. In making up recipes, I've attempted to give the amount of liquid at average temperature and humidity. You will find that when the skies are weeping outside or the humidity is high, the flour will already have absorbed some of this water and you can cut the amount of liquids by up to 3 tablespoons. The best way to do this is to hold back about that amount of water and add it in the bread machine after a few minutes of mixing if needed.

Learning to read the bread consistency is the "art" in bread making. By the hand-mixing method, the dough should be the consistency of thick cake batter. In a bread machine, the dough should round up in the pan and be shiny, not dull looking, not sloppy wet, nor should it form a heavy dough ball. If the dough is too wet, add sweet rice flour 1 tablespoon at a time until the correct consistency is obtained. When you turn out that perfect loaf, remember the consistency that you had and try to duplicate it next time. Only repeated baking can teach you to judge the correct consistency for the machine, climate, and altitude.

Some Simple Suggestions for Making Better Bread

Whether you were a skilled bread baker before the diagnosis or came to it—as I did—a rank beginner, there are different factors to consider when baking with gluten-free flours. The rice breads are most difficult and demanding, while the bean flour breads will act more like wheat. Both will need xanthan gum or another gum to achieve that "stretch" factor and keep the loaf from turning to crumbs. You will have greater success if you understand some of the problems.

BEFORE YOU START

1. Yeast is your most important ingredient. Be sure it is fresh, not outdated. Old yeast will turn out brickbats, not bread. Test any yeast that is nearing the expiration date by putting about 1 tablespoon into ½ cup of water with 1 teaspoon of sugar. If it doesn't foam up to double volume in 10 minutes, discard it and buy new yeast.

2. Measuring cups can vary, so use the same cup or style of cup for all measurements whether wet or dry.

INGREDIENTS

3. Water is an important ingredient. Check yours to see if it is acid or alkaline. In a city, you can call the water department to determine the pH factor. A 5.5 to 5.6 rating would be perfect for bread, but most city water has added alkaline, so we should add either vinegar, lemon juice, or a dough enhancer. If you can't discover your pH factor, try using bottled water. If you use orange juice as a liquid, you are adding more acid and may have to add a little baking soda. The egg whites in my recipes help to balance the pH factor. Softened water should not be used in bread, for it has a high sodium content.

4. Different brands and grinds of rice flour may require a variation in the amount of water or liquid in a recipe.

5. Lemon juice or dough enhancer added to a recipe to balance the pH factor both enhances the flavor and acts as a preservative.

6. Cottage cheese and ricotta cheese can be interchanged in recipes, but the taste will be slightly different. For the lactose intolerant, cubed tofu can substitute for the above cheeses, but remember that you are adding soy, which often calls for a decrease in liquids.

7. One teaspoon of unflavored gelatin added to the dry ingredients can add spring to the texture of your bread, but it is always optional.

8. When a recipe calls for melted butter or margarine, you can save time by cutting the butter or margarine into small chunks before adding it to the liquids.

9. Remember always to bring ingredients (except water) to room temperature before starting to bake, thus avoiding cooling the yeast too much. Cold eggs can be warmed by putting in a pan of warm water for a couple of minutes.

10. Freeze-dried coffee crystals can be replaced by GF instant coffee or regular fine-grind coffee in baking.

11. When experimenting with a recipe, change only one ingredient at a time.

12. Sugar or liquid sweetener: For machines, all the sugar can be added to the dry ingredients. Liquid sweetener (molasses, honey, etc.) should be added to the wet ingredients. If mixing by hand, reserve 1 teaspoon of sugar and add it to the water to make the yeast slurry. When converting a recipe from sugar to a liquid sweetener such as honey or molasses, cut down the amount of liquid (water) by the amount of sweetener added.

13. Milk powders retain the sugar (lactose) of the milk, so when replacing the dry milk powder in a recipe with a nondairy substitute, add about 2 extra tablespoons sugar to the recipe.

14. Baking at a higher elevation (over 2,500 feet) will require an addition of 1 to 2 tablespoons of water.

15. If the bread rises high and then falls, try reducing the amount of water by 1 or 2 tablespoons in the next batch. If that fails in a machine where you can't control the rising time, cut the yeast by ¼ to ½ teaspoon.

BREAD MACHINES

16. Use recipes developed and tested for our gluten-free flours and don't try to use those in the manual that came with the machine. The recipes will not work by simply exchanging rice flour for wheat flour.

17. Most of the gluten-free recipes for machines call for 3 cups of flour to fit the requirements of the large machine (1½ pounds). For the smaller (1 pound) machine, just cut the recipes down by a third.

18. Whipping the eggs or egg substitutes before adding to the liquids will give the bread a better texture.

19. If the dough rises so high it threatens to overflow the pan, poke it with a skewer to break up the bubbles. Keep poking with the skewer if necessary to prevent the rising and avoid a mess in the oven.

20. Fruit, nuts, and cereal can be added to the flour mix and put into the machine with the dry ingredients at the beginning of the mix cycle.

21. If your machine automatically preheats the ingredients, use water at room temperature. If it doesn't have a preheat cycle, use water that's about 80 degrees.

22. My recipes suggest blending dry ingredients and wet ingredients separately before placing in the machine. This has proved to be the most successful way of working with our flours. You do not have to completely premix the dough outside the machine if your machine is good for our heavy doughs.

    For placement in machines, incorporate yeast into the dry ingredients for round-pan models; place dry ingredients in the pan first, then liquids. For square upright or rectangular models, place wet ingredients in pan, then dry. The yeast should be placed in a well on top of the dry ingredients, although I've had good results mixing the yeast with the dry ingredients for most machines.

FOR ALL BREADS

For a more tender crust, rub the bread lightly with butter or margarine immediately after taking it from the oven or machine. Although you'll be

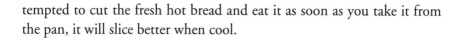

tempted to cut the fresh hot bread and eat it as soon as you take it from the pan, it will slice better when cool.

Choosing a Bread Machine for Gluten-free Flours

I know this is a problem for many of you, for my mail is filled with questions such as, What machine do you suggest buying? Why doesn't my machine turn out good bread?

I had planned to make this section a comparison of the many bread machines I've tested, but after working with many brands, I have to confess that I find only a few that turn out a really fine loaf of our bread. The other bakers I've talked to have much the same feeling. Although all of the machines will make bread, some require more work than others, and the outcome is less predictable. The best of the machines have strong paddles and can be programmed to one kneading and one rising (which is all our bread needs). Some will have a cycle that is similar to this, but many of the machines cannot be so programmed. Many have very weak paddles and you either have to mix the dough ahead of time or stir it with a rubber spatula while the machine is kneading.

I hadn't realized the vast differences between machines, because all my testing has been done on two machines. The recipes in *More from the Gluten-free Gourmet* were tested with the Zojirushi BBCC-S15, the ones in this book with my Welbilt Multilogic. I can recommend both of these, but they need some programming and have some drawbacks. They do have cool-down cycles, so I can put my ingredients in after the dishes are done in the evening, turn on the machine, and not worry about the bread. It will be cooled to cut for breakfast in the morning. *Warning!* Do not let the ingredients sit in the machine on a timed cycle, for our recipes contain fresh eggs.

Following are comparisons of machines I tested and found worked well with our heavy flours. Some are new; others are disappearing from the market. Three are expensive, two are moderately priced, and one is a good economy model. So you do have choices.

HOW TO MAKE THE BEST BREAD IN THE WELBILT MULTILOGIC

1. Program it by eliminating the second kneading, and use either 10 minutes of second rising or eliminate this entirely. (The directions for programming are in your manual.)
2. Have all ingredients (even water) at room temperature.
3. Load the dry ingredients (yeast included), turn on, and pour in the wet ingredients while the blade is rotating.
4. Remove the kneading blade after this kneading is finished to avoid the stir-down. I do this with plastic tongs to avoid scratching the paddle. This is messy and takes a bit of practice. (Be careful not to drop the blade into the "oven" section of your bread machine, as one baker confessed happened to her.)
5. Make a "cap" of aluminum foil to cover, shiny side down, the rounded glass top to keep the heat in after the paddle is removed.

The one feature that a lot of people don't like about this machine is that the shape of the loaf is round. I am now so used to working with a round loaf that the square one looks peculiar. A drawback is that production has stopped on this model and it may be hard to find.

HOW TO MAKE THE BEST BREAD WITH THE ZOJIRUSHI BBCC-S15

1. Have all ingredients at room temperature.
2. Load the wet ingredients first, then the dry ingredients, except for the yeast. Make a small well in the top of the flours for the yeast.
3. Turn machine on to Home Made Menu. I program this by watching the dough; when it has kneaded about 25 to 30 minutes, I bypass the Knead 2 and Rise 1 and go immediately to Rise 2. When the dough

has almost doubled in bulk, I press Bake and usually allow 60 minutes for baking before pressing Cool. Remember to press the Home Made Memory bar to keep this menu if you plan to use it again. You can always start with this, and if the rising or baking times need to be adjusted, change them as the bread bakes.

This machine has a cool-down cycle, so you don't have to worry about taking out the bread.

The feature that people don't like about this machine is that they must stay by the machine that first time to get the correct menu. Another aspect that bothers some owners is adjusting the liquid, since it is added first. I usually hold out a couple of tablespoons and add them if needed after about 5 minutes of mixing.

HOW TO MAKE THE BEST BREAD USING THE WEST BEND BAKERS CHOICE 41080

This is the Cadillac of bread machines, for it has two strong paddles, is shaped more like an oven than other machines, and makes the familiar rectangular-shaped loaf. The paddles even lie down after the knead cycle is over so there are no large holes in the bottom of the loaf. Although this machine cannot be programmed to remove the stir-downs, they come early in the cycle of rising and don't seem to affect the final product.

1. Program to Basic/Rapid and set the Bread Color on Medium.
2. Have all ingredients at room temperature.
3. Put in all but 1 to 2 tablespoons of the liquid.
4. Add the dry ingredients. Yeast may be put in a well on top or incorporated into the dry ingredients.
5. After pushing the On button, watch the dough texture and add more liquid, if needed, after a few minutes of kneading, until the dough mounds up slightly over each kneading bar and does not form separate balls.
6. Push the Off button and remove the pan as soon as possible after the signal, for there is no cool-down cycle.

This machine has a preheat cycle, so you don't have to worry about the temperature of the water. It has two knead bars, so all the dough is well mixed. It has an oven light that lets you see the bread without opening the lid and an Extend Rise button that lets you extend the rise time by 10 or 20 minutes as the bread is rising. The oven door swings open so you don't have to lift the pan from the top. And it has a Too Hot or Too Cold display if the oven is either before you start. Finally, the readout button counts down the time left for the complete baking cycle.

Some of its drawbacks are that it cannot be started the night before, as it has no cool-down cycle; nor can it be started in the morning and left while the baker is at work, for the bread will tend to become soggy if it stays in the machine too long after it finishes baking, although there is a keep-warm period.

The next three machines are all similar in appearance with upright rectangular pans. None have cool-down cycles, but all have a keep-warm period like the machine above. The paddles are strong and will work well with our flours. I have worked with all of these and find them most satisfactory. They require no mixing of the dough outside the pan and no stirring while the kneading cycle is in progress.

The Red Star is new on the market, and at an affordable price. It can be programmed separately for Dough or Bake only, as well as the complete cycle.

The Toastmaster Platinum 1199S has an extra-heavy pan and a Rapid cycle that works well with our flours.

The West Bend 41040 has a Basic/Rapid cycle that is good for our flours.

To make the best bread using the three models above, follow the directions for the West Bend Bakers Choice, but select the button that corresponds to the Basic/Rapid. You must put the wet ingredients in first and then the dry, putting the yeast either in a well on top or incorporating it into the dry ingredients. You will not be able to change the knead time, rise time, or bake time. Be sure to remove the bread as soon as possible after the baking is done, taking care not to burn yourself on the hot pan.

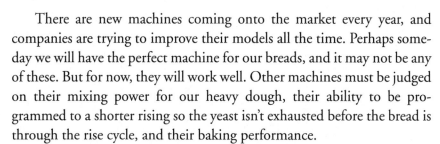

There are new machines coming onto the market every year, and companies are trying to improve their models all the time. Perhaps someday we will have the perfect machine for our breads, and it may not be any of these. But for now, they will work well. Other machines must be judged on their mixing power for our heavy dough, their ability to be programmed to a shorter rising so the yeast isn't exhausted before the bread is through the rise cycle, and their baking performance.

Yes, there is a lot to learn about bread making and I am always discovering new quirks. But I confess to feeling like a culinary Rembrandt when my bread turns out plump and crusty, looking like one of the pictures in my baking books.

FOR FURTHER READING

The Bread Machine Magic Book of Helpful Hints, by Linda Rehberg and Lois Conway. New York: St. Martin's Press, 1993.

FOR BREAD MACHINE HELP

Phone: Red Star Yeast & Products, 800-423-5040 (800-4-CELIAC).

Time-saving Mixes

Baking Mixes

Basic Cake Mix
    Featherlight Yellow Cake
    Low-Fat Cake
    Lactose-free, Soy-free Cake
    Low-Fat Chocolate Cake
Buttermilk Biscuit Mix
    Plain Biscuits
    Sweet Shortcake Biscuits
    Sweet Potato Biscuits
    Green Onion Biscuits
    Quick Cheese Muffins
Pancake and Waffle Mix
    Pancakes
    Waffles
Dream Pastry Mix
    Dream Pastry
    Easy Cream Cheese Pastry

Oil Crust
Mayonnaise Crust

Pasta Mixes

Pasta Base Mix
Mock Rice-A-Roni Mix

Soup Mixes

Creamed Soup Base
    Cream of Chicken Soup
    Cream of Mushroom Soup
    Cream of Tomato Soup
    Cheese Soup or Sauce
    Shrimp Soup or Sauce
    Tasty Cream Sauce
Onion Soup Mix

The last time I accidentally steered my cart down the crowded aisle of baking mixes in my neighborhood grocery, I wondered if anyone still buys flour and sugar and baking powder anymore to make their own baked goods. Probably not—no one has the time.

I came home thinking it wasn't fair. We who have to live gluten free are just as busy, and starting from scratch may often seem more trouble than a treat is worth. Some gluten-free mixes can be ordered or found in the health food stores, but they're expensive, and we have to take the trouble to order by phone or mail or look up that distant store. There's the additional problem that the mixes, while gluten free, can still contain some ingredient to which we may be allergic, such as lactose, soy, or corn.

With this in mind, I started creating more mixes you can stir up in your own kitchen to pull out when time is short. I have discovered that, with alterations, I can make my Buttermilk Biscuit Mix (page 55) into biscuits or muffins and even bases for quiches and meat pies. The Pancake and Waffle Mix turns out a great sponge cake.

To save all that measuring and whisking and flour on the kitchen floor when I want a pie, I put together a whole bag of the Dream Pastry Mix so I can make several different types of crusts with almost no trouble. And as for pasta, all I do is measure some liquid egg substitute or crack an egg and add with 1 tablespoon of oil to a cup of the Pasta Base Mix, then roll it out for homemade noodles or lasagne. After a lot of trials (with the results ending in the garbage disposal), I finally found the combination for a Basic Cake Mix that can be made with your choice of liquids, whether you desire a lactose-free cake, a soy-free one, or a cake that contains neither.

And if you've hungered for that box of Rice-A-Roni to stir up a quick rice and pasta dish, I've discovered we can even make this at home.

Because I use the Onion Soup Mix and the Powdered Soup Base from *More from the Gluten-free Gourmet* so much that they stand beside the salt and pepper by my kitchen stove, I have included them here. I've added two new flavors to the soup—cheese and shrimp. In this book you'll find a lot of recipes using these time-savers.

Many of the mixes start with GF Flour Mix. You can order this from a supplier listed on pages 376–81 or make your own. I mix up a large batch at a time.

THE FORMULA IS:	THIS CAN BE:
2 parts white rice flour	12 cups white rice flour
⅔ part potato starch flour	4 cups potato starch flour
⅓ part tapioca flour	2 cups tapioca flour

Basic Cake Mix

This is a basic mix that can be changed in many ways. Make a rich Featherlight Yellow Cake, a low-fat cake, or one both lactose and soy free. Flavor it with mocha, chocolate, or orange. Add spices or ginger. This quantity of mix will make four cakes, and it can be doubled easily. Store the mix in a plastic bag or plastic container with your regular flours for you to add the fresh eggs, shortening, and liquid when stirring up the cake.

5¼ cups GF Flour Mix	2½ teaspoons xanthan gum
8 teaspoons baking powder	2 teaspoons salt
2 teaspoons baking soda	2⅔ cups sugar
4 teaspoons powdered vanilla	2 tablespoons Egg Replacer

Whisk all ingredients together and store on pantry shelf.

FEATHERLIGHT YELLOW CAKE: Preheat oven to 350°. In a mixing bowl place 2 cups Basic Cake Mix.

Add: 1 egg plus 1 egg white (or ½ cup liquid egg substitute)
⅓ cup mayonnaise or Light Mayonnaise (page 366)
⅔ cup nondairy sour cream

Beat for about 1 minute on medium speed and turn batter into an 8″ square pan sprayed with vegetable spray. Bake 25 to 30 minutes. (See below for flavor variations.)

LOW-FAT CAKE: Preheat oven to 350°. In a mixing bowl place 2 cups Basic Cake Mix.

Add: 1 egg plus 1 egg white (or ½ cup liquid egg substitute)
2 tablespoons vegetable oil
2 tablespoons pear or apple sauce
½ cup low-fat milk or nondairy liquid

Beat for about 1 minute on medium speed and turn batter into an 8″ square pan sprayed with vegetable spray. Bake 25 to 30 minutes. (This is excellent with the Spiced Ginger Flavor.)

LACTOSE-FREE, SOY-FREE CAKE: Preheat oven to 350°. In a mixing bowl place 2 cups Basic Cake Mix.

Add:
- 1 egg plus 1 egg white
- 4 tablespoons melted margarine
- ⅓ cup citrus-flavored carbonated beverage (Sprite, etc.)

Beat for about 1 minute on medium speed and turn batter into an 8″ × 8″ pan sprayed with vegetable oil spray. Bake 25 to 30 minutes.

LOW-FAT CHOCOLATE CAKE: Preheat oven to 350°. In a mixing bowl place 2 cups Basic Cake Mix.

Whisk in:
- 3 tablespoons cocoa

Add:
- 1 egg plus 1 egg white
- 2 tablespoons vegetable oil
- One 2½-ounce jar baby pea puree
- ½ cup cherry cola

Beat for about 1 minute on medium speed and turn batter into an 8″ square pan sprayed with vegetable spray. Bake 25 to 30 minutes.

MOCHA FLAVOR: To any of the above recipes add 1 tablespoon instant coffee granules plus 2½ tablespoons cocoa to the dry mix before adding any liquid.

ORANGE FLAVOR: To the Basic Cake Mix add 1 tablespoon fresh orange zest before adding any of the liquids. This is especially good with the citrus-flavored carbonated beverage.

SPICE CAKE: To the Basic Cake Mix add 1½ teaspoons cinnamon, 1 teaspoon cloves, and ¼ teaspoon allspice before adding the liquids.

SPICED GINGER FLAVOR: To the Basic Cake Mix add 1 tablespoon finely chopped candied ginger before adding the egg and liquids.

Buttermilk Biscuit Mix

This gluten-free "Bisquick" can serve in any recipe that calls for biscuits, muffins, potpie toppings or for those "easy" dishes that rely on a self-rising prepared mix for the "easy." This formula makes 5 batches of biscuits.

2½ cups rice flour
1⅔ cups potato starch
3 tablespoons baking powder
2½ teaspoons baking soda
2½ teaspoons salt

¼ cup sugar (or to taste)
½ cup dry buttermilk powder
3 tablespoons Egg Replacer (optional)
1 cup less 1 tablespoon shortening

In a large mixing bowl, whisk together the rice flour, potato starch, baking powder, baking soda, salt, sugar, buttermilk powder, and Egg Replacer (if used). With a pastry blender, cut in the shortening until no lumps appear. Store in a 2-quart plastic bag or container in the refrigerator.

PLAIN BISCUITS: Preheat oven to 400°. To 1¼ cups Buttermilk Biscuit Mix add 1 egg (or ¼ cup liquid egg substitute) beaten with ¼ cup water for rolled biscuits or ⅓ cup water for light drop biscuits. Handle gently and roll out or drop as soon as the dough is moistened. Bake for 12 to 15 minutes. *Makes 8 biscuits.*

SWEET SHORTCAKE BISCUITS: Preheat oven to 400°. To 1¼ cups Buttermilk Biscuit Mix add 1 tablespoon sugar, 1 teaspoon vanilla, and 1 egg (or ¼ cup liquid egg substitute) beaten with ¼ cup water. Handling lightly, pat into rounds and put on a cookie sheet. Bake for 12 to 15 minutes. *Makes 8 biscuits.*

SWEET POTATO BISCUITS: Preheat oven to 400°. To 1¼ cups Buttermilk Biscuit Mix add 1 sweet potato, baked, peeled, and mashed. (I microwave mine.) Use 1 egg and add enough water to make a stiff dough. Roll or pat out and place on cookie sheet. Bake for 12 to 15 minutes. *Makes 8 to 10 biscuits.*

GREEN ONION BISCUITS: Preheat oven to 400°. To 1 cup plus 2 tablespoons Buttermilk Biscuit Mix add:

> **5 tablespoons chopped green onions**
> **2 tablespoons cornmeal**

Mix with 1 egg (or ¼ cup liquid egg substitute) and about ¼ cup cold water to make a dough stiff enough to roll out. Cut and place on cookie sheets. Bake for 12 to 15 minutes. *Makes 8 biscuits.*

QUICK CHEESE MUFFINS: Preheat oven to 350°. Prepare 12 muffin tins by greasing the bottoms only. To 2 cups Buttermilk Biscuit Mix add:

> **2 tablespoons sugar**
> **2 tablespoons chopped green onion**
> **¼ cup grated Parmesan cheese**

Mix together:

> **2 eggs, beaten slightly, or ½ cup liquid egg substitute**
> **½ cup mayonnaise**
> **¼ cup cold water**

Stir the liquids into the biscuit mix and drop into the prepared tins. Bake for 20 to 25 minutes. *Makes 12 muffins. Recipe may be halved for 6 muffins.*

Pancake and Waffle Mix

This simple mix can go from pancakes to waffles to cake with very little work. This is another staple on my shelf. It does not have to be refrigerated.

4 cups GF Flour Mix	4 teaspoons baking powder
1 cup buttermilk powder	2 teaspoons baking soda
¼ cup sugar	4 teaspoons Egg Replacer
1½ teaspoons salt	(optional)

Combine the ingredients and mix well. Store in an airtight container on the pantry shelf. *Makes 4 batches of pancakes, waffles, or cakes.*

PANCAKES: Beat together:

> 2 eggs
> 1 cup water
> 2 tablespoons oil

Place 1⅓ cups of the Pancake and Waffle Mix in a bowl. Add the egg mixture and beat until smooth. Do not overbeat.

Drop spoonfuls of the batter onto a hot greased griddle and cook until the top is full of tiny bubbles and the underside is brown. Flip and brown the other side. *Makes ten 4" pancakes.*

WAFFLES: Place in mixing bowl:

> 1⅓ cups Pancake and Waffle Mix
> 1 tablespoon sugar
> 3 tablespoons shortening

Cut in the shortening until the mixture is very fine.
In a small bowl, beat:

> 2 eggs
> 1 cup less 1 tablespoon water

Add these to the dry ingredients. Beat just until the batter is smooth. Do not overbeat. Pour enough batter to cover on a hot waffle iron, and cook until golden. *Makes 3 or 4 waffles.*

EASY SPONGE ROLL OR SPONGE CUPCAKES: See page 182.

Dream Pastry Mix

Make this mix and keep it handy for baking pies in a hurry. This is enough for 4 batches of Dream Pastry, which makes one 2-crust pie plus an extra crust. Use it for many of the recipes in the Pies and Pastries section.

2 cups tapioca flour	4 rounded teaspoons xanthan gum
2 cups cornstarch	2 teaspoons salt
1 cup potato starch flour	2 teaspoons sugar
4 cups sweet rice flour	

Mix well and place in coffee can or plastic bag. Store it with other flours. It does not need to be refrigerated.

TO MAKE DREAM PASTRY: You will need:

2¼ cups Dream Pastry Mix	1 tablespoon GF vinegar
½ cup (1 stick) margarine	¼ cup ice water
½ cup Butter Flavor Crisco	Sweet rice flour, for rolling
1 egg, cold	

Place Dream Pastry Mix in medium bowl. Cut in the margarine and Crisco in small pieces until you have shortening the size of lima beans (not cornmeal).

Beat the egg with a fork and add the vinegar and ice water. Stir into the flour mixture, forming a ball. You may knead this a bit since it can stand handling. Refrigerate the dough for an hour or more to chill.

Divide dough and roll out on a sweet rice–floured board (or on floured plastic wrap, for easier handling). Place in a pie tin. If using plastic wrap, remove it to the pie tin and invert the dough into the pan. Shape before removing the plastic. Bake as directed for the filling used.

For a baked shell, prick the pastry with a fork on sides and bottom. Bake the crust in a preheated 450° oven for 10 to 12 minutes or until slightly browned. Cool before filling. *Makes enough pastry for a 2-crust 9″ pie plus 1 pie shell.*

TO MAKE EASY CREAM CHEESE PASTRY: You will need:

> ⅓ cup Butter Flavor Crisco
> 1 ounce cream cheese
> 1 cup Dream Pastry Mix
> ¼ cup ice water

In a food processor, blend the shortening and cream cheese. Add the Dream Pastry Mix and process a few seconds. Add the water and process until the dough forms a ball.

Place the ball in the center of a 9″ pie tin and pat out with the fingers, covering the bottom and up the sides of the pan. For a precooked filling, bake the crust first in a preheated 425° oven for 6 to 8 minutes. The crust will not brown much. Cool before filling. For a pie that is to be baked, fill the unbaked crust and follow baking directions for the pie.

TO MAKE AN OIL CRUST: To 2 cups Dream Pastry Mix add:

> 3 tablespoons cold milk or nondairy liquid
>   blended with
> ⅔ cup vegetable oil

For a pie baked with the filling, bake at the temperature suggested in your recipe. For a baked shell, bake in a preheated 450° oven for 10 to 12 minutes or until slightly browned. Cool before filling. Makes 1 crust.

MAYONNAISE CRUST: To 1⅔ cups Dream Pastry Mix add:

⅔ **cup cold mayonnaise**

Blend well and press the crumbly mix into the pie tin. If using for a pie with precooked filling, bake 10 to 12 minutes at 450°. Cool before filling. If the pie is to be baked, just add the filling and bake at the temperature the recipe suggests.

Pasta Base Mix

With this dry mix on hand, it takes only a few minutes to add the eggs and oil to turn out fresh egg pasta for dinner. In experimenting with egg substitutes in the pasta, I've found they work very well.

2 cups tapioca flour	1 tablespoon salt
2 cups cornstarch	5 tablespoons xanthan gum
¾ cup potato starch flour	

Blend the flours, salt, and xanthan gum well. Store in a covered container in a dry place. *Makes 5 batches of pasta, each making 2 to 3 servings.*

TO MAKE PASTA: Put 1 cup Pasta Base Mix in a medium mixing bowl. Mix in ½ cup liquid egg substitute or 1 egg plus 1 egg white plus 1 tablespoon vegetable oil. Stir together until this forms a ball. Work with the hands, kneading gently on a cornstarch-covered board until the dough is firm and not at all sticky. Roll out as thin as possible, using more cornstarch to dust the board, and cut into desired shape—thin spaghetti, wide noodles, lasagne shape (2" × 6") or manicotti shape (4" squares). Or put the dough through an Atlas pasta cutter.

Cook the spaghetti or noodles in boiling salted water to which a few drops of cooking oil have been added for 10 to 12 minutes or until the pasta tests done. Follow recipe directions for other shapes.

Mock Rice-A-Roni Mix 400°

Add this gluten-free form of the familiar commercial Rice-A-Roni to your shelves as a quick standby. It'll take only minutes to make up a delicious baked or stove-top pilaf to accompany plain meats.

2 cups dried GF spaghetti broken into 1-inch lengths
4 cups white rice

Preheat oven to 400°.

Place broken spaghetti in a 9" × 13" baking pan. Bake in oven, stirring occasionally, until the pasta is a rich brown color, approximately 5 minutes. Let cool before mixing with the rice. Store in a plastic container on the kitchen shelf. *Makes 6 cups or enough for 4 recipes of Mock Rice-A-Roni (page 253).*

Creamed Soup Base

This base is a time-saver when a recipe calls for 1 can of creamed soup. I keep some on hand all the time so that it is now as handy for me as canned soups used to be. A few tablespoons of this plus water or other stock (see directions below) and you can have chicken soup, mushroom soup, tomato soup, cheese soup, shrimp soup, or a cream sauce.

For vegetarians, there are some vegetable soup bases on the market. Use one of these in place of the chicken soup base.

For the lactose intolerant, use the powdered baby formula Isomil (soy) or Pregestimil (corn) instead of Lacto-Free nondairy dry powder for the best flavor.

1 cup non-instant dry milk or nondairy substitute (see note above)	½ teaspoon pepper
	½ teaspoon salt
1 cup white rice flour	3 tablespoons GF powdered chicken soup base or
2 tablespoons dried minced onions	vegetable soup base

Combine all ingredients and mix well. Store in an airtight container on your pantry shelf. *This mix is the equivalent of 8 or 9 cans of soup.*

CREAM OF CHICKEN SOUP: Blend 3 to 4 tablespoons of Creamed Soup Base with ¼ cup cold water. Add 1 cup hot or cold water (or chicken stock) and cook, stirring, until the soup thickens. Use 3 tablespoons for thin soup, 4 for a thick soup.

CREAM OF MUSHROOM SOUP: Follow the instructions for Cream of Chicken Soup, using the liquid from one 4-ounce can of mushroom bits and pieces as part of the water (reserving the mushrooms). After the soup thickens, add the mushrooms.

CREAM OF TOMATO SOUP: Follow the instructions for Cream of Chicken Soup, using one 5.5-ounce can of V-8 juice as part of the liquid.

CHEESE SOUP OR SAUCE: Follow the instructions for Cream of Chicken Soup, using ¼ cup Creamed Soup Base. Add ¼ cup extra water. Stir in ½ to ⅔ cup grated Cheddar cheese before removing from the stove.

SHRIMP SOUP OR SAUCE: Follow the instructions for Cream of Chicken Soup. Use one 8-ounce bottle clam juice plus the ¼ cup water and add one 4½-ounce can broken shrimp (drained) or ½ cup cut-up, cooked shrimp, before removing from the stove.

TASTY CREAM SAUCE: Melt 1 tablespoon butter or margarine in a small saucepan and add 1 teaspoon chopped chives or 2 thinly sliced green onions before putting in the soup base. Add 1¼ cups hot water and cook as directed for Cream of Chicken Soup.

TO USE IN A CASSEROLE: If your casserole (scalloped potatoes, etc.) calls for canned soup and is to be baked over 1 hour, just tumble the Creamed Soup Mix with the ingredients and pour on 1¼ to 1½ cups hot water.

Onion Soup Mix

This mix works like that packet on the grocery shelf but contains less sodium and is definitely gluten free. When a recipe calls for 1 packet dried onion soup, use 2 tablespoons of this mix, increasing or decreasing to your taste. I use this frequently in recipes in this book.

½ teaspoon onion powder
½ teaspoon onion salt
½ teaspoon sugar
¼ teaspoon Kitchen Bouquet
   browning sauce

1 tablespoon vegetable oil
½ cup minced dehydrated onions
1 tablespoon potato starch flour

In a small bowl, combine the onion powder, onion salt, and sugar. Add the Kitchen Bouquet and oil. Stir until the seasonings are uniformly colored.

Add the dehydrated onion and mix thoroughly until an even color is achieved. This may take several minutes. Stir in the potato starch flour to keep the flakes separated. Store in a closed container on the kitchen shelf. *Makes ½ cup mix (four packets).*

Breads

Rice-based Yeast Breads

New Formula Yeast Bread
   Quick Granola Bread
   Sunflower Seed Bread
   Banana-Nut Bread
   Orange-Raisin Bread
   Date-Nut Bread
Bette's Best Rice Bread
Old-fashioned Potato Bread
Fat-free French Bread
   Sourdough French
Cranberry-Pecan Bread
Ploughman's Lunch Bread
Fruit Bread with Cardamom
Spiced Granola Bread
Lemon-Buttermilk Bread
Single-Rising Yogurt Bread

Rice-free Yeast Breads

Mock Graham Bread
Orange Rye Bread
Nut Butter Bread
Cinnamon-Raisin Nut Bread
Orange Bean Bread
   Apple-Lemon Bread
   Raisin-Nut Bean Bread
Sesame Bean Bread
Honey-Orange Bread with
   Sesame Seeds
Dark Mock Rye Bread
Rice-free Popcorn Bread
Arrowroot (or Corn Flour)
   Bread
Cornstarch Bread
   Melba Toast

Sourdough Breads

Sourdough Starter
Heavenly Honey Sourdough

Shaped Yeast Buns and Flatbreads

Salem Crumpets
  Onion Buns
  Sesame Seed Buns
  Pizza Crust
Focaccia

Self-Rising Breads

Applesauce Bread
Spiced Banana Loaf
Rice-free Graham Crackers

Breakfast Breads

Boston Brown Bread Muffins
Vegetable Garden Muffins
Fresh Apple Muffins
My Favorite High-Fiber
    Muffins
Spicy Corn Muffins
Bagels
  Cinnamon (or Cardamom)
    Raisin Bagels
  Onion Bagels
  Sesame Bagels
Breakfast Focaccia

Uses for Stale Bread

Toasted GF Bread Crumbs
  Buttered GF Bread Crumbs

Today's new nutrition pyramid uses breads and pastas as a base for good nutrition. That means that even if we can't eat wheat, we shouldn't abandon bread and subsist on rice cakes, as we often had to do when I was first diagnosed, over twenty years ago. Thank goodness, with the magic of xanthan gum and with a lot of experimentation—and valuable help from fellow celiacs—I've found that we can make breads of just about every other gluten-free grain, root, or bean that's ground into fine flour. Yes, beans, corn, arrowroot, tapioca, and soy do make excellent breads—in a variety of combinations.

The catch is, to have a variety we have to make our own. But with the wonderful time-saving bread machines on the market we can toss in the ingredients and have bread kneading, rising, and baking while we're out of the house or sleeping (I start mine after the dinner dishes are done and let it work while I sleep). Of course, if we have the time we can make bread using a heavy-duty mixer or, in some cases, a light handheld model. Whatever way it's made, the bread from beans, corn, or rice can be just as tasty as any traditional loaf.

And if you've been missing some of the old treats such as bagels or focaccia, they're waiting for you on the following pages. This chapter also contains some old favorites, such as a lighter sourdough, a fat-free French bread with a crust so crunchy one thinks of Paris, and several high-fiber bean breads so delicious I serve them with pride at luncheons and dinner parties.

As many of the breads in this section have only bread machine directions, here are my new directions for hand mixing breads if you do not have a bread machine. (These rules also apply to any bread recipes given for a bread machine in *More from the Gluten-free Gourmet*.)

Directions for Hand Mixing Breads

For best results, double the yeast and add two to three tablespoons more liquid to any bread machine recipe.

Prepare three small 3½″ × 7¼″ pans, or two 4¼″ × 8¼″ pans, or one large 5″ × 9¼″ bread pan as well as several muffin cups, by spraying them with vegetable oil spray and dusting them with rice flour. (This applies to recipes containing approximately 3 cups flour. Adjust the number of pans if using a 2-cup recipe.)

In a medium bowl, place all the dry ingredients except 1 teaspoon of the sugar. Dissolve this sugar in the amount of water called for in the recipe (the water should be lukewarm) and add the yeast. Set aside to foam. (If the recipe calls for a different liquid, such as orange juice, replace ½ cup of this liquid with water in which to dissolve the yeast.)

Break the eggs into the bowl of a heavy-duty mixer. Add the oil, melted shortening, or margarine, plus any liquid sweetener such as molasses or honey, and vinegar or dough enhancer. Using the heavy beater (not the dough hook), beat lightly on low speed. Add the yeast water. Add the flour mix gradually. (If you dump the flour in all at once, it will be all over the kitchen.)

Beat at the highest speed for 3½ minutes.

Spoon the dough directly into your prepared pans, filling them ⅔ full. The overflow from the large pan will make several muffins.

Let the dough rise until it is slightly above the top of the pan (or has doubled in bulk), 45 to 60 minutes for regular yeast, about 30 to 35 minutes for rapid-rising yeast.

Preheat oven to 400°. Bake the large loaf for approximately 1 hour, small loaves for 40 to 45 minutes, and rolls for about 25 minutes. Cover with foil after 15 minutes to avoid burning the top. To test breads for doneness, tap gently with finger. Bread will have a slightly hollow sound. Remove from pan immediately to cool. Enjoy!

If all of this seems just too much work for you or too time consuming, I'd be remiss not to mention that the list of suppliers of bread items is growing, and many of them are also making up mixes for both the bread machine and a heavy-duty mixer. These, too, are more tasty than ever before. See pages 376–81 for the long list of suppliers.

The recipes in this book often call for one of my three basic mixes: GF Flour Mix, Bread Flour Mix, or Light or Dark Bean Flour Mix. I keep all but the Bread Flour Mix in large quantities. The formulas for these are:

GF FLOUR MIX (can be stored in dry cupboard):

> 2 parts white rice flour
> ⅔ part potato starch flour
> ⅓ part tapioca flour

BREAD FLOUR MIX (must be stored in refrigerator or freezer):

> 1 part white rice flour
> 1 part brown rice flour
> ⅔ part potato starch flour
> ⅓ part tapioca flour

BEAN FLOUR MIX (can be stored in dry cupboard):

> 1 part light or dark bean flour
> 1 part cornstarch
> 1 part tapioca flour

New Formula Yeast Bread

(with Five Variations)

In this bread, developed from my original True Yeast Bread in The Gluten-free Gourmet, *I've lowered the cholesterol and sodium. I've also given directions for both the 1½-pound breadmaker and the 1-pound one. Use this as a basic formula for all your bread experiments with additions of seeds, nuts, or fruits. For a white bread use the GF Flour Mix; for more fiber use the Bread Flour Mix. For hand-mixing directions, see page 68.*

FOR 1½-POUND BREADMAKER

DRY INGREDIENTS

3 cups GF Flour Mix or
  Bread Flour Mix
2 tablespoons Potato Buds
2½ teaspoons xanthan gum
1 teaspoon unflavored gelatin
1 teaspoon salt
1 teaspoon Egg Replacer
  (optional)
¼ cup dry milk powder or
  nondairy substitute
¼ cup sugar

WET INGREDIENTS

1 egg plus 2 egg whites, or ⅔
  cup liquid egg substitute
3 tablespoons margarine,
  melted
1 teaspoon vinegar or dough
  enhancer
1 tablespoon molasses
1⅔ cups water
2¼ teaspoons (1 packet) dry
  yeast

FOR 1-POUND BREADMAKER

DRY INGREDIENTS

2 cups GF Flour Mix or
  Bread Flour Mix
4 teaspoons Potato Buds
1¾ teaspoons xanthan gum
⅔ teaspoon unflavored gelatin
⅔ teaspoon salt

WET INGREDIENTS

1 egg plus 1 egg white, or ½
  cup liquid egg substitute
2 tablespoons margarine,
  melted
⅔ teaspoon vinegar or dough
  enhancer

1 teaspoon Egg Replacer (optional)	2 teaspoons molasses
3 tablespoons dry milk powder or nondairy substitute	¾ cup plus 2 tablespoons water
3 tablespoons sugar	1¾ teaspoons dry yeast

In a bowl, combine the flour mix, Potato Buds, xanthan gum, gelatin, salt, Egg Replacer (if used), milk powder, and sugar. In another bowl, whisk the eggs slightly and add the margarine, vinegar, molasses, and water (at the temperature suggested by your breadmaker's manual). Place in the breadmaker in the order suggested on page 42. Add yeast to dry ingredients in round-pan breadmakers; put it in a well on top of flour in square upright or rectangular models. Use the setting for white bread with a medium crust.

QUICK GRANOLA BREAD: Add 1 cup crushed granola (or substitute ¾ cup crushed GF cereal plus ½ cup chopped dried fruit) to the dry ingredients. You may need 2 to 3 tablespoons extra water. (Add after mix starts kneading, to judge amount.)

SUNFLOWER SEED BREAD: Chop ½ cup sunflower seeds in food processor. Add to the dry ingredients. You may need 1 to 2 tablespoons additional water. (Add after mix starts kneading, to judge amount needed.)

BANANA-NUT BREAD: Replace white sugar with ⅓ cup brown sugar and add ⅓ cup nuts to the dry ingredients. To the wet ingredients add 1 large or 2 small mashed bananas. Lower water amount by 2 tablespoons.

ORANGE-RAISIN BREAD: Eliminate the dry milk powder. Cut the sugar to 3 rounded tablespoons. Add 1 teaspoon baking soda, ½ cup raisins, 2 tablespoons orange zest, and ¼ cup NutQuik or finely ground almonds to the dry ingredients. Replace the water with orange juice heated to the temperature your manual calls for. Use Light setting or cut baking time by 5 minutes.

DATE-NUT BREAD: Use Bread Flour Mix. Add ½ cup chopped dates, ½ cup chopped walnuts (or other nuts), and 1 teaspoon dried orange peel to the dry ingredients.

Bette's Best Rice Bread

If you don't like tapioca flour in your bread, try this all-rice recipe. The flavor is delicious, although the texture is not quite as springy as the New Formula Bread. If cholesterol is no problem for you, you may use 2 large eggs in place of the Egg Replacer.

Directions for making this bread with a heavy-duty mixer will be found on page 68.

FOR 1½-POUND BREADMAKER

DRY INGREDIENTS

1 cup fine brown rice flour
2 cups fine white rice flour
1 tablespoon xanthan gum
1 teaspoon Egg Replacer
1 teaspoon salt
¼ cup dry milk powder or nondairy substitute
½ cup sugar
1 teaspoon unflavored gelatin

WET INGREDIENTS

1 egg plus 2 egg whites, or ⅔ cup liquid egg substitute
4 tablespoons margarine, melted
1 teaspoon vinegar or dough enhancer
1 tablespoon molasses
1½ cups (scant) water
2¼ teaspoons (1 packet) dry yeast

FOR 1-POUND BREADMAKER

DRY INGREDIENTS

⅔ cup brown rice flour

1⅓ cups white rice flour

2 teaspoons xanthan gum

1 teaspoon Egg Replacer

¾ teaspoon salt

3 tablespoons dry milk powder

3 tablespoons sugar

⅔ teaspoon unflavored gelatin

WET INGREDIENTS

1 egg plus 1 egg white, or ½ cup liquid egg substitute

3 tablespoons margarine, melted

⅔ teaspoon vinegar or dough enhancer

2 teaspoons molasses

¾ cup plus 1 tablespoon water

1¾ teaspoons dry yeast or ⅔ yeast cake

In a bowl, combine the flours, xanthan gum, Egg Replacer, salt, milk powder, sugar, and gelatin. In another bowl, whisk the eggs slightly and add the margarine, vinegar, molasses, and water (at the temperature suggested in your breadmaker's manual). Place in breadmaker in the order suggested on page 42. Add yeast to dry ingredients for round pans; put it in a well on top for square upright or rectangular models. Use setting for white bread with a medium crust.

Old-fashioned Potato Bread

In this bread I found that old-fashioned taste of my mother's moist, fresh loaf made with fermented potato water, even though this recipe uses yeast. It takes just minutes to put together for your breadmaker. (Whirl the potato in your food processor to save time.) If you don't have a bread machine, follow the directions on page 68 for making bread by hand.

3 cups GF Flour Mix or Bread Flour Mix	¾ cup peeled and grated raw potato (approx. one fist-sized potato)
2½ teaspoons xanthan gum	
¼ cup nonfat dry milk powder or nondairy substitute	1 egg plus 2 egg whites
1½ teaspoons salt	3 tablespoons margarine or butter, melted
1½ teaspoons Egg Replacer (optional)	1 teaspoon vinegar or dough enhancer
3 tablespoons sugar	1¼ cups water
1 teaspoon unflavored gelatin	1½ teaspoons dry yeast

Combine flours, xanthan gum, milk powder, salt, Egg Replacer (if used), sugar, and gelatin. Stir in the potato.

Beat the eggs. Add melted margarine, vinegar, and water (warm or cool). Place ingredients in your breadmaker in the order suggested on page 42. Add yeast to dry ingredients in round-pan models; put it in a well on top in square upright or rectangular models. Use the setting for white bread with a medium crust.

Fat-free French Bread 400°

Finally, we've found a French bread that looks, tastes, and tears apart like real French bread. The crust is so crunchy you can almost smell the bread ovens of Paris. This recipe is quick and easy, for it needs only a simple handheld mixer or a heavy-duty mixer on medium speed. It's wonderful for the diabetic celiac since it takes only 1½ teaspoons of sugar.

2 cups plus 2 tablespoons GF Flour Mix	2 teaspoons quick-rising yeast
2½ teaspoons xanthan gum	1 teaspoon vinegar or dough enhancer
1½ teaspoons sugar	2 egg whites (room temperature)
1 teaspoon salt	1½ cups warm water (110°–115°)

Prepare a French bread pan by spraying with vegetable oil, or curve a doubled piece of heavy foil about the length of your cookie sheet to form a mold and spray this.

In the bowl of your mixer, combine the flour mix, xanthan gum, sugar, salt, and yeast. Whisk together to blend well. Add the vinegar, egg whites, and water. Beat at medium speed for 3 minutes. Spoon dough into the mold to almost the full length. Smooth the top. Cover and let rise for 15 minutes. Preheat oven to 400°.

Bake for 1 hour. Turn oven to 350° and bake 15 minutes longer. To eat it hot and crusty, tear it apart; it won't cut until it's cool. The bread keeps for several days but the crust gets more tender with time.

SOURDOUGH FRENCH: Add 1½ teaspoons Sourdough Starter (page 93) to the liquids before beating them in.

Cranberry-Pecan Bread

Dried cranberries and toasted pecans make this "party" bread so tasty your guests will never guess it's gluten free. Directions are for the bread machine. For hand mixing see page 68.

3 cups Bread Flour Mix
2½ teaspoons xanthan gum
½ cup dry milk powder or
    nondairy substitute
1 teaspoon salt
1 teaspoon unflavored gelatin
¼ teaspoon cloves
1 teaspoon cinnamon
1 tablespoon dried orange peel
2 teaspoons Egg Replacer
    (optional)

¼ cup dried cranberries,
    chopped
¼ cup toasted pecans, chopped
¼ cup sugar
1 egg plus 2 egg whites
1 teaspoon vinegar or dough
    enhancer
3 tablespoons margarine or
    vegetable shortening, melted
1⅔ cups water
2¼ teaspoons (1 packet) dry
    yeast

Blend together the Bread Flour Mix, xanthan gum, milk powder, salt, gelatin, cloves, cinnamon, orange peel, Egg Replacer (if used), cranberries, pecans, yeast, and sugar.

In a small bowl, beat the eggs slightly. Add the vinegar, melted margarine, and water (at the temperature suggested in your bread machine manual).

Place ingredients in the baking pan of the machine in the order suggested on page 42. Add yeast to dry ingredients in round-pan models; put it in a well on top in square upright or rectangular models. Use the setting for white bread with a medium crust.

Ploughman's Lunch Bread

With its flavor of onion and cheese, this bread reminds me of the wonderfully rich bread served with a Ploughman's Lunch in an English pub. It tastes great with cheese, strong meats, or soups and stews. See page 68 for hand-mixing directions.

3 cups Bread Flour Mix
2½ teaspoons xanthan gum
1 teaspoon salt
2 teaspoons Egg Replacer (optional)
½ cup dry milk powder or nondairy substitute
1 teaspoon unflavored gelatin
2 teaspoons dry mustard
3 tablespoons minced fresh onion
1 cup sharp Cheddar cheese, grated

1 teaspoon celery seeds
3 rounded tablespoons sugar
1 egg plus 2 egg whites, or ⅔ cup liquid egg substitute
3 tablespoons margarine, melted, or 3 tablespoons oil
1 teaspoon vinegar or dough enhancer
1⅔ cups water
2¼ teaspoons (1 packet) dry yeast

In a bowl, combine the flour mix, xanthan gum, salt, Egg Replacer (if used), milk powder, gelatin, mustard, onion, cheese, celery seeds, and sugar. In another bowl, beat the eggs and add the margarine, vinegar, and water (at the temperature suggested by your breadmaker's manual). Place in breadmaker in the order suggested on page 42. Add yeast to dry ingredients in round-pan models; put it in a well on top in square upright or rectangular models. Use the setting for white bread with a medium crust.

Fruit Bread with Cardamom

A tester added fruit and cardamon to my Basic Yeast Bread and came up with a delicious fruited treat, wonderful for breakfast toast.

Note: You can purchase fruit bits already chopped or cut your own. The bits usually are a mix of dried apricots, pears, apples, and prunes. Add a few chopped candied cherries for more color and flavor, if desired.

3 cups GF Flour Mix	¼ cup sugar
2½ teaspoons xanthan gum	1 egg plus 2 egg whites, or ⅔
1 teaspoon salt	cup liquid egg substitute
2 teaspoons Egg Replacer (optional)	3 tablespoons margarine or butter, melted
¼ cup dry milk powder or nondairy substitute	1 teaspoon vinegar or dough enhancer
1 teaspoon unflavored gelatin	1⅔ cups water (scant)
2 teaspoons cardamom	2¼ teaspoons (1 packet) dry
1 teaspoon dried lemon peel	yeast
¾ cup finely chopped mixed dried fruit	

In a bowl, combine the flour mix, xanthan gum, salt, Egg Replacer (if used), milk powder, gelatin, cardamom, lemon peel, fruit, and sugar.

In another bowl, whisk the eggs and add the margarine, vinegar, and water (at the temperature suggested by your breadmaker's manual). Place in the breadmaker in the order suggested on page 42. Add yeast to dry ingredients in round-pan models; put it in a well on top in square upright or rectangular ones. Use the setting for white bread with a medium crust.

Spiced Granola Bread

Sweet, spicy, and delicious—and wonderful for toast! The recipe calls for Bread Flour Mix but you can substitute my GF Flour Mix. I've given only bread machine directions. If you don't have a machine, follow hand-mixing directions, page 68.

1 cup GF cereal, crushed
3 cups Bread Flour Mix
1 teaspoon cardamom or cinnamon
1 teaspoon dried orange peel
2½ teaspoons xanthan gum
1½ teaspoons salt
½ cup dry milk powder or nondairy substitute
1½ teaspoons Egg Replacer (optional)

¼ cup sugar (slightly more if desired)
1 egg plus 2 egg whites
3 tablespoons Butter Flavor Crisco, melted
1 teaspoon vinegar, or 2 teaspoons dough enhancer
1⅔ cups water
2¼ teaspoons (1 packet) dry yeast

In a bowl, combine the crushed cereal, flour mix, cardamom, orange peel, xanthan gum, salt, milk powder, and Egg Replacer (if used). In another bowl, whisk the eggs slightly and add the melted shortening, vinegar, and water (at the temperature suggested by your breadmaker's manual). Place in breadmaker in order suggested on page 42. Add yeast to dry ingredients in round-pan models; put it in a well on top in square upright or rectangular ones. Use the setting for white bread with a medium crust.

Lemon-Buttermilk Bread

Light, tender, and chewy with a delicate lemon taste, this bread is great for eating plain with butter or margarine or in any kind of sandwich. The directions given are for the breadmaker. If you don't have one, follow the directions on page 68 for making bread by hand.

3 cups GF Flour Mix
2½ teaspoons xanthan gum
½ cup buttermilk powder
½ teaspoon baking soda
1½ teaspoons salt
2 teaspoons Egg Replacer
  (optional)
1 tablespoon lemon zest

5 tablespoons sugar
1 egg plus 2 egg whites
4 tablespoons margarine or
  butter, melted
3 tablespoons lemon juice
1⅔ cups water
2¼ teaspoons (1 packet) dry yeast

In a medium bowl, combine the flour mix, xanthan gum, buttermilk powder, baking soda, salt, Egg Replacer (if used), lemon zest, and sugar.

In another bowl, whisk the eggs lightly and add the melted margarine, lemon juice, and water (at the temperature suggested in your breadmaker's manual).

Place the ingredients in your breadmaker in the order suggested on page 42. Add the yeast to dry ingredients in round-pan models; place it in a well on top in square upright or rectangular ones. Use the setting for white bread with a medium crust.

Single-Rising Yogurt Bread 350°

If you don't have a breadmaker and want to make a quick loaf, this single-rising white bread is a good choice. It's light and chewy, and soy gives extra flavor. Stir it up, wait only 45 minutes for rising, then pop it into the oven.

1¾ cups GF Flour Mix	1 tablespoon dry yeast
¼ cup soy flour	¾ cup plain yogurt
1½ teaspoons xanthan gum	4 tablespoons (½ stick)
¼ teaspoon salt	margarine or butter, cut into
1½ teaspoons Egg Replacer	pieces
(optional)	2 eggs or ½ cup liquid egg
⅓ cup warm water	substitute
1 tablespoon honey	1 teaspoon dough enhancer
	(optional)

Grease and dust with rice flour a 4″ × 8″ loaf pan.

In a small mixing bowl, blend the flour mix, soy flour, xanthan gum, salt, and Egg Replacer (if used). Set aside.

Measure the water and stir in the honey. Add the yeast and let it dissolve.

Put the yogurt in a microwave-safe bowl and add the margarine. Microwave on Defrost for 3 minutes to melt the margarine and warm the yogurt. (Test to be sure it is just lukewarm.)

In the bowl of your mixer, place the yogurt and yeast water and add the eggs and dough enhancer (if used). Beat for a few seconds. Add the flour and beat on High for 2 minutes. Turn into your prepared loaf pan. Cover and let rise in a warm place for approximately 45 minutes or until doubled in size. Bake in a 350° preheated oven for 50 minutes or until the loaf tests done by sounding hollow when rapped. Turn out immediately onto a board to cool.

Mock Graham Bread

(Rice Free)

One of my basic breads. It tastes so much like my mother's graham bread that I feel I'm sitting in our old farm kitchen savoring the smell of her seven fresh loaves as she pulls them from the oven of the cast-iron wood range. Even then I must have been a celiac for, much as I loved the taste, her graham wheat bread always gave me a stomachache.

For hand-mixing directions, see page 68.

DRY INGREDIENTS

3 cups Light Bean Flour Mix (page 69)

½ cup popcorn flour

2½ teaspoons xanthan gum

1 teaspoon salt

3 tablespoons maple or brown sugar

1 teaspoon Egg Replacer (optional)

1 teaspoon unflavored gelatin

WET INGREDIENTS

1 egg plus 2 egg whites, or ⅔ cup liquid egg substitute

1 teaspoon vinegar or 2 teaspoons dough enhancer

3 tablespoons vegetable oil

2 tablespoons maple syrup (or honey)

1¾ cups plus 1 tablespoon water

2¼ teaspoons (1 packet) dry yeast

In a bowl, combine the flours, xanthan gum, salt, brown sugar, Egg Replacer (if used), and gelatin. In another bowl, whisk the eggs slightly and add the vinegar, vegetable oil, maple syrup, and water (at the temperature suggested in your breadmaker's manual). Place in the machine in the order suggested on page 42. Add yeast to dry ingredients for round-pan models; put it in a well on top for square upright or rectangular ones. Bake on Light or cut the baking time by 5 minutes from regular loaf.

Orange Rye Bread

(Rice, Soy, and Lactose Free)

At a national meeting, a group of celiacs who tasted my first try at this bread said, "Don't change a thing." This is a dark bread, but the flavor lends itself well to any sandwich filling. I've given only bread machine directions. Hand-mixing directions are on page 68.

3 cups Light or Dark Bean
  Flour Mix (page 69)
2½ teaspoons xanthan gum
1 scant teaspoon salt
1 teaspoon Egg Replacer
  (optional)
Zest of 1 orange or 2 teaspoons
  dried orange peel
3 tablespoons brown sugar
1 teaspoon unflavored gelatin
4 teaspoons caraway seeds

1 egg plus 2 egg whites,
  or ⅔ cup liquid egg
  substitute
1 teaspoon vinegar or 2
  teaspoons dough enhancer
3 tablespoons vegetable oil
3 tablespoons molasses
1½ cups orange juice
2¼ teaspoons (1 packet)
  dry yeast

Whisk together the bean flour mix, xanthan gum, salt, Egg Replacer (if used), orange zest, brown sugar, gelatin, and caraway seeds.

In another bowl, blend the eggs, vinegar, oil, molasses, and orange juice. Place in breadmaker in order suggested on page 42. Add yeast to dry ingredients in round-pan models; place it in a well on top in square upright or rectangular ones. Use the sweet bread cycle or, on a programmable machine, cut the baking time by 5 minutes from regular bread.

Nut Butter Bread

(Rice, Lactose, and Soy Free)

When this bean bread is toasted and served with jam, the very slight nut fla-vor is absolutely wonderful. It's also tasty eaten plain or with cheese. Try this with peanut, almond, macadamia, or mixed nut butters.

1 cup garbanzo bean flour
   or light bean flour
1 cup cornstarch
¾ cup tapioca flour
2½ teaspoons xanthan gum
¾ teaspoon salt
1 teaspoon unflavored gelatin
3 tablespoons maple or
   brown sugar
1 teaspoon Egg Replacer
   (optional)

1 egg plus 2 egg whites, or
   ⅔ cup liquid egg substitute
¼ cup nut butter (creamy or
   chunky): peanut, macadamia,
   or mixed nut
1 teaspoon vinegar or dough
   enhancer
1½ cups water
2¼ teaspoons (1 packet) dry
   yeast

In a bowl, combine the bean flour, cornstarch, and tapioca flour. Add the xanthan gum, salt, gelatin, brown sugar, and Egg Replacer (if used). In another bowl, whisk the eggs slightly and add the nut butter and vinegar. Whisk smooth. Add the water at the temperature suggested in your bread-maker's manual.

Place in the baking machine in the order suggested on page 42. Add yeast to dry ingredients for round-pan models; put it in a well on top for square upright or rectangular ones. Set on white bread at light crust. If you have a programmable breadmaker, cut the baking time to about 5 minutes less than what you used for a rice flour loaf.

Cinnamon-Raisin-Nut Bread 350°

(Rice and Lactose Free)

Smells wonderful while baking and tastes delicious. The bean flour mix is especially good in flavored breads. You don't need a breadmaker for this single-rising loaf, nor do you need a lot of time.

2 cups Light or Dark Bean
   Flour Mix (page 69)
1 tablespoon maple or brown
   sugar
1½ teaspoons xanthan gum
½ teaspoon salt
1 teaspoon dried orange peel
1 teaspoon cinnamon
2 teaspoons Egg Replacer
   (optional)
¼ cup raisins

¼ cup chopped nuts
⅓ cup lukewarm water
2 tablespoons honey
1 tablespoon dry yeast
¾ cup orange juice (lukewarm)
1 egg plus 1 egg white, or ½ cup
   liquid egg substitute
1 teaspoon vinegar or dough
   enhancer
3 tablespoons margarine or
   butter, melted

Spray a 4" × 8" loaf pan with vegetable oil spray.

In a small mixing bowl, blend the bean flour mix, brown sugar, xanthan gum, salt, orange peel, cinnamon, and Egg Replacer (if used). Stir in the raisins and nuts. Put aside.

In a measuring cup, mix the water and honey. Add the yeast and let dissolve. In the bowl of your heavy-duty mixer, place the yeast water and orange juice and add eggs, dough enhancer, and melted margarine. Using the heavy beater (not dough hook), beat for a few seconds. Add the flour mix and beat on High for 2 minutes. Turn into your prepared loaf pan. Cover and let rise in a warm place for approximately 1 hour (should about double in bulk). Bake in a preheated 350° oven for 50 minutes or until the loaf tests done by sounding hollow when rapped. Turn out immediately onto a board to cool.

Orange Bean Bread

(Rice, Soy, and Lactose Free)

Use gluten-free bean bread as a tasty alternative to rice bread. Try this loaf either as it is presented here or try the variations below. See the list of suppliers in the back of the book for the bean flours.

1 cup dark or light bean flour
1 cup cornstarch
¾ cup tapioca flour
2½ teaspoons xanthan gum
1 teaspoon salt
1 teaspoon dried orange peel
3 tablespoons brown sugar
1 teaspoon Egg Replacer
   (optional)

1 teaspoon unflavored gelatin
1 egg plus 2 egg whites, or ⅔
   cup liquid egg substitute
3 tablespoons margarine or
   butter, melted
1 teaspoon vinegar or dough
   enhancer
1⅔ cups orange juice
2¼ teaspoons (1 packet) dry
   yeast

In a bowl, combine the bean flour, cornstarch, and tapioca flour. Add the xanthan gum, salt, orange peel, brown sugar, Egg Replacer (if used), and gelatin. In another bowl, whisk the eggs and add the margarine, vinegar, and orange juice.

Place in the breadmaker in the order suggested on page 42. Add the yeast to the dry ingredients for the round-pan model; place it in a well on top for the square upright or rectangular ones. Set on white bread at light crust. If you have a programmable breadmaker, cut the baking time to about 5 to 10 minutes less than what you used for a rice flour loaf.

APPLE-LEMON BREAD: Change the peel to lemon peel and use apple juice in place of the orange juice.

RAISIN-NUT BEAN BREAD: Add 1 teaspoon cardamom or 1 teaspoon cinnamon, ⅓ cup raisins, and ⅓ cup chopped nuts.

Sesame Bean Bread

My favorite bread—the springy texture resembles wheat bread, while the mild grain flavor is perfect for sandwiches and toast. This stays fresh-tasting for several days. For hand mixing, see the directions on page 68.

DRY INGREDIENTS
- 3 cups Light or Dark Bean Flour Mix (page 69)
- 2½ teaspoons xanthan gum
- 1 teaspoon salt
- 1 teaspoon unflavored gelatin
- 3 tablespoons brown sugar
- 1 teaspoon Egg Replacer (optional)
- 2 tablespoons sesame seeds

WET INGREDIENTS
- 1 egg plus 2 egg whites
- 4 tablespoons margarine or butter, cut into pieces
- 1 teaspoon vinegar or dough enhancer
- 1 tablespoon molasses
- 1½ cups water (scant)
- 2¼ teaspoons (1 packet) dry yeast

In a medium bowl, combine the flour mix, xanthan gum, salt, gelatin, brown sugar, egg replacer (if used), and sesame seeds.

Beat the eggs slightly and add the margarine, vinegar, molasses, and water (at the temperature suggested by your machine's manual).

Place in the breadmaker in the order suggested on page 42. Add yeast to the dry ingredients for round-pan models; put it in a well on top for square upright or rectangular models. Use a Medium setting on your bread machine.

Honey-Orange Bread with Sesame Seeds

(Rice, Soy, and Lactose Free)

Taste this flavorful, high-protein loaf and you'll understand why testers call this wonderful!

1 cup garbanzo bean flour
1 cup cornstarch or arrowroot flour
1 cup tapioca flour
2½ teaspoons xanthan gum
1 teaspoon salt
1 tablespoon Egg Replacer (optional)
3 tablespoons brown sugar
1 teaspoon unflavored gelatin
4 teaspoons toasted sesame seeds

Zest of 1 orange or 2 teaspoons dried orange peel
1 egg plus 2 egg whites, or ⅔ cup liquid egg substitute
1 teaspoon vinegar, or 2 teaspoons dough enhancer
3 tablespoons vegetable oil
3 tablespoons honey or molasses
1⅔ cups orange juice (see note)
2¼ teaspoons (1 packet) dry yeast

In a medium bowl, mix together the bean flour, cornstarch, tapioca flour, xanthan gum, salt, Egg Replacer (if used), brown sugar, gelatin, sesame seeds, and orange zest.

In another bowl, beat the eggs slightly and add the vinegar, oil, honey, and orange juice (at the temperature suggested by your machine's manual).

Place in the breadmaker in the order suggested on page 42. Add the yeast to the dry ingredients for the round-pan models; put it in a well on top for the square upright or rectangular ones. Use the setting for sweet bread on a Light cycle. On a programmable machine, cut the baking time by 5 minutes.

Note: To heat the orange juice, put in microwave on High for about 35 to 45 seconds. Be sure to stir before testing the temperature.

Dark Mock Rye Bread

(Rice, Soy, and Lactose Free)

This very dark, flavorful bread will fool anyone into thinking it is made with wheat and rye, but look at the unusual flours! Use this with appetizers or as a wonderful accompaniment to soups and stews. I've given instructions for the bread machine. If you wish to make the bread by hand, follow the directions on page 68.

1 cup dark or light bean flour	1 egg plus 2 egg whites, or
¾ cup tapioca flour	⅔ cup liquid egg substitute
1 cup cornstarch	1 teaspoon vinegar, or 1
2½ teaspoons xanthan gum	tablespoon dough enhancer
1 teaspoon unflavored gelatin	3 tablespoons vegetable oil
1 teaspoon salt	3 tablespoons molasses
2 teaspoons dried orange peel	1⅔ cups water (scant)
4 teaspoons caraway seeds	2¼ teaspoons (1 packet) dry
2 tablespoons brown sugar	yeast
1 tablespoon freeze-dried coffee	

In a bowl, combine the flours and cornstarch, xanthan gum, gelatin, salt, orange peel, caraway seeds, brown sugar, and coffee. In another bowl, beat the eggs slightly and add the vinegar, oil, molasses, and water (at the temperature suggested by the breadmaker's manual.) Place in breadmaker in order suggested on page 42. Add the yeast to dry ingredients for machines with round pans; put it in a well on top for square upright or rectangular pans. Use the sweet bread cycle, or, on a programmable machine, cut the baking time by 5 minutes from that used for regular bread.

Rice-free Popcorn Bread

Surprisingly, this does not taste like a corn bread but more like an old-fashioned whole wheat bread. I've given two choices for one of the flours: either cornstarch or arrowroot flour. The arrowroot keeps the bread fresh-tasting longer, but for either, the bread slices can be brought back to just-baked freshness by microwaving for about 25 to 35 seconds. See the suppliers on pages 376–81 for the popcorn flour.

1 cup popcorn flour
1 cup arrowroot flour or cornstarch
⅔ cup potato starch flour
⅓ cup tapioca flour
1 teaspoon Egg Replacer (optional)
2½ teaspoons xanthan gum
1 teaspoon salt
1 teaspoon unflavored gelatin

½ cup non-instant dry milk powder or nondairy substitute
1 egg plus 2 egg whites
1 teaspoon vinegar or dough enhancer
¼ cup vegetable oil
¼ cup honey
1½ cups water (scant)
2¼ teaspoons (1 packet) dry yeast

In a medium bowl, combine the flours, Egg Replacer (if used), xanthan gum, salt, gelatin, and milk powder. In another bowl, beat the egg and whites slightly and add the vinegar, oil, honey, and water (at the temperature suggested by your breadmaker's manual). Place in your breadmaker in the order suggested on page 42. Add the yeast to the dry ingredients for machines with round pans; put it in a well at top for square upright or rectangular pans. Set at medium crust. For hand-mixing directions, see page 68.

Arrowroot (or Corn Flour) Bread

(Rice Free)

This wonderfully soft white bread was created especially for those who cannot have wheat and are allergic to rice. It is great for sandwiches when fresh and for toasting anytime. Although it dries out more quickly than rice bread, it can taste like fresh if microwaved for about 25 seconds. For hand-mixing directions, see page 68.

1 cup arrowroot (or corn) flour
1 cup cornstarch
⅔ cup potato starch flour
⅓ cup tapioca flour
2 tablespoons Potato Buds
2½ teaspoons xanthan gum
1 teaspoon salt
1 teaspoon unflavored gelatin

½ cup non-instant dry milk powder or nondairy substitute
1 egg
1 teaspoon vinegar or dough enhancer
¼ cup vegetable oil
3 tablespoons honey
1½ cups water (scant)
2¼ teaspoons (1 packet) dry yeast

In a medium bowl, combine the flours, Potato Buds, xanthan gum, salt, gelatin, and dry milk. In another bowl, beat the egg slightly and add the vinegar, oil, honey, and water (at the temperature suggested by your breadmaker's manual). Place in your breadmaker in the order suggested on page 42. Add the yeast to the dry ingredients for machines with round pans; put it in a well at top for square upright or rectangular pans. Set at white bread on medium crust.

Cornstarch Bread 450°

(and Melba Toast)

"Closest thing we have to Wonder Bread," one celiac raved. Then she told me about the fantastic Melba toast she makes from the bread. She's right on both counts. Eat the bread the day you make it and use the rest for the toast. Carry this as a snack, use it for hors d'oeuvres, have enough for any trip (it keeps so well), or just slather it with jam and crunch it for breakfast. This doesn't take a breadmaker or even a heavy-duty mixer. Make this in one hour!

Note: If you want a rice-free bread, eliminate the rice flour and reduce the water by 2 tablespoons. The flavor may be varied by using, in place of the ground pecans, 1 teaspoon dill, ⅓ cup dried apple fiber (available in health food stores), or other kinds of nuts.

2½ cups cornstarch	¼ cup sugar
⅓ cup potato starch flour	1½ teaspoons xanthan gum
2 tablespoons sweet rice flour	3 tablespoons finely ground
2 tablespoons dried egg white	pecans or walnuts
or 1 large egg white	2 cups hot water (about 120°)
4½ teaspoons (2 packets) dry	2½ tablespoons vegetable oil
yeast	1½ teaspoons salt

In the bowl of your mixer, combine the cornstarch, potato starch flour, sweet rice flour (if used), dried egg white, yeast, sugar, xanthan gum, and ground pecans or walnuts. Whisk to mix. Add the water (mixed with the egg white if using fresh egg) and beat vigorously about 2 minutes on Medium if using a heavy-duty mixer, 3 to 4 minutes on High with a hand-held mixer. Cover and let stand 15 minutes. The dough will be very thin. While waiting, spray two 4¼″ × 8¼″ loaf pans with vegetable oil spray. Pre-heat oven to 450°.

Add the vegetable oil and salt, beating until smooth and well mixed. Pour batter into the prepared pans and let rise, covered, about 20 minutes, until the batter is just level with the top of the pan.

Bake for 25 minutes or until golden brown. Cover with a towel and let cool for 10 minutes. Turn out to cool. This bread is so soft it cannot be sliced until cooled to room temperature. If you don't eat it all on the first day, store in the freezer or make the following Melba toast.

MELBA TOAST: When the loaf is cooled, cut the crusts from all sides of loaf, slice the bread thin, cut slices to desired size. Place in a single layer on a cookie sheet. Bake at 200° to 225° until dry and very light brown (about 1 hour). Cool and store in an airtight container. Keeps well for 1 month.

[Adapted from a recipe by R. W. Shortridge received at the 1992 Kansas City celiac meeting.]

Sourdough Breads

If you're hungry for the smell and taste of real sourdough, hunger no more. Our rice flour lends itself well to sourdough breads and makes a fine sourdough starter. Keeping a starter going is the real secret of having sourdough any time you wish. The starter is made, fermented, and then replenished with each use, or once a week if you haven't baked sourdough in that time. Just discard about ¾ cup old starter and add ½ cup lukewarm water and ¾ cup rice flour to what's in the crock. The older the starter, the more taste the bread will have.

The starter should be made at least one day before you plan to bake. Then it can be stored in its crock or glass jar (never metal or plastic) in the kitchen or placed in the refrigerator. If refrigerated, it should be pulled out at least 10 hours before baking, or the night before. I bake so often, I leave my starter out on the kitchen drainboard except when I am going on vacation. Then I freeze it and let it come back to life as soon as I return.

SOURDOUGH STARTER:

> 2¼ teaspoons (1 packet) dry yeast
> 1 cup lukewarm potato water (or water)
> Pinch of sugar
> 1½ cups white rice flour

In a 1- or 1½-quart glass jar or pottery crock, dissolve the yeast in the potato water. Add the sugar and rice flour. Let the jar sit out until fermented (1 to 3 days), stirring every few hours. This will bubble up and ferment and then die down with a skim of liquid on the top. Be sure to stir well before using. The consistency should be about that of pancake batter.

Replenish by feeding the remaining starter with either ½ cup (or 1 cup) lukewarm water and ¾ cup (or 1½ cups) rice flour, as needed each time you bake.

Heavenly Honey Sourdough

(Lactose Free)

This flavorful variation of my original Simply Super Sourdough from More from the Gluten-free Gourmet *was created from suggestions of several testers. Note that the amount of yeast is lowered. The amount of water will differ according to the consistency of the starter.*

3 cups GF Flour Mix or
   Bread Flour Mix
½ cup cornstarch
2½ teaspoons xanthan gum
1 teaspoon salt
1 teaspoon Egg Replacer
   (optional)
1 teaspoon unflavored gelatin

1 egg plus 2 egg whites
1 teaspoon dough enhancer or
   vinegar
¾ cup Sourdough Starter
¼ cup vegetable oil
¼ cup honey
1⅓ cups water (save back
   some and use as needed)
1½ teaspoons dry yeast

Mix together the flour mix, cornstarch, xanthan gum, salt, Egg Replacer (if used), and gelatin. Whisk the eggs and dough enhancer slightly and add the starter, oil, honey, and most of the water.

Place in the breadmaker in the order suggested on page 42. Add the yeast with the dry ingredients in round-pan models; put it in a well on top for square upright or rectangular ones. If the dough is too stiff, add water 1 tablespoon at a time until the right consistency is achieved. Use the setting for white bread with a medium crust.

Salem Crumpets   375°

My original crumpet recipe was revised by a reader to include some garbanzo bean flour, which made it more tasty and even more filling. I simplified her recipe to use my Bean Flour Mix. This recipe makes 6 crumpets. It can easily be doubled, but don't increase the yeast, which may be either rapid rising or regular. See directions at the end for a pizza crust.

¾ cup GF Flour Mix
¾ cup Light Bean Flour Mix
   (page 69)
1 teaspoon xanthan gum
1½ teaspoons baking powder
1½ teaspoons Egg Replacer
   (optional)
½ teaspoon salt
1½ tablespoons vegetable oil

¼ cup liquid egg substitute or
   1 egg
½ teaspoon vinegar or dough
   enhancer
1½ tablespoons brown or maple
   sugar
1 cup water (barely warm)
2¼ teaspoons dry yeast (1 packet)

On a cookie sheet, place 6 English muffin rings and spray with vegetable oil spray.

In a small bowl, whisk together the two flour mixes, xanthan gum, baking powder, Egg Replacer (if used), and salt. Set aside.

In a larger mixing bowl, place the oil, egg substitute, vinegar, and 1 tablespoon of the brown sugar. Measure the water and add the rest of the sugar to it. Drop in the yeast to dissolve.

Beat the egg-oil mix slightly with a handheld mixer at low speed, adding the yeast water. Beat in half the flour. With a spoon, stir in the remaining flour and beat until smooth. Pour the batter into the prepared rings. Cover and let rise until the batter doubles, 40 to 50 minutes for regular yeast, 20 to 25 minutes for rapid-rising. Turn the oven to 375° to preheat.

Bake for 18 to 20 minutes or until browned lightly and pulled slightly from the rings. *Makes 6 crumpets.*

ONION BUNS: Add 1 tablespoon Onion Soup Mix (page 63) to dry ingredients.

SESAME SEED BUNS: Add 2 teaspoons sesame seeds to dry ingredients.

PIZZA CRUST: Spray a baking sheet or 15″ round pizza pan with vegetable oil spray. Preheat oven to 425°.

Mix the batter as above, pour onto the prepared baking sheet, and spread with a spatula to a 12½″ circle, allowing the edges to stay slightly thicker. Spread on your pizza sauce and add the toppings. Bake for 25 to 30 minutes. *Makes 6 servings.*

Focaccia   400°

Enjoy the compliments from family or guests when you serve this easily made Italian flat bread with soups, stews, or salads.

2 teaspoons sugar	½ teaspoon salt
1 cup lukewarm water	1 egg, or ¼ cup liquid egg
2¼ teaspoons (1 packet)	substitute
dry yeast	3 tablespoons olive oil, divided
1 cup rice flour	Onion salt (optional)
½ cup tapioca flour	2 tablespoons Parmesan cheese
1½ teaspoons xanthan gum	Optional toppings: sun-dried
1 tablespoon minced onion	tomatoes, sliced olives, other
1 teaspoon fennel seed	cheeses (or see next page)

Spray a 10″ × 15″ jelly roll pan or a 9″ × 15″ flat cake pan with vegetable oil spray. Put sugar in water and add yeast. Set aside.

Whisk together the rice flour, tapioca flour, xanthan gum, minced onion, fennel, and salt. Set aside.

In the bowl of a heavy-duty mixer, blend the egg, 1 tablespoon of the oil, and the yeast water. Add the flour mix and beat on High for 2 minutes. Pour the very thin dough into prepared pan and spread to cover. Top with the remaining oil dribbled on, a dash of onion salt, if desired, and the Parmesan cheese. Cover and let rise, 20 to 25 minutes for rapid-rising yeast, 45 to 50 minutes for regular yeast. Preheat oven to 400°.

Bake for 20 to 25 minutes or until slightly browned. Cut into squares to serve. Best served warm. *Makes 9 to 12 servings.*

FRESH VEGETABLE TOPPING: Slice 2 fresh tomatoes and 1 onion over the olive oil. Sprinkle on salt, pepper, and fresh rosemary. Drizzle a bit more olive oil over all.

Applesauce Bread   350°

(Low Fat, Low Sugar)

A nut bread you can eat without feeling guilty. Use this moist, chewy bread as brunch treat, dinner dessert, or nibbling snack. Toasting the nuts before chopping enhances flavor. Sweetened applesauce can be substituted.

1¾ cups GF Flour Mix	¾ teaspoon baking soda
¼ cup soy flour	¼ cup toasted walnuts, chopped
1½ teaspoons Egg Replacer	(see note)
(optional)	½ cup liquid egg substitute, or
½ teaspoon xanthan gum	1 egg plus 1 egg white
1 teaspoon apple pie spice	½ cup brown sugar
¼ teaspoon salt	1½ cups unsweetened applesauce
2 teaspoons baking powder	

Preheat the oven to 350°. Spray an 8½″ × 4½″ × 2¾″ loaf pan with vegetable oil spray and sprinkle with rice flour. Toast the nuts and chop fine.

In a mixing bowl, blend the flour mix, soy flour, Egg Replacer (if used), xanthan gum, apple pie spice, salt, baking powder, baking soda, and chopped nuts.

In a medium bowl, beat the egg substitute with the brown sugar. Add the applesauce and blend. Pour into the flour mix and stir until well blended. Spoon the batter into the pan and bake 45 to 50 minutes or until a pick inserted in the center comes out almost clean. Cool slightly and turn out. When cool, wrap airtight and store at room temperature. (The flavor is better if stored overnight.)

Note: To toast nuts, sprinkle in a shallow pan and place in a 350° oven for 7 to 10 minutes or until they are slightly browned. Cool before chopping.

Spiced Banana Loaf   350°

(High Fiber, Low Cholesterol)

Wonderfully delicious and different. Bean flour flavors the bread and gives it more fiber. Use the dark bean flour for a mocha taste, the garbanzo flour for a more delicate nutty flavor.

⅔ cup light, dark, or garbanzo bean flour	1½ teaspoons apple pie spice
⅔ cup cornstarch	⅓ cup (⅔ stick) margarine
½ cup tapioca flour	⅔ cup brown sugar
½ teaspoon xanthan gum	1 egg plus 2 egg whites, or
¾ teaspoon baking soda	⅔ cup liquid egg substitute
1¼ teaspoons cream of tartar	1 teaspoon vanilla
½ teaspoon salt	1 cup ripe bananas, mashed

Preheat oven to 350°. Spray a 9″ × 5″ loaf pan with vegetable oil spray.

In a medium bowl, blend the bean flour, cornstarch, tapioca flour, xanthan gum, baking soda, cream of tartar, salt, and apple pie spice.

In a large mixing bowl, cream the margarine and brown sugar. Beat in the eggs gradually, until the mixture is fluffy. Add the vanilla. Beat in the flour mix alternately with the banana until the batter is smooth. (If batter seems too thick, thin with 1 to 2 tablespoons orange or apple juice.) Pour batter into prepared pan and bake for 50 to 55 minutes, or until loaf springs back to the touch. Let cool a few minutes in pan and then remove to cool on rack before slicing. *Makes 1 loaf.*

Rice-free Graham Crackers 325°

A grahamlike cracker for those who can't have rice—and for all the rest of us. Like the Mock Graham Crackers in More from the Gluten-free Gourmet, *these travel well and are a good substitute for cookies; the crumbs make a tasty pie crust. For added flavor, sprinkle cinnamon sugar on some before baking.*

3 cups Light Bean Flour Mix	¾ cup (1½ sticks) margarine
2 tablespoons popcorn flour	or butter
(optional)	¼ cup honey
1 teaspoon xanthan gum	1 cup brown sugar
1½ teaspoons salt	1 teaspoon vanilla
1 rounded teaspoon cinnamon	⅛ to ¼ cup water
2½ teaspoons baking powder	

In a medium bowl, whisk together the flour mix, popcorn flour (if desired), xanthan gum, salt, cinnamon, and baking powder. Set aside.

In a large mixing bowl, beat together the margarine, honey, brown sugar, and vanilla. Add the dry ingredients alternately with the water, using just enough moisture to hold the batter in a dough ball that will handle easily. Refrigerate for at least 1 hour.

Preheat the oven to 325°. Lightly grease two 12″ × 15½″ baking sheets.

Using half the dough, work in more cornstarch if necessary to form a ball that isn't sticky. (The dough can take handling.) Roll out on cornstarch-dusted plastic wrap to a rectangle about ⅓″ thick. Transfer to the prepared baking sheet by placing it over the dough, holding the wrap, and flipping the whole. Complete rolling out the dough until it covers the sheet about ⅛″ thick, like pastry dough. Cut with a pastry wheel into 3″ squares. Prick each square with a fork 5 times.

Bake for about 30 minutes, removing the crackers around the edges if they get too brown.

Repeat with the other half of the dough. *Makes about 5 dozen crackers.*

Boston Brown Bread Muffins   400°

A high-fiber muffin with great flavor! These easy-to-mix muffins will give you the taste of old-fashioned steamed Boston brown bread in just minutes. This dough is very thin but rises and bakes into moist, rich muffins. I cut the eggs by using Egg Replacer, but instead you can add 1 extra egg and cut the buttermilk by ¼ cup.

DRY INGREDIENTS

1½ cups Light Bean Flour Mix
½ cup cornmeal
½ teaspoon xanthan gum
¼ cup maple or brown sugar
1¼ teaspoons baking soda
2 teaspoons Egg Replacer
½ cup raisins

WET INGREDIENTS

¼ cup liquid egg substitute or
  1 egg, beaten
1 cup buttermilk
¼ cup molasses
¼ cup vegetable oil

Preheat the oven to 400°. Spray 12-muffin tin with vegetable oil.

In a mixing bowl, whisk together all the dry ingredients. In a smaller bowl, beat the egg substitute (or egg) and add the rest of the wet ingredients. Mix well.

Pour the liquids into the dry mix and stir together until all the flour is wet. Don't beat. Spoon into the prepared muffin tins and bake for 15 minutes. *Makes 12 muffins.*

Vegetable Garden Muffins   400°

(Salt Free)

The vegetables might come straight from the garden, but the flavor is out of this world! To save time, chop the carrots and onions together in the food processor. These are a great accompaniment to stews and soups or good eaten alone with cheese.

2 cups GF Flour Mix	¼ cup finely chopped green
½ teaspoon xanthan gum	onions
4 teaspoons baking powder	½ cup finely chopped or grated
1 teaspoon baking soda	carrots
1 teaspoon salt-free seasoning	2 eggs or ½ cup liquid egg
1½ teaspoons Egg Replacer	substitute
(optional)	2 tablespoons vegetable oil
2 teaspoons sugar	1 cup yogurt (nonfat is fine)

Preheat the oven to 400°. Spray 12 large muffin cups with vegetable oil spray.

In a large mixing bowl, combine the flour mix, xanthan gum, baking powder, baking soda, salt-free seasoning, Egg Replacer (if used), sugar, onions, and carrots.

In a small bowl, beat the eggs slightly. Add the oil and yogurt. Stir into the flour mixture until just moistened. Spoon into muffin cups. Bake 25 to 30 minutes until golden brown and a tester inserted into center comes out clean. *Makes 12 2½" muffins.*

Fresh Apple Muffins 400°

Apples, bran, and spices are combined for great flavor in this heart-healthy muffin.

1½ cups crushed GF cereal flakes

1¼ cups GF Flour Mix

½ teaspoon xanthan gum

¼ cup brown sugar

1 tablespoon baking powder

½ teaspoon baking soda

2 teaspoons Egg Replacer (optional)

1 teaspoon apple pie spice

1 apple, peeled and grated

⅔ cup skim milk or nondairy liquid, thinned

4 tablespoons corn oil margarine, melted

¼ cup liquid egg substitute or 2 egg whites, beaten slightly

Preheat oven to 400°. Spray 12 large muffin cups with vegetable oil spray.

In medium bowl, combine the cereal, flour mix, xanthan gum, brown sugar, baking powder, baking soda, Egg Replacer (if used), and apple pie spice.

In another bowl, blend the apple, milk, margarine, and liquid egg. Stir this into the flour mix until just blended. Spoon the batter into the prepared muffin cups. Bake for 25 minutes. *Makes 12 2½″ muffins.*

My Favorite High-Fiber Muffins 425°

(Rice Free)

I ran out of bread at our remote island cabin when I had a dozen guests, so I served these muffins instead. They were so popular I served them again and again, as breakfast muffins and as a sweet cake base for frozen yogurt or whipped cream. To save time, I chop the carrots in a food processor.

1½ cups Light or Dark Bean
    Flour Mix (see page 69)
½ cup crushed GF cereal
1 teaspoon cinnamon
½ teaspoon nutmeg
¾ teaspoon baking soda
2 teaspoons baking powder

1 cup finely chopped or
    grated carrots
⅓ cup raisins or dried cranberries
½ cup liquid egg substitute
¼ cup brown sugar
¼ cup vegetable oil
⅔ cup orange juice

Preheat the oven to 425°. Spray vegetable oil in 18 muffin cups or line them with a paper liner, sprayed.

In a large bowl, combine flour mix, cereal, cinnamon, nutmeg, baking soda, baking powder, grated carrots, and raisins. Mix well.

Beat the liquid egg with the brown sugar and add the oil and orange juice. Combine with the dry mixture, mixing until the ingredients are moistened. Do not beat. Fill the prepared cups ⅔ full. Bake for 20 to 25 minutes. Serve hot or cold. *Makes 18 2½″ muffins.*

Spicy Corn Muffins   425°

Green onions and cayenne pepper combine for a great flavor treat. Serve these with stews, soups, or salads to spark up a meal. These can be made ahead, for the flavor seems even better the second day.

1 cup GF Flour Mix
½ teaspoon xanthan gum
¾ cup yellow cornmeal
1½ teaspoons baking powder
2 teaspoons Egg Replacer
    (optional)
1 teaspoon salt

1 teaspoon baking soda
¼ teaspoon cayenne pepper
⅔ cup liquid egg substitute
1 cup yogurt
¼ cup vegetable oil
½ cup finely sliced green onions

Heat oven to 425°. Spray 12 2½″ muffin cups with vegetable oil spray.

In a medium bowl, blend flour mix, xanthan gum, cornmeal, baking powder, Egg Replacer (if used), salt, baking soda, and cayenne pepper.

In large mixing bowl, beat the egg substitute slightly with a wire whisk. Add the yogurt and oil and whisk. With spoon, stir in the flour mix until just blended. Stir in the green onions. Spoon into prepared muffin cups. Bake 15 minutes or until tester comes out clean. Serve hot from the oven or cool to serve later. *Makes 12 2½" muffins or 16 2" muffins.*

Bagels
425°

I had never eaten a bagel before my diagnosis (not so surprising in the Pacific Northwest of the sixties), so when a fellow celiac asked for a recipe, I was stumped. Finally, in a baking book, I discovered one for regular flours and worked from there. Non-celiac tasters say this is delicious and very close to a wheat bagel. It's really easy to make with a heavy-duty mixer (a KitchenAid or another of the same power) and your bread hook. I use rapid-rising yeast to cut the rising time, but regular yeast works just as well.

FOR 8 BAGELS

2 cups GF Flour Mix	½ teaspoon vinegar or dough
2 teaspoons xanthan gum	enhancer
Scant teaspoon salt	2 tablespoons vegetable oil
2 teaspoons sugar	2 tablespoons honey
1 tablespoon dry yeast	¾ cup warm water
1 egg plus 1 egg white	Up to ⅓ cup sweet rice flour
	or rice flour for mixing

FOR 12 BAGELS

3 cups GF Flour Mix	¾ teaspoon vinegar or dough
1 tablespoon xanthan gum	enhancer
1 teaspoon salt	3 tablespoons vegetable oil
1 tablespoon sugar	3 tablespoons honey
1 tablespoon dry yeast	1 cup plus 1 tablespoon warm water
1 egg plus 2 egg whites	Up to ½ cup sweet rice flour
	or rice flour for mixing

In bowl of a heavy-duty mixer, place the flour mix, xanthan gum, salt, sugar, and yeast. With dough hook attached, turn mixer to Low to blend ingredients.

In a small bowl, whisk the egg and extra white slightly with the vinegar or dough enhancer. Add the oil, honey, and water. Pour into the flour mix and beat on High for 4 minutes. (This should form a dough ball. If too thin, add the extra sweet rice flour 1 tablespoon at a time until the dough sticks together in a ball. The weather, humidity, and altitude will make the difference in how much extra flour is added.)

Prepare 2 cookie sheets by spraying with vegetable oil and sprinkling lightly with cornmeal. Form bagels by dividing dough into 8 (or 12) pieces. Working with oiled hands, roll into balls larger than golf balls but smaller than tennis balls. Flatten the balls to about ½" thick. Create the hole by poking a finger through center and enlarging. Place on cookie sheets, cover with plastic wrap, and let rise until they are puffy and almost doubled in bulk, about 1 hour or slightly more for regular yeast, 30 to 40 minutes for rapid-rising yeast.

Ten minutes before they have finished rising, preheat oven to 425°.

In a large pan, bring 3 inches of water plus 1 teaspoon sugar to a boil. Drop in the bagels, 4 at a time. Cook 1 minute, turning at 30 seconds. Drain and replace on cookie sheet. Repeat, keeping the water at a low boil. Bake 20 minutes. Cool slightly before eating. *Makes 1 dozen bagels.*

Note: To freshen old bagels, slice before microwaving for 30 seconds on High. They will taste like they've just come from the oven.

CINNAMON (OR CARDAMOM) RAISIN BAGELS: Add 1 teaspoon cinnamon (or cardamom) and ½ cup raisins to the dough.

ONION BAGELS: Add 1½ to 2 tablespoons GF Onion Soup Mix (page 63) to the dough.

SESAME BAGELS: Add 1 teaspoon sesame seeds to the dough, and before rising, sprinkle the dough with toasted sesame seeds.

Note: This recipe makes a light bagel. For a heavy, doughy bagel, replace the 1 egg plus whites with 2 whole eggs plus 1 extra yolk for 8 bagels, 3 whole eggs plus 2 extra yolks for 12 bagels.

Breakfast Focaccia   375°

This Italian flatbread in a sweetened version is perfect with coffee for breakfast or brunch. I've used 1½ cups of Mock Apple Pie Filling (page 174), but if you don't have this, use 2 apples peeled, cored, and sliced with ¼ cup sugar and a dash of cinnamon and cloves. Cook in a microwave-safe bowl for 3 minutes on High. Other toppings could be peaches, cherries, or pears prepared as above. Or use canned crushed pineapple, drained.

1½ cups GF Flour Mix	½ teaspoon vinegar or dough
1 teaspoon xanthan gum	enhancer
1½ teaspoons baking powder	5 tablespoons margarine or
½ teaspoon salt	butter, melted (divided)
1½ teaspoons Egg Replacer	1 cup lukewarm water
(optional)	2¼ teaspoons (1 packet) dry
1 teaspoon dried lemon peel	yeast
3 tablespoons sugar (divided)	cinnamon sugar for topping, if
1 egg or ¼ cup liquid egg	desired
substitute	

Spray a 9" × 13" pan with vegetable oil spray.

In a small bowl, whisk together the flour mix, xanthan gum, baking powder, salt, Egg Replacer (if used), and lemon peel. Set aside.

In a mixing bowl, place all but 1 teaspoon of sugar, the egg, vinegar, and 3 tablespoons of the margarine. Place the rest of the sugar in a measuring cup and add the water. Stir in the yeast.

With a handheld mixer on low speed, beat the egg mixture. Add the yeast water and beat in half of the flour. With a spoon, stir in the remaining flour and beat until smooth. Pour the batter into the prepared pan, spreading to cover the bottom. Brush the top with the remaining 2 tablespoons of melted margarine and top with the apple pie filling. If desired, sprinkle on 1 or 2 teaspoons of cinnamon sugar. Cover and let rise until doubled in bulk, 20 to 25 minutes for rapid-rising yeast, or 40 to 50 minutes for regular yeast. Preheat oven to 375°.

Bake for 20 to 25 minutes or until the top is slightly browned. Cut into 3" squares and serve warm from the oven or reheat in the microwave. *Makes 9 servings.*

Toasted GF Bread Crumbs 225°

So handy on the shelf or in the freezer! You'll find this a great way to save any stale bread. I use these to mix with melted butter to top casseroles, as the base for several dressings, or to mix with sugar, cinnamon, and butter as a mock graham cracker crust for pies, cheesecakes, and other desserts calling for a cookie or graham cracker crust.

Save the bread until you have at least half a loaf. Then crumble it fine onto a baking sheet with raised sides. Place in a preheated 225° oven and bake for 1 to 2 hours, stirring every half hour. When slightly browned and almost dry, turn off heat and let finish drying in the oven. This will take several hours or overnight.

Store in closed container on kitchen shelf or, for perfect freshness, place in freezer bags and store in freezer. They may be poured directly from the bag and used with no thawing.

BUTTERED GF BREAD CRUMBS: For casserole toppings, melt about 2 tablespoons margarine or butter for each ½ cup of toasted crumbs and tumble together in a plastic bag. These add to the looks and taste of many casseroles.

Cakes

Sheet Cakes

Featherlight Yellow Cake
Featherlight Mocha Cake
Caramel-Pecan Cake
Pineapple or Peach Upside-Down Cake

Quick Dump Cakes

Pineapple-Nut Cake
Cranberry Cake

Bundt or Angel Food Cakes

Mocha-Banana Bundt Cake
Yogurt Chocolate Cake
Chocolate-Cherry Bundt Cake

Lighter Cakes

A Lighter Chiffon Cake
Guilt-free Carrot and Plum Cake
Light Gingerbread

Cakes from Mixes

Devil's Delight Chocolate Cake
Butterscotch-Rum Pudding Cake
Caramel-Pecan Pudding Cake
Chocolate and Apple Loaf
Zesty Lemon Cake
Easy Black Forest Cake
Pineapple Upside-Down Cupcakes

Rice-free Cakes

Chocolate Rum Cake
Simply Super Carrot Cake
Fruit Cocktail Torte with Bean
    Flour

No-Bake Cakes and Cheesecakes

No-Bake Fruitcake
Mocha Cheesecake
Light Lemon Cheesecake
No-Bake Pineapple Cheesecake

Icings and Frostings

Butterscotch Icing
Coffee Icing
Orange Cream Frosting
Fluffy White Frosting

Sauces and Fillings

Mock Raspberry Filling (or
    Jam)
Raspberry Sauce

*I*n this chapter I show you how to make cakes that are easier and healthier!

The quick featherlight cake easily converts into four different flavors and rivals any cake made with wheat in taste and texture. Several "dump" recipes require only one bowl, a handheld mixer, and a few minutes of your time.

For those who want healthier cakes, try one made with bean flour, or take an old favorite that has been lightened. Since rice flour has a tendency to make pudding out of a cake lightened with applesauce, my testers and I worked hard to discover formulas that turn out light, fluffy cakes using some applesauce while cutting sugar, eggs, and oil. We all agree that these cakes are better than before.

If you still hesitate to start from scratch, there are now many GF mixes offered from some of the suppliers listed on pages 376–81. These usually come two pouches to a box. Each pouch contains approximately 13½ ounces, or 1½ cups. The recipes here were tested with Dietary Specialties cake mixes, but you may substitute any GF cake mix, using approximately 1½ cups as 1 pouch. Stir up the mixes plain or use them, as I do, to create some excitingly different cakes.

Many of the recipes call for my GF Flour Mix. This may be ordered from one of the suppliers, or you can mix your own:

2 parts white rice flour
⅔ part potato starch flour
⅓ part tapioca flour

Others call for the Light or Dark Bean Flour Mix (see page 32). Never again hunger for cake when it is so easy to stir one up.

Featherlight Yellow Cake

Take only minutes to mix a cake so light and tasty no one will guess it's gluten free. If you're in a hurry, serve it with whipped cream or fresh fruit. If you're making ahead, frost it with your favorite icing.

Note: When nondairy sour cream is unavailable, replace with soy-based nondairy creamer plus 1 tablespoon GF vinegar. For the soy intolerant, use regular sour cream but cut the flour by ¼ cup.

1¼ cups GF Flour Mix	1 teaspoon powdered vanilla
2 teaspoons baking powder	2 eggs or ½ cup liquid egg
½ teaspoon baking soda	substitute
½ teaspoon xanthan gum	⅔ cup sugar
½ teaspoon salt	⅓ cup mayonnaise
1 teaspoon Egg Replacer	⅔ cup nondairy sour cream
(optional)	(see note above)

Preheat oven to 350°. Spray an 8″ square cake pan with vegetable oil spray.

Whisk together the flour, baking powder, baking soda, xanthan gum, salt, Egg Replacer (if used), and powdered vanilla. Set aside.

In a large mixing bowl, beat the eggs and sugar until light and foamy. With mixer on Low, blend in flour mix, beating only until smooth.

Stir in the mayonnaise and sour cream until well blended. Do not beat. Pour the batter into pan and bake for 30 to 35 minutes or until the top springs back and the sides pull slightly from the pan. May be served immediately or cooled and frosted.

Double the recipe for a two-layer round cake or a 9″ × 13″ flat cake.

FEATHERLIGHT MOCHA CAKE: To the egg and sugar mix, add 1 square melted semisweet chocolate, and replace the vanilla with 1 tablespoon freeze-dried coffee crystals. Frost with Mocha Icing.

CARAMEL-PECAN CAKE: Replace white sugar with dark brown sugar, replace vanilla flavoring with either caramel flavoring or GF vanilla, butter, and nut flavoring. Add ½ cup chopped pecans. Frost with Butterscotch Icing (page 133).

PINEAPPLE OR PEACH UPSIDE-DOWN CAKE: Melt ⅓ cup margarine or butter in the ungreased baking pan. Scatter on ½ cup (or less) brown sugar. Arrange canned pineapple slices or peach halves (cut side down) over the sugar mix, using one 28-ounce can. Pour cake batter over the fruit and bake, adding 4 to 5 extra minutes baking time. Serve warm or cold topped with whipped cream or nondairy whipped topping, if desired.

Pineapple-Nut Cake   350°

A true "dump" cake that takes only minutes to mix but turns out moist and flavorful. Serve this with whipped cream or your favorite fruit frosting. This makes a large cake and may be halved to bake in an 8″ × 8″ pan. Use 1 egg plus 1 egg white in place of the eggs, and use one 8-ounce can of pineapple. Cut the baking time to approximately 25 minutes.

2 cups GF Flour Mix	¾ cup liquid egg substitute
½ teaspoon xanthan gum	or 3 eggs
1 tablespoon Egg Replacer	½ cup chopped nuts (optional)
(optional)	1 teaspoon vanilla
1½ cups sugar	One 20-ounce can crushed
2 teaspoons baking soda	pineapple (undrained)

Preheat oven to 350°. Spray a 9″ × 13″ pan with vegetable oil spray.

In a mixing bowl, blend together the flour mix, xanthan gum, Egg Replacer (if used), sugar, and baking soda. Add the egg substitute, nuts (if used), vanilla, and pineapple. Beat with a spoon until liquid and dry ingredients are thoroughly combined. Pour into the prepared pan and bake 45 minutes, or until golden and the sides of the cake pull away from the pan. Serve warm or cold with whipped cream or nondairy topping, but cool before frosting. *Makes 12 servings.*

Cranberry Cake 350°

Light, moist, and so good it needs no frosting, this tasty "dump" cake could be made in one bowl by just dumping in all the ingredients, but I find mixing the dry ingredients separately gives a better texture. The recipe can be halved for baking in a 9" square pan. To substitute for the sour cream, use nondairy liquid creamer plus 1 tablespoon vinegar.

3 cups GF Flour Mix	2 eggs
1½ teaspoons xanthan gum	1¼ cups sugar
1 teaspoon salt	⅓ cup orange juice concentrate
2 teaspoons baking soda	1 can whole berry cranberry
1 teaspoon dried orange peel	sauce
1 teaspoon Egg Replacer	½ cup mayonnaise
(optional)	¾ cup nondairy sour cream

Preheat oven to 350°. Spray a large tube pan with vegetable oil spray and dust with rice flour.

In a medium bowl, blend together the flour mix, xanthan gum, salt, baking soda, orange peel, and Egg Replacer (if used). Set aside.

In a mixing bowl, beat together the eggs, sugar, orange juice concentrate, and the cranberry sauce. Add the flour mixture and the mayonnaise and sour cream. Beat until mixed. Do not overbeat. Pour into prepared pan and bake for one hour or until the tester comes out clean. Let cool in pan before removing to cake plate. Serve plain to accompany fruit or top with whipped cream.

Mocha-Banana Bundt Cake 350°

Chocolate, coffee, cinnamon, and bananas combine for a marvelous flavor. Yogurt and egg whites keep it light and moist. An easy-to-mix cake so good that it needs no frosting, but if you wish you can drizzle on a thin powdered sugar icing for looks; make it with lime or lemon juice for a tart contrast. Note: This cake needs no xanthan gum.

1¾ cups GF Flour Mix	½ teaspoon salt
¾ cup sugar	3 ripe bananas, peeled
¼ cup cocoa	½ cup dark corn syrup
1 tablespoon freeze-dried coffee	½ cup yogurt
1 teaspoon cinnamon	¼ cup vegetable oil
1 teaspoon Egg Replacer (optional)	2 teaspoons GF vanilla
2 teaspoons baking soda	4 egg whites

Preheat oven to 350°. Spray a 12-cup bundt pan with vegetable oil spray.

In a large mixing bowl, blend the flour mix, sugar, cocoa, coffee, cinnamon, Egg Replacer (if used), baking soda, and salt.

In a food processor, puree the bananas (should yield 1½ cups). Put them into a medium bowl and add the corn syrup, yogurt, oil, and vanilla. With a spoon, beat this mixture into the flour mix until well blended.

Whip the egg whites until stiff. Gently fold them into the batter and pour this into the prepared pan. Bake 55 to 60 minutes or until a tester inserted into the center comes out clean. Cool 10 minutes before inverting the pan over your cake plate. If using an icing, drizzle this on the still-warm cake. *Makes 16 to 20 servings.*

Yogurt Chocolate Cake 350°

This deliciously delicate chocolate bundt cake is a lightened variation of a recipe sent to me by Beth Hillson from The Gluten Free Pantry. For a richer, darker chocolate version, increase the sugar to 2 cups and the cocoa to ¾ cup.

2 cups GF Flour Mix	½ cup (1 stick) margarine or butter
1 teaspoon xanthan gum	½ cup cocoa
2 teaspoons baking powder	¾ cup liquid egg substitute, or
1 teaspoon baking soda	1 egg plus 2 egg whites
1 teaspoon Egg Replacer	1⅓ cups sugar
(optional)	½ cup plain yogurt
Pinch of salt	2 teaspoons GF vanilla
1 cup boiling water	

Preheat the oven to 350°. Spray a bundt or tube pan with vegetable oil spray and dust with rice flour.

In a medium bowl, blend the flour mix, xanthan gum, baking powder, baking soda, Egg Replacer (if used), and salt. Set aside.

In a large mixing bowl, combine the water, margarine, and cocoa and stir until the margarine is melted.

In a small bowl, beat the egg substitute until foamy. Add this with the sugar to the cocoa mixture, and beat well with a wooden spoon. Beat in the dry ingredients until smooth. Add the yogurt and vanilla and mix well. The batter should be fairly thin. Pour into the prepared pan and bake 50 minutes or until a tester comes out clean. Let cool slightly before turning onto a serving plate. The cake can be dusted with confectioners' sugar, frosted with your favorite frosting, or drizzled with a thin icing of confectioners' sugar mixed with milk or lemon juice. *Makes 16 to 20 servings.*

CHOCOLATE-CHERRY BUNDT CAKE: For a wonderful variation of the above cake, soak 1 cup of dried cherries in ⅓ cup kirsch overnight. Add them to the batter with the yogurt.

A Lighter Chiffon Cake   325°–350°

By reducing the number of egg yolks and using Junior apricots to replace some of the oil in the Orange Chiffon Cake from The Gluten-free Gourmet, *I came up with a delicious, lower-cholesterol, lower-fat apricot-flavored cake. The texture is still light, and I think the flavor superb.*

2 cups GF Flour Mix	3 eggs plus 4 egg whites
1 cup sugar	¾ cup orange juice
1 tablespoon baking powder	2 teaspoons orange zest
2 teaspoons Egg Replacer (optional)	One 6-ounce jar Junior apricots
	3 tablespoons vegetable oil
1 teaspoon salt	½ teaspoon cream of tartar

Preheat oven to 325°. Line the bottom of a large tube pan or 13″ × 9″ pan with waxed paper. (Do not grease.)

Separate eggs, placing the whites in a large metal or ceramic bowl (not plastic). Retain 3 egg yolks. Save or discard the other 4.

In a large mixing bowl, blend the flour mix, sugar, baking powder, Egg Replacer (if used), and salt. Make a well and add in order: the 3 egg yolks, orange juice, orange zest, apricots, and oil. Beat with a spoon until smooth.

With a clean beater, whip the egg whites and cream of tartar until very stiff peaks form. Pour the batter into the egg whites and fold with a rubber spatula until just blended. Pour into the prepared pan. Bake the tube pan for 55 minutes, then turn temperature to 350° and bake for 10 minutes longer. Bake the oblong pan at 350° for 45 to 50 minutes.

Frost if desired with your favorite icing or drizzle with a glaze of powdered sugar mixed with 1 tablespoon soft margarine and orange juice to the desired consistency.

Guilt-free Carrot and Plum Cake   350°

(Lactose, Soy, and Cholesterol Free)

A taste treat the whole family will love. Use four 2½-ounce jars baby prunes plus enough water to make 1¼ cups if you don't want to bother with the puree-ing process.

2 cups brown rice flour	1 tablespoon pumpkin pie spice
1 scant teaspoon xanthan gum	1 teaspoon dried lemon peel
1 cup sugar	One 16-ounce can plums, with some juice
2 teaspoons baking soda	¾ cup liquid egg substitute
2 teaspoons baking powder	3 tablespoons vegetable oil
½ teaspoon salt	3 cups grated carrots

Heat oven to 350°. Spray a bundt pan with vegetable oil spray and dust with rice flour.

In a large mixing bowl, combine flour, xanthan gum, sugar, baking soda, baking powder, salt, spice, and lemon peel. Set aside.

Drain the plums, reserving the juice; pit them and puree them in the food processor, adding enough of the reserved juice to make 1¼ cups. Combine the puree, egg substitute, and oil beating to mix well. Stir into the flour mixture along with the grated carrots. Pour batter into prepared pan and bake for 1 hour and 10 minutes or until a tester comes out clean. Cool in pan 10 minutes before turning out.

If desired, while still warm, drizzle on a thin icing of confectioners' sugar mixed with fruit juice.

Light Gingerbread 350°

This very light gingerbread tastes like the ones my mother used to make, but the ingredients are certainly different! This recipe is for a small 8" square cake. Double the recipe for a 9" × 13" cake and add 10 to 15 minutes to the baking time. Notice this is a rice-free cake.

½ cup light or dark bean flour	½ cup sugar
½ cup cornstarch	¼ cup honey
¼ cup tapioca flour	4 tablespoons (½ stick)
1 teaspoon baking soda	margarine
1 teaspoon pumpkin pie spice	½ cup boiling water
¼ teaspoon xanthan gum	1 egg plus 1 egg white, or ½ cup liquid egg substitute

Preheat oven to 350°. Spray an 8" square cake pan with vegetable oil spray.

In a medium bowl, blend together the bean flour, cornstarch, tapioca, baking soda, pumpkin pie spice, and xanthan gum.

In a large mixing bowl, put the sugar, honey, margarine, water, and egg. Beat slightly. Add the flour mixture and beat well. Pour batter into the prepared pan and bake for about 30 to 40 minutes, or until a tester comes out clean. Serve plain, with sweetened whipped cream, or a simple lemon sauce.

Devil's Delight Chocolate Cake 350°

No one will ever guess this moist, rich chocolate cake came from a mix. Stir it up in minutes.

1 pouch Dietary Specialties chocolate cake mix	½ cup mayonnaise
2 rounded tablespoons cocoa	⅔ cup cherry cola (water may be substituted)
1 egg plus 1 egg white	½ teaspoon almond flavoring

Preheat oven to 350°. Spray an 8″ square baking pan with vegetable oil spray.

In a large mixing bowl, blend the cake mix and cocoa. In a small bowl, beat the eggs slightly and add the mayonnaise, cola, and almond flavoring. With electric mixer at medium speed, beat the liquids into the flour mix until blended. Pour into the prepared pan and bake 35 to 40 minutes or until a tester inserted in the center comes out clean. Cool and frost with your favorite frosting. (The Coffee Icing on page 133 is excellent.) *Makes 9 servings.*

Note: For a large cake, use the whole box of mix (2 pouches), double the other ingredients, and bake in a large tube pan that has been sprayed with vegetable spray and dusted with rice flour. Bake approximately 50 to 55 minutes or until a tester comes out clean.

Butterscotch-Rum Pudding Cake   350°

Here's another cake from a mix that's as good as it sounds. Make it in minutes from a box of GF white cake mix.

1 pouch Dietary Specialties white cake mix	1 cup brown sugar
1 egg	1⅔ cups cola, heated to boiling
½ cup water plus 2 tablespoons	2 tablespoons rum
1 teaspoon GF butterscotch or caramel flavoring	2 tablespoons margarine or butter

Preheat oven to 350°.

Batter: In a large bowl, mix the cake mix with egg and water according to the directions on the box. Add the butterscotch flavoring. Pour into an ungreased 8″ square pan.

Sauce: Sprinkle the brown sugar over the batter. Heat the cola but remove from stove to add rum and margarine. Pour the liquid gently over the batter.

Bake for 45 to 50 minutes or until the cake top springs back to the touch. Serve in bowls with the sauce (which will be on the bottom). Top with whipped cream or nondairy topping if desired.

CARAMEL-PECAN PUDDING CAKE: Follow recipe above but eliminate the rum and sprinkle on ½ cup chopped pecans before pouring on the hot liquid.

Chocolate and Apple Loaf 350°

This ultra-moist fruit and chocolate loaf will never taste like cake from a mix.

3 medium apples, peeled,
cored, and sliced
¾ teaspoon apple pie spice
2 teaspoons sugar
1 pouch Dietary Specialties
chocolate cake mix

1 egg plus 1 egg white
½ cup cola or water
1 teaspoon almond flavoring
Whipped cream, nondairy
whipped topping, frozen
yogurt, or ice cream for topping

Preheat oven to 350°. Spray a 9″ × 5″ loaf pan with vegetable oil spray and dust with rice flour.

In a microwave-safe bowl, mix the apple slices, apple pie spice, and sugar. Microwave on High for 4 minutes.

Pour the cake mix into a mixing bowl. Add the egg, egg white, cola, and almond flavoring. Beat on medium speed 1 minute.

Pour half the batter into the bottom of the prepared pan. Gently lay on the apple slices. Top with the rest of the batter. Bake for 40 to 45 minutes. Let cool in pan for 10 minutes before unmolding onto a cake plate. Slice and serve warm or cold with your preferred topping.

Zesty Lemon Cake 350°

This tasty recipe from my past is still a favorite in the family. I've cut the time of mixing by using a prepared mix. If you use mayonnaise, Light Mayonnaise (page 366) works well.

1 pouch Dietary Specialties
white cake mix
1 egg plus 1 egg white
¼ cup mayonnaise (optional)
½ teaspoon dried lemon peel

½ cup plus 2 tablespoons lemon-
lime soda (Sprite, Squirt, etc.)
One 3-ounce package lemon gelatin
1 cup boiling water

Preheat oven to 350°. Spray an 8″ square cake pan with vegetable spray.

In a large mixing bowl, place cake mix, egg, egg white, mayonnaise (if using), lemon peel, and soda. Beat on medium speed for 1 minute. Pour into the prepared pan and bake 35 to 40 minutes or until tester comes out clean.

While the cake is still hot, poke holes with a large meat fork at ½-inch intervals. Dissolve the gelatin in the cup of boiling water and pour it carefully over the hot cake. Cool and place in refrigerator.

If desired, frost with your favorite frosting. (The Orange Cream Frosting on page 134 is excellent if you replace the orange with lemon.) Or serve with a dab of whipped topping, ice cream, or frozen yogurt.

Easy Black Forest Cake 350°

A GF cake mix and a can of cherries combine for this wonderful treat.

One 17-ounce can dark cherries, drained (save juice)	1 pouch Dietary Specialties chocolate cake mix
2 tablespoons GF Flour Mix	1 egg plus 1 egg white
1 tablespoon sugar	½ cup plus 2 tablespoons of
1 teaspoon cinnamon	reserved juice

Preheat oven to 350°. Spray an 8½″ × 4½″ × 3″ loaf pan with vegetable oil spray and dust thoroughly with rice flour.

Cut drained cherries in half. Mix together the flour mix, sugar, and cinnamon. Tumble gently into cherries.

In a medium mixing bowl, place the cake mix, eggs, and juice. Beat on medium speed for 1 minute. Gently fold in the cherries. Pour into the prepared pan and bake for 40 to 45 minutes or until a tester comes out clean. Cool for a few minutes before turning onto a cake plate. Slice and serve with a whipped topping, ice cream, or frozen yogurt.

Pineapple Upside-Down Cupcakes 350°

Stir up these cupcakes in minutes from a white cake mix and have an instant dessert. Make enough to store in the freezer in single serving packets and have dessert whenever you want to pull one out. They reheat in the microwave to taste fresh-baked.

One 8-ounce can crushed
   pineapple
4 tablespoons (½ stick)
   margarine or butter
7 tablespoons brown sugar

1 pouch Dietary Specialties white
   cake mix
Whipped topping (optional)

Heat oven to 350°. Drain the pineapple, reserving the juice.

Melt the butter in the microwave or in small saucepan. Remove from heat. Add the sugar and drained pineapple. Spoon into a 12-cup muffin tin, about 1 tablespoon to each cup.

Mix the cake according to directions on the package, using the reserved juice as part of the liquid. Spoon over the pineapple mix in the muffin tins. Bake 20 to 25 minutes or until cupcakes shrink from the sides of the pan and a toothpick inserted in center comes out clean. Cool in pan for 10 minutes and then turn out. Serve warm or at room temperature. Top, if desired, with whipped topping. *Makes 12 cupcakes.*

Chocolate Rum Cake

350°

(Rice Free)

Two favorites from my other books are combined in this tender, flavorful new cake created especially for a celiac who's allergic to rice. If you don't have the bean flour, the cake will turn out well by replacing the flours with 2½ cups of GF Flour Mix (page 33).

⅞ cup light or dark bean flour
⅞ cup cornstarch
¾ cup tapioca flour
½ teaspoon xanthan gum
½ cup unsweetened cocoa
3½ teaspoons baking powder
2 teaspoons baking soda
1 teaspoon cinnamon
1 teaspoon salt
2 teaspoons Egg Replacer
  (optional)

¾ cup (1½ sticks) margarine
1½ cups sugar
3 eggs plus 2 egg whites, or
  1 cup liquid egg substitute
⅓ cup rum, brandy, or water
2 cups grated zucchini
½ cup strong coffee
1 cup chopped walnuts
  or pecans (optional)

Preheat oven to 350°. Spray a bundt pan with vegetable oil spray and dust with rice flour.

In a medium bowl, blend the bean flour, cornstarch, and tapioca flour. Add the xanthan gum, cocoa, baking powder, baking soda, cinnamon, salt, and Egg Replacer (if used) and blend again. Put aside.

In large mixing bowl, beat margarine and sugar with electric beater until smooth. Beat in eggs, one at a time, until fluffy. With mixing spoon, stir in the rum and zucchini.

Stir in the flour mix with the coffee until well blended. Add nuts, if used. Pour batter into the prepared pan and bake 50 to 55 minutes or until the cake begins to pull from the pan sides and springs back when pressed with a finger. Let cool in pan about 10 minutes before inverting onto cake plate to finish cooling. Top if desired with a thin glaze of 1½ cups powdered sugar thinned with coffee or lemon or lime juice.

Simply Super Carrot Cake

(Rice Free)

This may be one of the best carrot cakes you've tasted and, like all carrot cakes, it stays moist for days. Frost the cake or serve it with whipped cream. Double the recipe for a crowd.

½ cup light or dark bean
  flour
½ cup cornstarch
½ cup tapioca flour
½ teaspoon xanthan gum
1 teaspoon baking powder
1 teaspoon baking soda
1 teaspoon cinnamon
1 teaspoon vanilla
¼ teaspoon ground ginger
1½ teaspoons Egg Replacer
  (optional)

½ teaspoon salt
2 eggs or ½ cup liquid egg
  substitute
¾ cup sugar
½ cup mayonnaise or Light
  Mayonnaise (page 366)
1½ cups grated carrots
3 tablespoons finely chopped
  pecans
3 tablespoons dried cranberries

Preheat oven to 350°. Spray an 8″ square pan with vegetable oil spray.

In a medium bowl, blend together the bean flour, cornstarch, tapioca flour, xanthan gum, baking powder, baking soda, cinnamon, vanilla, ginger, Egg Replacer (if used), and salt. Set aside.

In a large mixing bowl, beat the eggs until light. Add the sugar and mayonnaise and beat to blend. With a spoon, beat in the flour mix. Add the carrots, nuts, and cranberries and stir until blended. The dough will be quite thick. Spoon into the prepared pan and bake for 30 to 35 minutes or until a tester comes out clean. Cool before frosting.

If you double the recipe, use a 9″ × 13″ oblong pan and bake 45 to 50 minutes.

Fruit Cocktail Torte with Bean Flour 325°

(Rice Free, Cholesterol Free, High Fiber)

I tried this favorite standby with the new bean flour and discovered it's even better than before. With the egg substitute, it's now both fat and cholesterol free, so you can have your cake and eat healthy. The recipe can easily be doubled. Use a 9″ × 13″ pan for baking.

⅓ cup light or dark bean flour	½ cup liquid egg substitute,
⅓ cup cornstarch	beaten lightly
⅓ cup tapioca flour	One 17-ounce can fruit cocktail
1 cup sugar	1 teaspoon vanilla
1 teaspoon salt	½ cup brown sugar
1 teaspoon baking soda	½ cup chopped nuts

Preheat oven to 325°. Spray an 8″ square pan with vegetable oil spray.

In a large mixing bowl, blend together the bean flour, cornstarch, tapioca flour, sugar, salt, and baking soda.

Add the beaten egg substitute, fruit cocktail (juice included), and vanilla. Stir until well blended. Pour batter into prepared pan and sprinkle with the brown sugar and nuts. Bake 1 hour. Serve warm or cold topped with whipped cream or nondairy whipped topping.

No-Bake Fruitcake

When held to the light, the slices of this firm, not-too-spicy fruitcake look like stained glass. This is a large cake and keeps well, but the recipe can easily be halved. Don't save it just for Christmas but use it for a treat when traveling or hiking.

2½ cups dried GF cookie crumbs or crushed GF graham crackers

One 16-ounce carton candied fruit

One 8-ounce carton candied cherries

One 8-ounce carton candied pineapple

2 cups golden raisins

8 ounces fruit slice candy, diced

1¼ cups chopped cashews

1¼ cups chopped pecans or macadamia nuts

1½ cups chopped dates

One 14-ounce can sweetened condensed milk

In a very large mixing bowl, mix cookie crumbs with fruits, candy, and nuts. Stir in the milk. The mixture will be very stiff. Work with hands until the dough is evenly moistened and sticks together well.

Line 4 small (2½″ × 5″) bread pans with buttered foil long enough to pull up sides and over top. Pack the dough in tightly. Fold over foil to seal and refrigerate. Remove after 12 hours to slice and serve or store in refrigerator. To keep over 1 month, freeze. *Makes 4 loaves.*

If you prefer, roll the loaves into 2½″ rolls about 10 to 12 inches long. Wrap in buttered foil. *Makes 4 rolls.*

Mocha Cheesecake

An absolutely decadent taste with very little work. Cheescakes are made ahead and keep for several days, so they should be on any busy cook's list of quick and easy desserts. The crust suggested here makes this cake special, but you can use any GF cereal or cookie crust you wish.

CRUST

1½ cups GF cereal, crushed
¼ cup (½ stick) margarine or
   butter, melted
3 tablespoons brown sugar
¼ cup dried, shredded
   coconut, chopped finer
   in a food processor
¼ cup pecans, ground fine

FILLING

2 ounces semisweet chocolate
2 tablespoons heavy cream
Two 8-ounce packages cream
   cheese
⅔ cup sugar
2 eggs
1 cup sour cream or nondairy
   substitute
2 teaspoons freeze-dried coffee
   crystals
1 teaspoon vanilla

Preheat oven to 350°.

Crust: Combine ingredients in a plastic bag and tumble together. Pat into bottom of an 8″ springform pan, reserving about 2 tablespoons.

Filling: Break the chocolate and grate in food processor. In microwave-safe bowl, place chocolate and cream. Microwave on Defrost for about 2½ to 3 minutes to melt. Meanwhile place cream cheese and sugar in food processor. Blend until smooth. Add the eggs, one at a time, processing until blended. Add the sour cream, coffee crystals, vanilla, and melted chocolate. Blend until smooth. Pour into the crust, sprinkle on the reserved crust, and bake for 60 to 70 minutes. The center of the cake will not seem quite solid but will firm up while cooling. Remove from oven and cool before refrigerating.

Chill before serving.

Light Lemon Cheesecake   350°

(Egg Free, No Bake)

A very light cheesecake for the calorie conscious, egg free for the cholesterol counters. This can be made for the diabetic using the sugar-free gelatin. If you have Mock Sour Cream (page 368) use this in place of the sour cream substitute. Top this with the marmalade as shown below or make Raspberry Sauce (page 136).

CRUST

1½ cups GF dried cookie, graham cracker, or sweet bread crumbs

2 tablespoons margarine, melted

FILLING

One 6-ounce or two 3-ounce packages lemon gelatin

One 8-ounce package light cream cheese

1 cup sour cream substitute or fat-free sour cream

½ cup sugar

1 teaspoon vanilla

½ cup orange or kiwi marmalade for topping (optional)

Crust: Preheat oven to 350°. Mix the crumbs and margarine. Pat into a 9″ springform pan, reserving 2 tablespoons for topping if neither marmalade or Raspberry Sauce is used. Bake for 7 to 10 minutes. Let cool.

Filling: In a large mixing bowl, dissolve the gelatin in 2 cups boiling water. Add 1 cup ice water. Refrigerate until almost set, about 1 hour. Meanwhile beat together the cream cheese, sour cream, sugar, and vanilla.

When the gelatin is almost set, beat (with mixer at high speed) the cream cheese blend into the gelatin for 5 minutes. Pour into the prepared pan (sprinkle on the reserved crumbs, if desired) and refrigerate until set, about 4 hours.

To serve with topping rather than crumbs, thin the marmalade slightly with orange juice and spread on top of the cheesecake.

No-Bake Pineapple Cheesecake

My husband's favorite! By using the microwave, you can make this delightfully tart cheesecake in minutes, refrigerate a few hours, and serve. Or eat it the next day; it'll still taste fresh.

3 tablespoons GF cookie
   crumbs
2 cups low-fat plain yogurt
2 teaspoons powdered vanilla
1 egg or ¼ cup liquid egg
   substitute
⅔ cup sugar

¼ cup GF Flour Mix (or
   cornstarch)
One 8-ounce package cream
   cheese
One 8-ounce can crushed
   pineapple (undrained)
1 tablespoon cornstarch

Spray a 9″ pie plate with vegetable oil spray. Sprinkle in the cookie crumbs.

In food processor (or with a heavy beater), blend the yogurt, vanilla, egg, sugar, and flour mix. Cut up the cream cheese and add gradually. Blend until smooth. Pour into a microwave-safe bowl.

Microwave on High for 8 to 10 minutes, stirring every 2½ minutes, until the custard is the consistency of thick pudding. Remove and stir until smooth. Pour gently into the pie plate. Let cool while making topping.

Combine the pineapple (with juice) and the cornstarch in a microwave-safe bowl. Microwave on High for 1 minute or until boiling, stirring once. Boil 1 minute. Spread over the cheesecake and refrigerate for 3 hours before serving.

Butterscotch Icing

This frosting requires little cooking and turns out smooth every time.

5 tablespoons margarine or
butter
1 cup dark brown sugar

¼ cup cream or nondairy liquid
1 cup confectioners' sugar

Melt the margarine in a medium saucepan over medium heat. Add the sugar and stir until smooth. Pour in the cream and bring the mixture to a boil, stirring constantly. Stop stirring and allow to boil 3 minutes with only a couple of stirs to keep from burning. Cool to lukewarm.

Add the confectioners' sugar and beat until thickened. Spread immediately. If prepared ahead, let stand at room temperature to keep the icing spreadable.

Coffee Icing

A quick and easy coffee-flavored frosting for any cake. This is a large recipe, enough for two flat 9″ × 12″ cakes, two bundt or tube cakes, or an icing on the top and sides of a 2-layer cake. It keeps well in the refrigerator for a week or two and freezes for several months.

¼ cup margarine or butter (room
temperature)
3 ounces cream cheese (room
temperature)

1 tablespoon freeze-dried
coffee crystals
2 tablespoons hot water
3 cups confectioners' sugar

In a medium bowl, beat together the margarine and cream cheese until blended. Dissolve the coffee crystals in the hot water and beat in. With mixer on Low, add the confectioners' sugar and beat until well blended and light and fluffy. If necessary, add more sugar to bring the frosting to spreading consistency. *Makes approximately 2 cups.*

Orange Cream Frosting

This frosting, with the zesty orange taste, turns a simple cake into a party dessert. Stir it up in minutes. This is a small recipe, just enough for the top of a 9″ × 13″ cake. Double the ingredients for the filling, top, and sides of a 2-layer cake.

1 tablespoon margarine or butter	1 tablespoon orange juice
2 ounces cream cheese (softened)	1½ cups confectioners' sugar
1 teaspoon orange zest	(to desired consistency)

With handheld mixer, blend the margarine, cream cheese, and zest. Add the orange juice. Beat in the confectioners' sugar about ½ cup at a time until the frosting is spreading consistency. *Makes about 1½ cups.*

Fluffy White Frosting

This airy frosting from Kay Spicer's Full of Beans *cookbook (Mighton House, 1993) is less sweet than seven-minute frosting and much easier to make. This uses boiling corn syrup; the other requires cooking a sugar syrup to just the right temperature.*

½ cup light corn syrup	¼ teaspoon cream of tartar
1 egg white	1 teaspoon vanilla

In a small saucepan, bring the syrup to a boil over medium heat.

In a small mixing bowl, beat egg white and cream of tartar until soft peaks form. Beat in vanilla. Gradually beat in hot syrup and continue beating for about 3 minutes or until stiff and shiny. *Makes about 2 cups.*

Mock Raspberry Filling or Jam

A marvelous raspberry-tasting filling to use on the Chocolate Sponge Roll (page 185) or to fill any white cake. If you prefer, it's great as a jam on toast, pancakes, or waffles. If you don't have green tomatoes in your garden, buy tomatoes in the market. Pick the firm ones—they won't be ripe.

2½ cups peeled and diced
    green tomatoes (2 or 3)
2 cups sugar
Dash of salt

1 tablespoon lemon juice
One 3-ounce box raspberry
    gelatin

Place the tomatoes in a 2½-quart saucepan with the sugar and salt. Bring to a boil and cook for 10 minutes, stirring frequently. Remove from burner.

Add the lemon juice and stir in the gelatin. Return to stove and bring to a boil, stirring constantly. Boil 1 minute. Put in jars or refrigerator cups. Keeps refrigerated for up to 1 month. For longer, put in freezer containers and freeze. *Makes 3 cups.*

Raspberry Sauce

Try this for an elegant topping for simple cheesecake or to spoon over frozen yogurt or plain ice cream.

> One 10-ounce package frozen raspberries or
>   2 pint baskets fresh raspberries
> 3 tablespoons sugar
> 1 teaspoon fresh lemon juice

In a blender or food processor, puree the ingredients. Strain through a sieve to remove the seeds. Refrigerate until cold before serving, about 1 hour. *Makes about 1½ cups.*

Cookies

Bar Cookies

Velvet Brownies
Peanut Toffee Bars
   Chocolate Toffee Bars
   Butterscotch Chews
Frosted Fudge Squares
Pecan Pie Squares
Apricot Bars
Health Bars
Fruitcake Bars
No-Bake Granola Bars

Drop Cookies

Mock Oatmeal Cookies with
   Fruit and Spice
Taster's Choice Peanut Butter
   Cookies
   Almond Crisps

Crunchy Chocolate Drops
Hawaiian Fruit Drops
Chocolate Cherry Chews

Shaped Cookies

Vanilla Wafers
   Nutty Wafers
   Lemon Wafers
   Citron Wafers
White Chocolate and
   Macadamia Nut
   Biscotti
Mocha-Rum Biscotti
Sugar Cookies II

There is no reason not to keep that cookie jar filled. Baking cookies is the simplest of all gluten-free baking, and some of the recipes in this section are extra easy. Others, like the biscotti, might take a bit more time but keep so well they can be made weeks ahead.

I have included a couple of health bars and several high-fiber cookies made with a bean flour mix. In others I've cut the cholesterol and fat but left in all the flavor. If you don't believe it, try the Velvet Brownies (page 140), with only 2 tablespoons of fat in the recipe.

If you don't feel like starting from scratch, there are several excellent cookie mixes and ready-baked cookies that can be ordered from the suppliers listed in the back of the book.

A word of warning: All the cookies in this book taste so good the whole family will love them—so be prepared to bake often.

Many of the recipes start with my GF Flour Mix:

> **2 parts rice flour**
> **⅔ part potato starch flour**
> **⅓ part tapioca flour**

Velvet Brownies

(Low Fat, Low Cholesterol)

Eat these brownies with less guilt, for they use cocoa rather than chocolate and pear or pea puree or applesauce to replace some of the fat. My favorite is made with baby food pea puree.

⅔ cup GF Flour Mix
⅓ cup cocoa powder
½ teaspoon cinnamon
¼ teaspoon salt
2 egg whites
1 egg
¾ cup sugar

6 tablespoons baby food pear or pea puree or unsweetened applesauce
2 tablespoons vegetable oil
1½ teaspoons vanilla
Optional: 1 tablespoon chopped pecans, walnuts, or macadamia nuts

Preheat oven to 350°. Spray an 8″ × 8″ pan with vegetable oil spray.

In a measuring cup, combine the flour mix, cocoa, cinnamon, and salt. In a mixing bowl, whisk the egg whites and egg slightly. Add the sugar, puree, oil, and vanilla and whisk until blended, but don't overbeat. Pour into the prepared pan and sprinkle on the nuts (if used).

Bake until set and a tester comes out clean, about 25 minutes. Cool before cutting into 2″ squares. *Makes 16 brownies.*

Peanut Toffee Bars

These almost-candy, layered bars are so easy to make they should become a favorite in any home. If you don't have bread or cookie crumbs, substitute crushed GF cereal flakes. See below for other flavors.

1 stick plus 3 tablespoons margarine or butter, divided
1 cup GF dried bread or cookie crumbs
2 cups GF miniature marshmallows

¾ cup brown sugar, packed
1 teaspoon vanilla
1 cup peanut butter chips
1 cup chopped peanuts
One 14-ounce can sweetened condensed milk

Preheat oven to 350°. Line a 9″ × 13″ baking pan on the bottom and up the sides with aluminum foil. Spray with vegetable oil spray.

Melt 3 tablespoons of the margarine. Put in pan and sprinkle in the bread crumbs. Top with a layer of the marshmallows.

In a heavy saucepan, melt the remaining ½ cup (1 stick) margarine. Add the brown sugar and bring to a full boil, stirring constantly. Lower heat to medium and continute boiling 5 minutes, stirring occasionally. Remove from heat and add the vanilla.

Drizzle this over the marshmallows. Top with the peanut butter chips and the chopped peanuts. Drizzle the condensed milk over all. Bake for 35 minutes. Let cool before cutting into 1½″ squares. *Makes about 3½ dozen bars.*

CHOCOLATE TOFFEE BARS: For a change of taste, use chocolate chips instead of peanut butter chips and change the nuts to walnuts or pecans.

BUTTERSCOTCH CHEWS: Replace peanut butter chips with butterscotch and the peanuts with pecans or macadamia nuts.

Frosted Fudge Squares

A rich, fudgy bar cookie that can be a full dessert. This "dump" recipe uses only one bowl with no sifting or beating. Use a microwave-safe bowl for the cookie base and the same unwashed bowl for the frosting. If allergic to soy, replace the two flours with ½ cup GF Flour Mix. The fudge squares won't be as moist but will still taste wonderful.

COOKIE BASE

⅓ cup rice flour plus 1 tablespoon
⅓ cup soy flour less 1 tablespoon
¼ cup cocoa
¾ cup sugar
¼ teaspoon salt
½ teaspoon cinnamon (optional)
6 tablespoons softened margarine
1 teaspoon vanilla
2 eggs, or ½ cup liquid egg
   substitute
½ cup chopped nuts (optional)

FROSTING

2 tablespoons cocoa
2 tablespoons milk or
   nondairy liquid
2 tablespoons margarine
1 cup powdered sugar

Cookie: Preheat oven to 375°. Spray a 9″ square cake pan with vegetable oil spray.

In a microwave-safe bowl or saucepan, dump the rice flour, soy flour, cocoa, sugar, salt, cinnamon, margarine, vanilla, and eggs or egg substitute. Stir until well blended. Add the nuts (if used) and stir again. Pour into the prepared cake pan and bake for approximately 17 minutes.

Frosting: While cookie is baking, dump into same bowl the cocoa, milk, and margarine. Microwave on Defrost for 3 minutes. Beat in the powdered sugar, adding more if necessary to get a spreadable consistency. Spread on the warm cake. When cool, cut into either 1″ × 2″ or 2″ squares. *Makes 16 2″ squares or 32 smaller ones.*

Pecan Pie Squares 350°

"This tastes like pecan pie but is so easy!" wrote my friend Mary when she sent this recipe. She was right. This is not a low-calorie cookie—a single square can serve as a full dessert. I found it a real crowd pleaser. If you don't have sweet rice flour use all GF Flour Mix.

CRUST

1¼ cups GF Flour Mix
¼ cup sweet rice flour
½ teaspoon salt
3 tablespoons sugar
6 tablespoons (¾ stick)
    margarine or butter

FILLING

2 eggs, very lightly beaten
¾ cup sugar
¾ cup corn syrup (light or dark)
1½ tablespoons margarine or
    butter, melted
¾ teaspoon vanilla
1¼ cups coarsely chopped pecans

Preheat oven to 350°. Spray a 7½″ × 11½″ pan with vegetable oil spray.

Crust: With mixer or food processor, beat the flours, salt, sugar, and margarine until crumbly (mixture will be dry). Press firmly into pan. Bake 20 minutes or until light golden brown.

Filling: Mix all the ingredients except the pecans until well blended. *Do not beat!* Stir in the pecans. Pour the filling gently over the crust and spread evenly. Bake until the filling is set (about 25 minutes). Cool. Cut into 1½″ squares. *Makes 35 squares.*

Double the recipe and use a jelly roll pan (15½″ × 10½″) for 70 squares.

Apricot Bars

Combine apricots and orange for a tangy taste. If you top the bars with frosting, you've got a full dessert. The Dream Pastry Mix makes the best crust, but you can substitute my GF Flour Mix if desired.

Note: You may replace the jar of Junior baby apricots with ⅔ cup cut-up dried apricots boiled in water to cover for 10 minutes.

CRUST
1 cup Dream Pastry Mix (page 58)
2 tablespoons sugar
5½ tablespoons margarine or butter

FILLING
¾ cup brown sugar
½ cup liquid egg substitute or 2 eggs
One 6-ounce jar Junior apricots
½ cup walnuts, chopped

½ cup shredded coconut
1 teaspoon almond flavoring
2 tablespoons GF Flour Mix (page 139)
1 teaspoon fresh orange zest

FROSTING (OPTIONAL)
2 tablespoons margarine or butter
2 teaspoons fresh orange zest
1½ cups powdered sugar
2 tablespoons orange juice
½ cup walnuts, chopped (optional)

Preheat oven to 375°. Spray an 8″ square or a 7″ × 11″ baking pan with vegetable oil spray.

Crust: In medium mixing bowl, combine the pastry mix, sugar, and margarine, cutting until crumbly. Pat into the bottom of prepared pan. Bake 20 minutes.

Filling: In the same bowl, stir together the brown sugar and liquid egg substitute. Add the apricots, walnuts, coconut, almond flavoring, flour mix, and orange zest. Stir until combined. Spread evenly over the baked crust. Return to oven and bake for 25 minutes or until the filling pulls gently away from the pan. Remove from oven to cool before adding the optional frosting.

Frosting: In a medium bowl, beat the margarine and orange zest with an electric mixer. Gradually beat in the powdered sugar. Add the orange juice, a little at a time, until the frosting is of a consistency to spread easily over the cooled bars. Sprinkle the walnuts on top. Cut into 1″ × 2″ bars. *Makes 30 bars.*

Health Bars 325°

The combination of cereal, nuts, and fruit makes these a most healthy addition to your cookie repertory. If desired, substitute applesauce for the apricot sauce.

4 cups crushed GF cereal flakes
1½ cups sliced almonds, crushed
One 6-ounce package mixed
    fruit bits or ¾ cup chopped
    dried fruit

¾ cup Junior baby apricots
¾ cup corn syrup
3 tablespoons almond butter,
    peanut butter, or
    margarine

Preheat oven to 325°. Spray a 15″ × 10″ jelly roll pan with vegetable oil spray.

In a large bowl, stir together the cereal, crushed almonds, and fruit bits.

In a small saucepan, cook together the apricot sauce, corn syrup, and margarine for about 4 minutes. Pour it into the cereal blend and mix thoroughly.

Spread the batter in the prepared pan and bake for 20 minutes. Let cool before cutting into bars. *Makes 4 dozen bars.*

Fruitcake Bars

Easy to make and delicious! Just put the ingredients in the pan in layers and bake.

Note: Dates that come already chopped may have wheat flour added to prevent them from sticking together. Buy whole pitted dates to be safe.

6 tablespoons margarine or butter

1½ cups dried GF cookie or bread crumbs

1 cup dried, shredded coconut

2 cups candied fruitcake mix or candied fruit

1 cup whole pitted dates, chopped (see note above)

1 cup nuts, chopped

One 14-ounce can sweetened condensed milk

Preheat oven to 350°.

Melt the margarine in a 15″ × 10″ jelly roll pan. Sprinkle the dried crumbs evenly over the melted margarine. Add in layers the coconut, candied fruitcake mix, dates, and nuts. Press the mixture with hands to even it over the pan. Drizzle on the sweetened condensed milk to cover the top evenly. Bake for 25 to 30 minutes. Cool in pan before cutting into small bars. *Makes about 4½ dozen bars.*

No-Bake Granola Bars

A high-energy, high-fiber bar suitable for carrying hiking, skiing, or to other active sports. I usually wrap these separately and freeze to have ready for travel. You may substitute almond or other nut butters for the peanut butter.

4 cups crushed GF flaked cereal	1 cup chopped dried fruit
1½ cups sliced almonds, crushed	1 cup peanut butter
1 cup semisweet chocolate chips (optional)	¾ cup light corn syrup

Spray a 15″ × 10″ jelly roll pan with vegetable oil spray.

In a large mixing bowl, blend the cereal, almonds, chocolate chips (if used), and dried fruit.

In a small saucepan, combine the peanut butter and corn syrup. Cook, stirring constantly, until hot and smooth, about 5 minutes. Pour the hot syrup over the cereal mix and blend well. Press the batter into the prepared pan. Refrigerate for about 15 minutes or let stand for an hour or so. Cut into bars. *Makes 4 dozen bars.*

Mock Oatmeal Cookies with Fruit and Spice

350°

An old favorite sparked up with grated apple and spices could be a popular lunchbox treat; or serve these with canned fruit to top off a meal. These are good keepers and travel well.

1 cup crushed sliced almonds	1 stick plus 2 tablespoons margarine
1¼ cups GF Flour Mix	
¼ cup sweet rice flour	1 cup plus 2 tablespoons dark brown sugar
¾ teaspoon baking soda	
1¼ teaspoons apple pie spice	1 egg
¼ teaspoon salt	½ cup grated apple
	1 cup dried fruit bits

Preheat oven to 350°. Spray 2 cookie sheets with vegetable oil spray.

In a large bowl, blend the almonds, flour mix, sweet rice flour, baking soda, apple pie spice, and salt.

In a large mixing bowl, beat the margarine and sugar with electric mixer until fluffy. Beat in the egg and apple. Add the dry ingredients and mix until well combined. Stir in the fruit bits. Drop by rounded teaspoonfuls onto the prepared sheets, about 2 inches apart. Bake about 10 minutes or until the cookies are a light golden. *Makes about 4½ dozen cookies.*

Taster's Choice Peanut Butter Cookies
350°

One non-celiac exclaimed, "This is absolutely the best cookie I've ever eaten!" Although not as low in fat as many of my cookies, this crunchy cookie is high in fiber and protein.

½ cup light or dark bean flour
¾ cup cornstarch
1 cup crushed GF cereal flakes
¾ cup sliced almonds, crushed
2 teaspoons baking soda
1 cup (two sticks) margarine or butter, melted

¾ cup brown sugar
¾ cup granulated sugar
2 teaspoons vanilla
1 cup creamy peanut butter
½ cup liquid egg substitute or 2 eggs

Preheat oven to 350°.

In a medium bowl, whisk together the bean flour, cornstarch, cereal, almonds, and baking soda. Set aside.

In a large mixing bowl, beat together the margarine, sugars, vanilla, peanut butter, and egg substitute. Stir in the flour mixture until well blended. Drop by teaspoons onto ungreased cookie sheets. Bake for 15 minutes or until browned and crisp. *Makes 7 dozen 2" cookies.*

ALMOND CRISPS: Another wonderful cookie! Replace the peanut butter with 1 cup almond butter (found in specialty food stores and large supermarkets).

Crunchy Chocolate Drops 350°

An easy drop cookie that starts with a cake mix. Use Dietary Specialties Chocolate Cake Mix or any other GF chocolate cake mix measuring about 1½ cups. Raisins or other dried fruit bits may be substituted for the chocolate chips.

1 pouch GF chocolate cake mix
1 cup (2 sticks) margarine or
 butter, melted
2 eggs or ½ cup liquid egg
 substitute, beaten lightly
1 cup coconut

1 cup GF cereal flakes,
 crushed
1 cup sliced almonds, crushed
¾ cup semisweet chocolate
 chips

Preheat oven to 350°.

In a large mixing bowl, combine the cake mix, melted margarine, and eggs. Mix well. Stir in the coconut, crushed cereal, almonds, and chocolate chips. Drop the batter by teaspoonfuls onto ungreased cookie sheets. Bake for 10 to 12 minutes. *Makes 5 to 6 dozen 1½″ cookies.*

Hawaiian Fruit Drops

An easy drop cookie, made from a cake mix, this keeps and travels well. A great lunch box treat. See below for other suggested flavors.

½ cup ricotta cheese

½ cup (1 stick) margarine or butter, softened

⅓ cup brown sugar

1 egg or ¼ cup liquid egg substitute

½ teaspoon dried lemon peel

1 pouch Dietary Specialties white cake mix

½ cup chopped macadamia nuts

One 8-ounce can crushed pineapple, well drained

Preheat the oven to 375°.

In large mixing bowl, cream the ricotta cheese, margarine, and sugar. Add the egg and dried lemon peel. Add all the cake mix except ½ cup to the batter. Stir thoroughly. Mix the remaining cake mix with the fruit and nuts. Stir into the batter.

Drop onto ungreased cookie sheets by the teaspoonful 2 inches apart. Bake for 10 to 12 minutes. Remove from cookie sheet while still hot. *Makes 5½ dozen 1½″ cookies.*

For other flavors: Omit the macadamia nuts and crushed pineapple and add dried cherries and walnuts with 1 to 2 tablespoons fruit juice or dried cranberries and pecans with 1 to 2 tablespoons fruit juice.

Chocolate Cherry Chews

(Rice Free)

This recipe for a delicious rice-free cookie was contributed by Beth Hillson of the Gluten Free Pantry. She suggested the soy flour—I substituted light bean flour (great!). Her recipe called for dried cherries. I often use dried apricots. These keep well and stay chewy to the end.

Note: If using the bean flour, increase the milk to 4 tablespoons.

1 cup soy flour or light bean flour
½ cup potato starch flour
¼ cup cornstarch
½ teaspoon xanthan gum (optional)
½ teaspoon baking soda
¾ cup (1½ sticks) margarine or butter
1 cup granulated sugar

½ cup brown sugar
1 teaspoon vanilla
2 tablespoons milk or nondairy liquid (4 if bean flour is used)
2 egg whites
⅓ cup cocoa powder
1 cup toasted pecans or walnuts
1 cup dried cherries or apricots, cut up

Preheat oven to 350°. Lightly grease 2 cookie sheets.

In a medium bowl, whisk together soy (or bean) flour, potato starch flour, cornstarch, xanthan gum (if used), and baking soda. Set aside.

In a large mixing bowl, cream the margarine, add the white and brown sugars, and beat until fluffy. Add the vanilla, milk, and egg whites and beat well. Mix in the cocoa until just incorporated. Fold in the flour mixture, add nuts and cherries (or apricots). Do not beat.

Drop by rounded teaspoonfuls onto the prepared cookie sheets. Bake 10 to 12 minutes. They may seem a little soft but this keeps them chewy. Wait a few seconds before removing. *Makes 5 dozen 2" cookies.*

Vanilla Wafers 375°

The recipe for these simple vanilla wafers was sent to me from Australia—along with the "custard powder" called for in the original recipe. Since most of us aren't familiar with custard powder, I experimented and came up with this recipe, which tastes like the original. This is a crisp cookie and can be used whenever a recipe calls for crushed vanilla wafers. They are excellent plain or baked with added nuts, lemon zest, or chopped citron.

1 cup white rice flour	1 teaspoon baking powder
¼ cup soy flour	½ cup (1 stick) margarine or butter
½ cup cornstarch	½ cup plus 1 tablespoon sugar
½ teaspoon salt	1 egg
2 teaspoons powdered vanilla	

Preheat oven to 375°.

In a small bowl, combine the rice flour, soy flour, cornstarch, salt, vanilla powder, and baking powder. Set aside.

Cream the margarine and sugar. Beat in the egg. Add the dry ingredients and mix until it forms a dough that's like pastry dough. Shape this into balls a bit smaller than a walnut and place on an ungreased cookie sheet 3 inches apart. Flatten with a moist fork to about ⅛" thick as you would for peanut butter cookies. Bake 6 to 10 minutes or until done and slightly browned. *Makes 4 dozen 1½" cookies.*

NUTTY WAFERS: Add ½ cup finely chopped nuts to the batter. Pecans and walnuts are the most flavorful.

LEMON WAFERS: Eliminate the vanilla. Replace with 1 teaspoon lemon flavoring and 1 teaspoon freshly grated lemon zest.

CITRON WAFERS: Add 1 teaspoon dried orange peel and ½ cup finely chopped citron to the batter.

White Chocolate
and Macadamia Nut Biscotti

350°/325°

My guests practically fought over these—and they were just as tasty a month later. I've never tested how long these keep but Marco Polo carried biscotti on his overland journey to China. Biscotti, although baked twice, are really easy to make—and well worth the double baking. Using the food processor to chop the nuts and grate the chocolate saves time and work.

¾ cup macadamia nuts	½ cup (1 stick) margarine or butter
4 ounces white chocolate	½ cup sugar
1¾ cups GF Flour Mix	2 tablespoons kirsch
¼ cup sweet rice flour	1 teaspoon rum-nut-butter
1 tablespoon baking	flavoring or 1 teaspoon vanilla
powder	3 eggs or ¾ cup liquid egg
¾ teaspoon xanthan gum	substitute
¼ teaspoon salt	¼ cup cream or nondairy liquid

Preheat oven to 350°. Spray 2 baking sheets with vegetable oil spray.

Place nuts in a shallow pan and bake for 8 to 10 minutes or until lightly browned. Remove and let cool slightly.

Reduce oven temperature to 325°. Place the nuts in a food processor and chop fine. Remove to a bowl and use the processor to chop the white chocolate.

In a medium bowl, blend together the flours, baking powder, xanthan gum, and salt. Set aside.

In a large mixing bowl, cream the margarine and sugar. Add the kirsch and other flavoring. Beat in the eggs, one at a time. Add the cream. Mix the flour into the creamed dough, stirring until well blended. Fold in the nuts and chocolate.

Divide the dough into 3 sections. With each, form a log on the sheets, about ½″ high, 2½″ wide, and almost the length of the pan. Bake at 325° for about 25 minutes or until lightly browned, reversing the position of the sheets in the oven halfway through baking.

Remove and cool for about 5 minutes. Slice diagonally across the logs in ½″ slices. Lay these slices on their sides on the baking sheets and return to the oven for 10 to 12 minutes, again reversing the position of the sheets halfway through baking.

Let cool and store airtight for up to 1 month. Or freeze for later use. *Makes about 4 dozen cookies.*

Mocha-Rum Biscotti   350°/325°

A real taste treat in a cookie that keeps and travels well. I've suggested cashews, but you can substitute the more traditional almonds.

¾ cup cashews	½ cup sugar
2 ounces semisweet chocolate	2 tablespoons rum
1¾ cups GF Flour Mix	1 tablespoon freeze-dried coffee crystals
¼ cup sweet rice flour	3 eggs or ¾ cup liquid egg substitute
1 tablespoon baking powder	
½ teaspoon xanthan gum	2 tablespoons cream or nondairy liquid
½ teaspoon salt	
½ cup (1 stick) margarine or butter	

Preheat oven to 350°. Spray 2 baking sheets with vegetable oil spray.

Place cashews in a shallow pan and bake for 8 to 10 minutes or until lightly browned. Remove and let cool slightly.

Reduce oven temperature to 325°. Place the nuts in a food processor and chop fine. Turn the nuts into a bowl and use the food processor to chop the chocolate.

In a medium bowl, whisk together the flours, baking powder, xanthan gum, and salt. Set aside.

In a large mixing bowl, cream the margarine and sugar. Add the rum and coffee crystals. Beat in the eggs, one at a time, then the cream. Add the flour mix to the creamed dough, mixing until well blended. Fold in the nuts and chocolate.

Divide the dough into 3 sections. With each, form a log on the sheets, about ½″ high, 2½″ wide and almost the length of the sheet. Bake at 325° for about 25 minutes or until lightly browned, reversing the position of the sheets in the oven halfway through baking.

Remove and cool for about 5 minutes. Slice diagonally across the logs into ½″ slices. Lay these slices on their sides on the baking sheets and return to the oven for 10 to 12 minutes, again reversing the position of the sheets halfway through baking.

Let cool and store airtight for up to 1 month, or freeze for later use. *Makes about 4 dozen cookies.*

Sugar Cookies II 375°

(Rice Free)

This is not a quick and easy recipe, but I've had so many calls for revising my original sugar cookie recipe from The Gluten-free Gourmet *that I've included it here. Kathy of California suggested the addition of xanthan gum and the refrigerating of my original recipe to make the rolling and cutting easier.*

1½ cups potato starch flour	1 teaspoon salt
⅔ cup cornstarch	1½ cups sugar
⅔ cup tapioca flour	1 cup Butter Flavor Crisco
2 teaspoons baking powder	4 egg yolks
1 teaspoon xanthan gum	2 teaspoons vanilla

Preheat oven to 375°. Spray 2 cookie sheets with vegetable oil spray.

In a medium mixing bowl, whisk together the potato starch flour, cornstarch, tapioca flour, baking powder, xanthan gum, and salt. Set aside.

In a large mixing bowl, cream the sugar and shortening. Add the egg yolks and vanilla. Add flour mix to the bowl and work the dough with your hands until you can form balls. Refrigerate for several hours or overnight.

Roll out cooled dough on wax paper to about ⅛" thick. Cut into desired shapes and transfer to the cookie sheets. Bake for 8 to 10 minutes. Sprinkle with sugar before baking or frost after cooling. *Makes 6 dozen 2" cookies.*

Pies and Pastries

Pastry and Pie Crusts

Baker's Best Bean Pastry
Bean Flour Oil Crust
Cream Cheese Pastry
Very Best Cereal Crust

Baked Pies

Fruit Dream Pie
Yogurt Peach Pie
Easy Apple-Yogurt Pie
Brownie Pie
Chocolate Caramel Pie with
    Walnuts
Pineapple Pie with Coconut
    Batter Topping

Refrigerator Pies

Quick Cranberry Pie
Key Lime Pie

Pineapple Cheese Pie
Sour Cream–Raisin Pie

Crisps

Peach and Plum Crisp
    End-of-Fruit-Basket Crisp

Pie Fillings

Lighter Basic Cream Pie Filling
    Banana Cream Pie
    Pineapple Cream Pie
    Coconut Cream Pie
Mock Apple Pie Filling
    Apple Crisp
    Open-Faced Apple Pie
    Hawaiian Crisp

With the introduction of Donna Jo's Dream Pastry in my last book, *More from the Gluten-free Gourmet,* I thought I'd given you all the pie crusts you needed to eat well. That was proved when a celiac in Wyoming wrote that she had won Grand Champion in a pie-baking contest pitting her Dream Pastry pie against pies with wheat crusts.

But we are always discovering something new. In this chapter you'll not only find new uses for Donna Jo's excellent formula, you'll also discover that the new rice-free bean flours make more than breads, cakes, and pastas. They also make a tasty, flaky pie crust that handles even more easily than Donna Jo's Dream Pastry.

For those who can't have rice, this is wonderful, and for those who want to rotate their diet, this will add one more item. For the rest of us, it's another great-tasting pie crust.

For fillings, I've included a few special pies and lightened several of my favorites. Remember, you can always use your own favorite fruit fillings by substituting gluten-free flours such as tapioca, sweet rice flour, or cornstarch in the thickening. My GF Flour Mix can be used in exact proportion to the amount of wheat flour called for. For a quick pie, many of the packaged pie filling mixes are gluten free, but always read the ingredients list, since companies often change formulas without changing the packaging.

For real convenience in pie making see the recipe for Dream Pastry Mix on page 58.

Baker's Best Bean Pastry

Now we have a new wheat-free pastry that rivals any other in taste and tenderness. It handles well and browns beautifully.

Note: If you can handle rice flour, substituting ¼ cup sweet rice flour for ¼ cup of the Light Bean Flour Mix will produce a more delicate crust. Roll out the pastry on sweet rice flour.

2 or 2¼ cups **Light Bean Flour Mix** (page 32)

¼ cup sweet rice flour (optional; see note above)

1 teaspoon baking powder

1 teaspoon xanthan gum

½ teaspoon salt

2 teaspoons brown or maple sugar

⅓ cup margarine

⅓ cup Butter Flavor Crisco

1 small egg, or 3 tablespoons liquid egg substitute

1 tablespoon vinegar

3 tablespoons ice water

Cornstarch for rolling (sweet rice flour may be used)

In a medium bowl, whisk together the Bean Flour Mix, rice flour (if used), baking powder, xanthan gum, salt, and sugar. Cut in the margarine and Crisco in small pieces until you have shortening the size of lima beans (not cornmeal).

Beat the egg with a fork and add the vinegar and ice water. Stir into the flour mixture, forming a ball. Refrigerate an hour or so to chill.

Divide dough into 2 halves and roll the first half out onto a board dusted with cornstarch or sweet rice flour (or on dusted plastic wrap for easier handling). Transfer to a pie tin. Fill the pie and roll the second half of the dough. Place the second crust over the filling, seal the edges, and bake as directed for the filling used.

For a baked pie shell, prick the pastry with a fork on sides and bottom. Bake in a preheated 425° oven for about 12 to 14 minutes. Cool before filling. *Makes one 2-crust pie or 2 pie shells.*

Bean Flour Oil Crust

Try this for a delicate, flaky, delicious, and easy crust for a one-crust pie. This can be filled before baking or baked and then filled.

1½ cups Light Bean Flour Mix (page 32)	1 teaspoon salt
1 teaspoon baking powder	½ cup vegetable oil
1½ teaspoons sugar	3 tablespoons cold milk or nondairy liquid

In a medium bowl, whisk together the flour mix, baking powder, sugar, and salt. Pour oil into a measuring cup and whisk in the cold milk with a fork until the two are blended. Pour into the flour mix and stir until the mass is crumbly and almost sticks together.

Pat the mixture into a 9″ or 10″ oiled pie tin. Form a medium-thick crust, shaping the edges and fluting the top, if desired.

If the pie is to be filled and baked, pour the filling in gently and bake according to the filling recipe.

When using a cooked filling, bake the crust in a preheated 400° oven for 13 to 15 minutes. Cool before filling.

Cream Cheese Pastry

So quick, so easy—with a melt-in-the-mouth texture. All you do is blend in your food processor and pat into the pan. Of course, if you wish to double the recipe and roll out a top crust, you must roll this as a regular pastry dough.

Note: You can also use 1 cup Dream Pastry Mix in place of the sweet rice flour, cornstarch, tapioca flour, xanthan gum, and salt.

½ cup sweet rice flour	½ teaspoon salt
¼ cup cornstarch	⅓ cup Butter Flavor Crisco
¼ cup tapioca flour	1 ounce cream cheese
½ teaspoon xanthan gum	¼ cup ice water

Mix together the sweet rice flour, cornstarch, tapioca flour, xanthan gum, and salt. Set aside.

In the food processor, blend the Crisco and cream cheese. Add the flour mix and process a few seconds. Add the water and process until the dough forms a ball.

Place in center of a 9″ pie tin and pat out with the fingers, covering the bottom and up the sides of the pan, pressing the edge tops into a design. If the filling is to be baked with the crust, fill and bake at the temperature suggested for the filling. If the filling is already cooked, then bake the crust in a preheated 425° oven for 6 to 8 minutes or until the crust is slightly brown and tests done. Cool before filling.

For a 2-crust pie, double the recipe and use half the dough for the bottom, pressing into the pan. Fill. Roll the rest of the dough between sheets of plastic film to the size desired. Remove the top plastic sheet and use the remaining one to reverse the dough onto the filling. Bake at the temperature suggested for the filling (usually 375° for about 1 hour).

Very Best Cereal Crust

Cereal crusts are simple to make for a one-crust pie. Any gluten-free dry cereal can be crushed and used in your pie or cheesecake crust, but this combination of rice and corn is my favorite. For an extra special crust, add the optional ¼ to ½ cup of finely ground nuts or coconut to the mix.

1 cup GF rice flakes, crushed
1 cup GF corn flakes, crushed
3 tablespoons sugar, white or
   brown
½ teaspoon cinnamon (optional)

3 tablespoons margarine
   or butter, melted
¼ to ½ cup finely ground
   nuts or coconut (optional)

Crush the cereal in a plastic bag. Dump in the sugar, cinnamon (if used), and the melted butter and mix all together. Pour into a 9″ pie tin and press across the bottom and up the sides. For a cheesecake, press into the bottom of a 9″ or 10″ springform pan.

If the pie or cheesecake is to be baked, add the filling and bake according to the recipe. If the filling is already cooked, bake the crust in a preheated 375° oven for 6 to 8 minutes or until it is slightly browned. Cool before filling.

To reduce fat: Use 2 tablespoons margarine and 1 tablespoon water.

Fruit Dream Pie

A delicious, open-faced layered fruit pie that takes just minutes to put together. This uses frozen prepared fruit so you don't have any peeling or cutting.

    2 cups frozen sliced fruit (rhubarb, peaches, or berries)
    One 9" Cream Cheese Pastry crust (page 162) or any GF crust,
        prebaked
    3 tablespoons tapioca flour
    ½ cup sugar (or to taste), divided
    ½ cup liquid egg substitute, or 2 eggs
    ½ cup milk or nondairy liquid
    1 teaspoon vanilla

Preheat the oven to 350°.

Remove the frozen fruit from freezer to thaw slightly while mixing the other layers.

Place a mix of the tapioca flour and ¼ cup of the sugar in the pie shell. Place the fruit in the shell. Beat together the eggs, milk, vanilla, and remaining sugar. Pour the mixture over the fruit. Bake for approximately 40 minutes or until a knife inserted in the center comes out clean. Cool before serving. *Makes 6 servings.*

Yogurt Peach Pie 350°

This creamy-tasting fresh peach pie should bring raves from your family or guests. Use the Very Best Cereal Crust for both crust and topping to make it easy as well as tasty.

1 Very Best Cereal Crust
(page 163)

FILLING
4 fresh peaches, peeled and
sliced
1 cup sugar, divided
2 tablespoons GF Flour Mix
1 egg, beaten slightly

1 cup nonfat yogurt
1 teaspoon vanilla

TOPPING
⅓ cup reserved crust mix
⅓ cup brown sugar
4 tablespoons margarine or
butter

Preheat oven to 350°.

Reserve ⅓ cup of the crust mix before patting the rest into a 9″ pie pan.

Filling: Slice the peaches into a bowl and sprinkle with ¼ cup of the sugar. In another bowl, combine the remaining sugar, flour mix, and egg. Fold in the yogurt and vanilla. Stir this mixture into the peaches and pour into the prepared crust.

Topping: Add the brown sugar to the reserved crust mix and cut in the margarine until the texture is crumbly. Sprinkle this over the filling. Bake for 1 hour. Cool before serving, and store any remaining in refrigerator. *Makes 6 servings.*

Easy Apple-Yogurt Pie

425°–350°

Delicious and quick to make, this creamy apple pie with a rich, crumbly topping is a wonderful finale for any meal. Serve it hot or cold to your family or for company. If you are lactose intolerant, substitute nondairy sour cream for the yogurt.

1 recipe Oil Crust (page 59)
2 to 3 apples, peeled, cored,
    and diced (2 cups)
2 tablespoons GF Flour Mix
⅛ teaspoon salt
¾ cup sugar
1 teaspoon apple pie spice

¼ cup liquid egg substitute
    or 1 egg
1 cup low-fat plain yogurt
1 tablespoon lemon juice
¼ cup (½ stick) margarine or
    butter
½ cup brown sugar

Preheat oven to 425°.

Press ¾ of the prepared crust mix into a deep 9″ pie tin. Reserve the rest for topping.

In a mixing bowl, tumble the apples with the flour mix, salt, sugar, and apple pie spice. Mix together the egg substitute, yogurt, and lemon juice. Add to the apples and pour into the prepared crust.

For the topping, mix together the remaining crust mix, margarine, and brown sugar until it is the consistency of crumbs. Sprinkle on top of the filling. Bake for 15 minutes at 425°. Reduce heat to 350° and bake 30 minutes longer. Serve warm or cold. *Makes 6 to 8 servings.*

Brownie Pie

400°–350°

This quick-and-easy fudgy pie can be stirred up and baked in minutes, for it makes its own crust, a thin creamy filling, and a firm top. It's low in cholesterol and so moderate in calories you can add a touch of low-fat ice cream or frozen yogurt for topping.

¼ cup margarine
⅔ cup dark brown sugar
½ cup liquid egg substitute
¼ cup buttermilk
¼ cup GF Flour Mix

⅓ cup cocoa powder
1 teaspoon vanilla
¼ teaspoon salt
Optional: Low-fat ice cream
    or frozen yogurt for topping

Preheat oven to 400°. Spray an 8″ pie pan with vegetable oil spray.

Melt margarine. Pour into a medium mixing bowl and stir in sugar. Add the remaining ingredients and stir until well blended. Pour into the prepared pan and bake for 15 minutes. Decrease oven temperature to 350° and bake 5 minutes more or until set. Cool slightly before serving. Top with your favorite topping, if desired. *Makes 8 servings.*

Chocolate Caramel Pie with Walnuts

350°

This is the ultimate in desserts, but easy to make and serves many since the pie is so rich.

One 9″ Very Best Cereal Crust
    (page 163)
3 tablespoons margarine or butter
½ cup semisweet chocolate pieces
3 eggs, or ¾ cup liquid egg
    substitute

1 cup dark corn syrup
¾ cup brown sugar
1 teaspoon vanilla
1 cup coarsely chopped
    walnuts

Prepare the pastry but do not bake. Preheat oven to 350°.

Melt the margarine. Place chocolate in food processor and whirl until fine.

In large mixing bowl, beat eggs (or egg substitute) until light. Add the corn syrup, brown sugar, vanilla, and melted margarine. Stir together until blended. Fold in the walnuts and chocolate. Pour gently into the pie shell and bake for 50 to 55 minutes or until a knife inserted in the center comes out clean. Cool before serving. *Makes 8 to 10 servings.*

Pineapple Pie with Coconut Batter Topping

325°

A pie with the mingled flavors of the tropics. This requires one large, sweet, ripe pineapple, so when I find one at the fruit market, I plan on this treat. The most flavorful crust is the Cream Cheese Pastry (page 162), but any unbaked crust works well.

1 unbaked pie crust	¾ cup liquid egg substitute,
1 large pineapple, peeled, cored,	or 3 eggs
and cut into tidbits (about	4 tablespoons margarine
3½ cups)	or butter, melted
1 cup sugar, divided	½ cup flaked coconut
3 tablespoons sweet rice flour	⅓ cup macadamia nuts,
¼ teaspoon salt	chopped

Prepare the crust and place in a 9″ pie tin. Preheat oven to 325°.

Place pineapple in crust and sprinkle on ⅓ cup of the sugar.

In a medium bowl, whisk together the remaining sugar, rice flour, and salt. Beat the eggs slightly and add to the sugar mixture. Add the margarine. Blend well. Add the coconut and macadamia nuts and pour the batter over pineapple. Bake about 1 hour and 15 minutes or until brown and the center is firm. Cool before serving. *Makes 8 servings.*

Quick Cranberry Pie

This is a tasty, easy pie for the winter holidays. You will need one baked pie crust. For a rich taste use the Cream Cheese Pastry crust (page 162). For a lighter pie, use a cereal crust (page 163).

One 9″ crust, baked
1 cup plain yogurt (nonfat or
   regular, or ½ cup yogurt
   and ½ cup sour cream, or
   nondairy substitute
1 to 3 tablespoons sugar
   (to taste)
1 teaspoon powdered vanilla

One 12-ounce package
   cranberries
1 tart cooking apple, peeled
   and cored
½ cup raisins
½ cup orange juice
1 teaspoon cinnamon
3½ tablespoons sugar

In a medium bowl, mix yogurt (or yogurt and sour cream) with sugar and vanilla. Pour into the prepared crust. Refrigerate to set while cooking the fruit.

Wash and pick over the cranberries. Place them and the apples in food processor and chop. (Do not puree.)

In a 2-quart saucepan, heat the fruit, raisins, orange juice, and cinnamon. Add 1 to 2 tablespoons of the sugar and bring to a boil. Turn to simmer and cook for approximately 8 to 10 minutes or until the fruit is tender. Stir occasionally. Sweeten with the remaining sugar to taste. Then cool.

Pour the sauce gently over the yogurt filling and refrigerate until serving. *Makes 6 to 8 servings.*

Key Lime Pie

This no-bake Key lime pie is egg free and has a light, delicate taste. To make it even lighter, the cream cheese can be changed to reduced-fat cream cheese or Yogurt Cream Cheese (page 369). For those who don't want the added lactose of dairy milk, I made this with condensed goat's milk, thinned.

Any prepared GF crust is good, but if you have any cookie crumbs, try tumbling 1 cup of them with 2 tablespoons melted butter to pat into the pie tin. You won't have to bake this.

1 GF crust, baked	One 8-ounce package cream
1 envelope (¼ ounce) unflavored	cheese, softened
gelatin	½ to ⅔ cup sugar (to taste)
1¾ cups milk (divided)	½ cup Key lime juice
(goat's milk is excellent)	

In a small saucepan, sprinkle the gelatin over ½ cup of the milk. Let stand a few minutes before placing over low heat until the gelatin is dissolved. Stir constantly.

In a medium bowl, beat the cream cheese and the sugar until fluffy. Add the remaining milk and the gelatin mixture. Blend in the lime juice. Pour into the prepared pie shell and refrigerate until set. About 2 hours. *Makes 6 to 8 servings.*

Pineapple Cheese Pie   250°

(Low Sugar, Low Fat)

A molded pie made from canned crushed pineapple, this can be made with sugar substitute or regular sugar. This keeps well, so it can be made ahead. If using bread crumbs add 2 tablespoons sugar and 1 teaspoon cinnamon.

Note: You may boil some of the drained juice to replace the water.

CRUST

1¼ cups GF bread or cookie
   crumbs
2 tablespoons water
1 tablespoon vegetable oil

FILLING

1 envelope unflavored gelatin
2 tablespoons cold water

¼ cup boiling water
½ cup low-fat ricotta cheese
¼ cup nonfat milk or nondairy
   liquid
1 teaspoon vanilla
2 tablespoons sugar
One 20-ounce can crushed
   pineapple in natural juice,
   drained

Preheat oven to 250°. Combine ingredients for the crust in a plastic bag and mix. Turn into a 9″ pie tin and press evenly to form a crust. Bake 15 minutes. Cool.

Sprinkle the gelatin into the cold water in a small bowl and allow to stand about 5 minutes. Add the boiling water and stir to dissolve.

In the food processor, place the cheese, milk, vanilla, sugar, and pineapple. Mix slightly. Add the softened gelatin and blend until almost smooth. Pour into the cool crust and refrigerate until firm. About 3 hours. *Makes 6 servings.*

Sour Cream–Raisin Pie

So easy, so good! This can be stirred up in minutes and put in the refrigerator for an hour or more before serving. It also keeps well, so it can be made a day ahead. One of the easiest and best shells for this is the Very Best Cereal Crust (page 163).

One 9″ pie shell, baked
⅔ cup golden raisins
2 cups milk (no substitute)
1 package GF instant vanilla
   pudding mix
1 teaspoon rum (optional)

⅓ cup sour cream or nondairy
   substitute
½ cup chopped pecans
1 cup whipped cream or
   nondairy whipped topping

In small bowl, place raisins and pour on hot water to plump. Drain after 15 minutes.

In a medium mixing bowl, make up the pudding mix following directions on the package. Add the rum (if used). Place in the refrigerator until it thickens.

Remove and add the sour cream, pecans, and raisins. Fold in the whipped cream or topping. Pour into the pie shell and refrigerate (1 to 24 hours). *Makes 8 servings.*

Peach and Plum Crisp   350°

The combination of peach and plum makes this rosy-colored crisp excitingly different in taste. Serve it plain or with ice cream, frozen yogurt, or a whipped topping.

FILLING	TOPPING
4 fresh peaches	¾ cup GF Flour Mix
6 fresh plums	2 tablespoons sweet rice flour
¾ cup sugar	½ cup brown sugar, packed
1 tablespoon GF Flour Mix	6 tablespoons (¾ stick)
1 tablespoon lemon juice	margarine or butter
	1 teaspoon dried orange peel

Preheat oven to 350°. Spray an 8" square pan with vegetable oil spray.

Filling: Peel and pit the peaches. Slice into large bowl. Pit the plums and slice into ¼" wedges. Add the sugar, flour mix, and lemon juice and tumble gently. Let stand while preparing topping.

Topping: Combine the flours, brown sugar, margarine, and orange peel until mixture is crumbly.

Spoon the filling into prepared pan and sprinkle on the topping. Bake for about 45 minutes until the fruit is tender and the topping is brown. Serve warm or cold. *Makes 6 to 8 servings.*

END-OF-FRUIT-BASKET CRISP: Don't have enough of any single fruit for a crisp? Then peel and slice any combination of peaches, apples, pears, plums, apricots, or nectarines to make enough to fill an 8″ square pan almost full. Tumble with sugar, GF flour mix, and lemon juice as shown above and add the topping. Any combination is delicious. (Plum, nectarine, and apricot skins may be left on.)

Lighter Basic Cream Pie Filling

This extra-light cream pie filling will certainly appeal to anyone watching cholesterol or weight. But it's also so good my guests and testers prefer it to my original cream filling. Use this with bananas, pineapple, or coconut. Prepare a crust for a 9″ pie (cereal or bread crumbs with added sugar make an excellent low-fat crust).

Note: You may substitute all milk (not fat free) or all nondairy liquid or goat's milk for the combination called for here.

1 baked 9″ pie shell	2 tablespoons dark rum
2 tablespoons GF Flour Mix	½ cup liquid egg substitute
¼ cup plus 2 tablespoons sugar	½ teaspoon vanilla or vanilla,
Dash salt	butter, and nut flavoring
½ cup fat-free evaporated milk	1 tablespoon margarine or
¾ cup milk (see note above)	butter

In a medium saucepan, blend flour mix, sugar, and salt. Mix the two milks and add the rum. Stir this in slowly to form a paste. Add the rest of the milk and the egg substitute. Cook over medium heat, stirring constantly, until it simmers. Continue stirring and cook 1 to 2 minutes longer. Remove from heat and stir in the vanilla and margarine. Follow the directions for any of the following pies.

BANANA CREAM PIE: Cool the filling. Line the baked pie shell with 2 bananas cut into ¼" slices. Pour the filling over the bananas. Chill and decorate with whipped cream or nondairy whipped topping fluted around the edges.

PINEAPPLE CREAM PIE: Add an 8-ounce can crushed pineapple, drained, to the cream filling before pouring into the baked pie shell. Chill and decorate as above.

COCONUT CREAM PIE: Preheat oven to 425°. Add 1 cup sweetened flaked coconut to the pie filling while it is still hot. Pour into the baked shell. Top with a meringue of 2 egg whites beaten stiff with 2 tablespoons sugar. Drizzle on a couple of tablespoons of coconut. Bake until meringue browns. Watch carefully—don't let the meringue get too dark.

Mock Apple Pie Filling

Delicious! Don't pass this by if you or your neighbor finds a hidden zucchini on the vine too big to eat as a vegetable. One very large zucchini will make enough for 4 quarts of slices. This recipe makes enough for several pies or crisps, so you can freeze some for desserts next winter.

To prepare the zucchini, cut lengthwise in quarters. Cut quarters into lengthwise slices about as wide at the outside as apple eighths. Scrape out the seeds and pith. Peel and then slice like apple slices.

4 quarts zucchini slices	3 cups sugar
5 tart cooking apples, cored, peeled, and sliced	4 teaspoons cinnamon
	1 teaspoon nutmeg
½ cup water	1 teaspoon salt
3 tablespoons lemon or lime juice	

Place all ingredients in an extra-large cooking pot (or 2 pots to begin) and bring to a boil. Turn heat to low and cook until the zucchini slices are translucent and when tasted (this is the fun part), taste exactly like apple. The mixture will cook down to about half its original volume, so the pots can be combined at the halfway point in cooking. When cooked, set aside to cool and package for freezing in 3 to 4 packages or use some as shown below.

APPLE CRISP: Place 3 cups in an 8″ × 8″ pan. Top with a blend of:

> ⅔ cup GF Flour Mix
> ⅓ cup brown sugar
> 2½ tablespoons butter or margarine
> ½ cup chopped nuts (optional)

Bake at 350° for 30 minutes. Serve plain either warm or cold or topped with ice cream, yogurt, or whipped topping. *Makes 6 to 8 servings.*

OPEN-FACED APPLE PIE: Pour 2½ cups into a prepared 9″ pie crust. Top as above or if using a cereal crust replace half the flour with crushed cereal. Bake at 350° for approximately 30 minutes. *Makes 6 servings.*

HAWAIIAN CRISP: In a 9″ square pan place 3 cups mix combined with one 20-ounce can crushed pineapple, drained. Top as above but use macadamia nuts either in the filling or in the topping. *Makes 9 servings.*

Desserts

Baked and Shaped Desserts

Egg-free Cheese Tart
Apple Delight
Apple Dessert Bars
Easy Sponge Roll or Sponge
    Cupcakes
Chocoholic's Delight
Chocolate Sponge Roll with
    Raspberry Cream Filling
  Mocha Roll
  Mocha Roll with
    Macadamia-Rum Filling
Peach Cobbler with Rum and
    Walnuts
Baked Prune Whip

No-Bake Desserts

Raspberry-Rum Trifle
Fruit Pizza

Puddings and Sauces

A Lighter Plum Pudding
Quick Bread Pudding
Five-Minute Pineapple Sauce

Confections

Creamy Pralines
Peanut Butter Fudge
Coconut–Macadamia Nut
    Brittle
  Peanut or Pecan Brittle
Peanut Butter Crunch
Ginger-Macadamia Chips
Jeweled Squares

I've learned to avoid the bakery sections of the delis in my neighborhood grocery, to tear my gaze from the dessert cart when dining out, and to hold my breath as I walk past those pastries behind glass at the coffee shop in the mall. But at home I like to enjoy a sweet at the end of a meal.

Sometimes it's as simple as a bowl of fruit or pudding. Other times my husband and I splurge on a high-calorie treat. Before that, the meal might be soup and bread to even out the calorie count.

You'll find in this section a variety of desserts to match any meal. Most of them are easy to prepare or can be made ahead. Some are old favorites lightened for today's diet-conscious eaters. All of them are gluten free, and all are tasty enough for the whole family and for guests.

Since the celiac and wheat allergic must be suspicious of many candy bars, chocolates, and other shaped or dipped confections because wheat flour may be used on the conveyer belt in the processing, I've added five simple confections in this chapter to satisfy that sweet tooth.

Egg-free Cheese Tart

Make an elegant dessert in a few minutes when only the crust is baked. This tart can be dressed up with fresh fruit, decorated with a twist of orange or lime, or served plain. Use a 9" pie tin or springform pan, and vary the crust with the nut of your choice.

CRUST

2 cups GF flaked cereal

⅔ cup brown sugar

4 tablespoons (½ stick) margarine or butter, melted

½ cup finely chopped nuts (cashew, pecan, coconut, or macadamia)

FILLING

One 15-ounce carton (or 2 cups) ricotta cheese

2 tablespoons lime or lemon juice

½ cup confectioners' sugar

Fruit for topping (optional)

Preheat oven to 375°.

Crush the cereal in a plastic bag. Add brown sugar, melted margarine, and nuts. Pat mixture into pie tin or springform pan, reserving 3 tablespoons for topping. Bake for 6 minutes. Cool to room temperature before filling.

Blend the cheese, juice, and confectioners' sugar in food processor or with an electric mixer. Spoon into tart shell. Top with sprinkle of remaining crust mix.

Serve immediately or refrigerate until serving. Top with fresh, sweetened fruit (strawberries, raspberries, peaches) or decorate with a twisted slice of lime or orange (including peel). *Makes 6 servings.*

Apple Delight

Not a cake, not a pie, but a little of both. And so simple to toss together. This recipe calls for apple slices, but you could substitute 2½ cups of fresh sliced peaches, pineapple, plums, or pitted cherries.

Note: If you use the Mock Apple Pie Filling (page 174), eliminate the sugar and spice in the recipe. If you prefer, 1½ cups of the Buttermilk Biscuit Mix (page 55) plus 1½ tablespoons sugar will work in this recipe.

1 pouch Dietary Specialties white cake mix	½ cup sugar
½ cup (1 stick) margarine or butter	1 teaspoon apple pie spice
½ cup sweetened shredded coconut	1 cup sour cream or nondairy substitute
3 apples, peeled, cored, and sliced (see note above)	1 egg

Preheat oven to 350°.

Pour cake mix into bowl and cut in the margarine and coconut as you would for a pie crust. Press into an ungreased 9″ × 13″ pan. Bake for 10 minutes.

Mix the sliced apples with the sugar and apple pie spice. Layer over the baked crust. Blend the sour cream and egg. Distribute evenly over the apple slices. Bake for 25 minutes. Serve hot or cold, plain or with whipped topping, ice cream, or frozen yogurt. *Makes 12 servings.*

Apple Dessert Bars 350°

This apple dessert uses nuts for crunch and yogurt for zip.

2 cups Dream Pastry Mix
  (page 58)
1 cup brown sugar
2 tablespoons margarine
¼ cup pecans or walnuts,
  chopped
1 teaspoon baking soda
1½ teaspoons apple pie spice
⅛ teaspoon salt

1 teaspoon vanilla
1 cup low-fat yogurt
¼ cup liquid egg substitute or
  1 egg
3 tart cooking apples, peeled,
  cored, and chopped
Optional toppings: whipped
  cream, ice cream, or frozen
  yogurt

Preheat oven to 350°. Spray a 9″ × 13″ baking pan with vegetable oil spray.

In large mixing bowl, combine Dream Pastry Mix and brown sugar. Cut in the margarine. Remove 2 cups to pat into the prepared baking pan and sprinkle with the chopped nuts.

To the rest of the flour mix, whisk in the baking soda, apple pie spice, and salt. Add the vanilla, yogurt, and liquid egg substitute and beat well. Stir in the chopped apples. Spread over the prepared crust and bake for 40 minutes or until browned and the apples are tender-crisp. Serve either warm or cold, with or without topping. *Makes 12 servings.*

Easy Sponge Roll or Sponge Cupcakes 375° or 400°

With Pancake and Waffle Mix (page 57) on hand (or using one of the mixes from the suppliers listed on pages 376–81) you can quickly stir up several different desserts ranging from those delicious spongy shortcake muffins seen in the stores during berry season to a dazzling whipped-cream-and-fruit-filled sponge roll.

2 tablespoons tapioca flour

½ cup plus 2 tablespoons Pancake and Waffle Mix (page 57)

3 eggs or ¾ cup liquid egg substitute

⅓ cup sugar

Preheat oven to 375° or 400° (according to the recipes below) and prepare pans accordingly.

Blend tapioca flour and Pancake and Waffle Mix. Set aside.

In a large mixing bowl, beat the eggs until thick. Slowly add the sugar and beat for 3 to 4 minutes or until light and fluffy. Add the pancake mix and beat on low speed until just combined. Pour into the prepared pans and bake according to the recipes below.

SPONGE ROLL: Preheat the oven to 375°. Line a 10″ × 15″ jelly roll pan (or a 9″ × 13″ flat cake pan) with wax paper and lightly grease it. Pour in the sponge batter and bake for 12 to 15 minutes for the jelly roll pan or 15 to 18 minutes for the cake pan, or until the top springs back when gently touched.

Immediately invert onto a smooth tea towel dusted with confectioners' sugar. Remove the wax paper. Roll the cake and towel together. Let cool, unroll, and spread with desired filling. This is excellent with whipped cream or nondairy whipped topping spread with fresh fruit. Roll again (without the towel), dust the top with confectioners' sugar (if desired), and refrigerate until serving time. To serve, slice in 1″ to 1½″ slices. *Makes 6 to 8 servings.*

SPONGE CUPCAKES: Preheat oven to 400°. Spray large (3″) muffin cups with vegetable oil spray and lightly dust with rice flour. Spoon the batter into the tins until half full. Bake for 8 to 10 minutes or until the top springs back after being lightly pressed. Serve these split, topped with fresh fruit or plain. *Makes 8 large cupcakes or 12 to 14 smaller ones.*

Chocoholic's Delight

This chocolate torte with its crispy outside and a rich fudgy-tasting inside has been lightened, but none of the flavor is lost. Serve this topped with a dab of whipped topping and some fresh fruit or with a fruit-flavored frozen yogurt. You'll need only a small slice unless you are a true chocoholic. (Almonds may be substituted for the hazelnuts.)

2 squares semisweet chocolate	¼ teaspoon cream of tartar
2 eggs plus 2 egg whites	3 tablespoons Light Bean
1 cup sugar, divided	Flour Mix (page 32) or
⅓ cup Dutch-style cocoa	GF Flour Mix
½ cup boiling water	¼ cup hazelnuts, ground
2 tablespoons apricot brandy	Topping as desired
¼ teaspoon almond extract	

Preheat oven to 375°. Line the bottom of an 8" springform pan with wax paper and spray with vegetable oil spray.

In food processor, chop the chocolate to fine consistency. Break the eggs, putting all the whites into the bowl of your mixer and reserving 2 egg yolks.

In large mixing bowl, combine ¾ cup of sugar, cocoa, and the finely ground chocolate. Stir in the boiling water until the chocolate is melted. Add the brandy, the almond extract, and the egg yolks. Beat with a spoon until blended.

Add the cream of tartar to the egg whites and beat at medium speed until soft peaks are formed. Slowly add the remaining ¼ cup sugar while beating. Beat just until the egg whites form stiff peaks. (Do not overbeat until dry.)

Gently beat the flour and hazelnuts into the chocolate batter. Fold in the egg whites, one at a time. Spoon into the prepared pan and bake 35 to 40 minutes or until a tester comes out only slightly moist. Cool before inverting onto a cake plate. Peel off the paper. Serve with whipped topping and fresh fruit or with frozen yogurt or ice cream. *Makes 12 to 16 servings.*

Chocolate Sponge Roll
with Raspberry Cream Filling

This is not hard to make, but serve this dessert roll at your most elegant party and watch the raves. It can be made ahead, for it keeps several days in the refrigerator if you use nondairy whipped topping. The filling suggested here may be changed to simple whipped cream or nondairy whipped topping or any other flavored jam. Try apricot; it's wonderful.

⅔ cup Light or Dark Bean
   Flour Mix (page 32) or
   GF Flour Mix
3 tablespoons Dutch-style
   cocoa
1 teaspoon baking powder
¼ teaspoon salt
1 teaspoon dried orange peel
1 cup liquid egg substitute, or
   4 eggs

¾ cup sugar
Powdered sugar to sprinkle on
   towel before wrapping roll
1 cup raspberry jam or Mock
   Raspberry Filling (page 135)
1 cup sweetened whipped
   cream or nondairy whipped
   topping

Preheat the oven to 400°. Line the bottom of a 10″ × 15″ jelly roll pan with wax paper and spray with vegetable oil spray.

In a medium bowl, whisk together the flour mix, cocoa, baking powder, salt, and orange peel. Set aside.

In a large bowl, beat the liquid egg substitute with electric mixer at Medium, adding the sugar slowly. Beat about 5 minutes or until the mixture is thickened. Fold in flour mix gently until all is mixed in. Spread the batter evenly in the prepared pan and bake 8 to 10 minutes or until the cake springs back when lightly touched.

On a clean, smooth-textured kitchen towel, sprinkle 2 to 3 tablespoons of powdered sugar. Rub it into the weave so the cake will not stick. Invert the cake onto the towel and peel off the wax paper. If the edges of the cake are crisp or dry, trim these off. Roll the cake and the towel together, making sure the towel separates the sections of cake. Let cool.

When cool, unroll and spread the cake with the jam or filling. Top with the whipped cream and reroll just the cake into a roll. Wrap this in aluminum foil and refrigerate until serving. Slice in 1¼" slices. *Makes 8 servings.*

If desired, spread only with the filling or jam and top the slices with the whipped cream.

MOCHA ROLL: Add 1 tablespoon freeze-dried coffee crystals with the cocoa.

MOCHA ROLL WITH MACADAMIA-RUM FILLING: In this dessert the filling is baked with the roll. Prepare the pan as above. Mix this filling:

12 ounces light cream cheese	3 tablespoons rum (or milk)
½ cup sugar	1 cup finely chopped macadamia
1 egg, or ¼ cup liquid egg	nuts, pecans, or cashews
substitute	

Cream the cheese and sugar until smooth. Beat in the egg and rum until blended. Stir in the nuts. Spread evenly into prepared pan.

Top with mocha cake batter and bake at 375° for 20 minutes or until top springs back when lightly pressed.

Remove and invert onto a clean, smooth-textured towel dusted with powdered sugar. While still warm, roll up the cake, but don't roll up the towel with it. Cool, wrapped in the towel. Remove to either foil or plastic and wrap to refrigerate until ready to serve. (This keeps for several days.) Cut in slices and serve with a dollop of whipped topping or frozen yogurt if desired. *Makes 8 servings.*

Peach Cobbler
with Rum and Walnuts

A no-fuss dessert that tastes like you took a lot of time for your company. If you don't have the Biscuit Mix, substitute GF Flour Mix and add a tablespoon or more of margarine to get the correct feel to the streusel topping.

5 cups peeled and sliced
    peaches or two 16-ounce
    packages frozen peaches,
    thawed and drained
¼ cup rum
½ cup brown sugar
1 tablespoon lemon juice
½ cup chopped walnuts

TOPPING
¾ cup Buttermilk Biscuit Mix
    (page 55)
½ cup crushed sliced almonds
½ cup brown sugar
4 tablespoons (½ stick)
    margarine or butter
½ teaspoon cinnamon

Preheat oven to 375°.

In a large bowl, combine peaches, rum, brown sugar, lemon juice, and walnuts. Place in a 9″ × 13″ × 2″ pan or large casserole.

For topping, combine the biscuit mix, crushed almonds, brown sugar, margarine, and cinnamon. Work with your fingers until the mix resembles coarse meal. Sprinkle over the peaches and bake for 45 minutes. Serve warm topped with ice cream, frozen yogurt, whipped cream, or nondairy whipped topping. *Makes 10 to 12 servings.*

Baked Prune Whip 350°

Here is a light and airy "prune" whip, a favorite from the past, modernized and brought up to healthier standards. Apricots may be substituted for the plums, or, for variety, try using fresh raspberries or blackberries. You will need about 1½ cups of the mashed berries.

One 16-ounce can plums, drained and pureed	2 teaspoons lemon juice
1 teaspoon fresh grated lemon peel	6 tablespoons powdered sugar (divided)
	4 egg whites

Preheat oven to 350°. Spray a 2-quart casserole with vegetable oil spray.

In a small bowl, combine pureed plums, lemon peel, lemon juice, and 3 tablespoons of the powdered sugar.

Add remaining sugar to the egg whites and beat until stiff. Gently fold in the prune mixture. Pile lightly into the baking dish and bake for 20 to 30 minutes. *Makes 6 servings.*

Raspberry-Rum Trifle

Easy party fare! Use leftover yellow cake, then add the jam and a simple pudding from a box. Use vanilla flavor for a trifle with raspberry or cherry jam and the lemon for one with apricot jam. For the lactose intolerant, substitute the custard as shown below.

Note: If you prefer not to use rum, double the amount of orange juice.

One package GF instant
    pudding (vanilla or lemon),
    prepared, or cook the
    custard below
1 yellow cake layer (or leftover
    cake)
¼ cup dark rum (optional, see
    note above)

¼ cup orange juice
1 cup raspberry (or other) jam
    or Mock Raspberry Filling
    (page 135)
Sliced bananas, kiwi, etc.
    (optional)
Whipped cream or nondairy
    whipped topping

CUSTARD
2 tablespoons GF Flour Mix
6 tablespoons sugar
Dash of salt

½ cup liquid egg substitute
1½ cups nondairy liquid
1 teaspoon vanilla

Prepare pudding according to package directions, or prepare custard as follows: In a medium saucepan, blend flour mix, sugar, and salt. Blend together the egg substitute and nondairy liquid. Stir a little of this into the flour mixture to form a paste. Add the rest slowly. Cook over medium heat, stirring constantly, until the custard simmers. Continue stirring and cook 1 to 2 minutes longer. Remove from heat and add the vanilla. Cool.

To assemble trifle: Into a large clear bowl (or trifle bowl), tear half the cake into about 1″ pieces. Mix the rum and orange juice and sprinkle half onto the cake. Top with dabs of the jam (using ½ cup). If using fruit, put in half the fruit. Pour on half the pudding or custard. Repeat. Refrigerate for several hours (or overnight) before serving. Top with whipped cream or nondairy whipped topping. *Makes 8 to 10 servings.*

Fruit Pizza

A simple but elegant-looking dessert that can be made ahead. Use any crust you prefer. I like one of the easy cereal crusts for contrast in textures, but the cream cheese crust makes a richer party dessert.

One 9″ baked GF pie crust

FILLING
One 8-ounce package cream cheese
¼ cup confectioners' sugar
1 teaspoon GF vanilla or almond flavoring

TOPPING
Any combination of sliced fresh kiwi, papaya, peach, pineapple, and berries

GLAZE
1 cup fruit juice (pineapple, orange, apple, or other)
3 tablespoons cornstarch
⅓ cup sugar (less if the juice is sweet)
1 tablespoon lemon juice

Filling: Soften the cream cheese and combine it with the sugar and vanilla or almond flavoring. Pour into the prepared crust.

Topping: Arrange the fruit in an attractive pattern on the filling. Circles are easy.

Glaze: In a small saucepan, combine the juice, cornstarch, sugar, and lemon juice. Cook over medium heat, stirring constantly until thickened. Spoon over fruit while hot. Refrigerate 2 hours or until ready to serve. *Makes 8 servings.*

A Lighter Plum Pudding

It's traditional for me to bring plum pudding to Christmas family gatherings. This new, cholesterol-free version made the same hit as my old family recipe laced with suet. It's delicious with bean bread and Bean Flour Mix but still very tasty with any other GF bread and regular GF flour mix. To cut fat even more, I serve this with the Pineapple Sauce on page 193 rather than the traditional whipped cream or hard sauce. Make this ahead, for it keeps for up to 3 weeks in the refrigerator.

1½ cups GF bread, in small
pieces
⅔ cup evaporated skim milk or
nondairy liquid, thinned
¾ cup GF Flour Mix or Light
or Dark Bean Flour Mix
(page 32)
¼ teaspoon xanthan gum
2½ teaspoons apple pie spice
1 teaspoon baking soda
¼ teaspoon salt

3 egg whites, slightly beaten
⅔ cup brown sugar
¼ cup vegetable oil
¼ cup orange juice
½ teaspoon GF vanilla
¾ cup dried prunes, snipped
¾ cup dried apricots, snipped
½ cup dried cranberries
Whipped cream, nondairy
whipped topping, or
Orange Sauce or Pineapple
Sauce (optional)

Spray a 6½-cup pudding mold (or a 2-pound coffee can) with vegetable oil spray. Prepare a steamer by placing a rack in a large kettle and filling with about 1″ to 1½″ of water. Bring water to a boil.

In a large mixing bowl, place the bread and cover with the milk. Let soak. In a medium bowl, blend the flour mix, xanthan gum, apple pie spice, baking soda, and salt. Set aside.

With a fork, break up the bread pieces until the texture is like mush. Add the egg whites, brown sugar, oil, orange juice, and vanilla. Stir in the fruit pieces and the flour blend.

Pour the mixture into the mold and cover with its cover or with foil (pressing tightly down sides and fastening with a rubber band). Place mold in water and cover kettle. Steam about 2½ to 3 hours or until a tester inserted in the center comes out clean. (You may have to add more boiling water during this time.)

Remove from water and let stand for 10 minutes before unmolding. Serve with whipped cream, nondairy whipped topping, Orange Sauce, or Pineapple Sauce. *Makes 8 to 10 servings.*

Note: This freezes well and can be made ahead of the holiday baking.

Quick Bread Pudding 350°

Use up that stale bread in this delicious dessert, served either hot or cold. Put this together in minutes and vary to suit your taste. Increase the milk by ½ cup for a creamy pudding. Raisins may be substituted for the other dried fruit. Add a bit of lemon zest. Use either brown or white sugar. Or, for a delightfully rich pudding, use a GF flavored nondairy liquid and one of the sweeter breads. The Lemon-Buttermilk Bread (page 80) is wonderful.

2 cups GF bread, crumbled	1 teaspoon vanilla or almond
¼ cup dried cranberries or	extract or vanilla, butter,
cherries	and nut flavoring
2 cups milk or nondairy	½ teaspoon cinnamon
liquid	2 eggs, or 1 egg plus 1 egg white,
4 tablespoons (½ stick)	or ½ cup liquid egg substitute
margarine or butter	Whipped cream or nondairy
½ cup sugar (or to taste)	whipped topping

Preheat oven to 350°. Spray an 8″ square baking dish or a 1½-quart casserole with vegetable oil spray.

Spread the crumbled bread on bottom. Top with the dried cranberries or cherries.

In a medium saucepan over low heat, combine milk, margarine, sugar, vanilla or flavoring, and cinnamon. Heat until the margarine melts. Remove from heat and pour over the bread. Beat the eggs slightly and pour into the baking dish. Stir slightly. Bake for 45 minutes. Serve warm or cold with whipped cream or nondairy whipped topping. *Makes 6 servings.*

Five-Minute Pineapple Sauce

A flavorful sauce to serve with bread puddings, over plain cakes, or with the Lighter Plum Pudding.

½ cup sugar
1 tablespoon cornstarch
One 6-ounce can pineapple juice
   plus 2 tablespoons water

1 tablespoon margarine or
   butter
1 tablespoon lemon juice
1 teaspoon dried lemon peel

In a small saucepan, blend sugar and cornstarch. Stir in the pineapple juice and water, margarine, lemon juice, and lemon peel. Bring to a boil and simmer until thickened and clear, about 5 minutes. *Makes 1 cup.*

    This keeps well in the refrigerator for up to a week. Reheat to serve.

Creamy Pralines

An easy candy that always turns out. A fellow celiac from Louisiana brought these to a conference and I was hooked! You will need a candy thermometer for the best results and a deep saucepan so the candy won't bubble over.

1 cup brown sugar
1 cup sugar
1 cup buttermilk
¾ teaspoon baking soda

½ teaspoon salt
1½ cups chopped pecans
2 tablespoons margarine or
    butter

In a deep, large saucepan, place brown sugar, sugar, buttermilk, baking soda, and salt. Mix well and bring to a boil over medium heat, stirring constantly. Continue cooking until the mixture reaches 210° on a candy thermometer.

Add the pecans and margarine and continue cooking until thermometer reaches 230°. Remove from heat and cool for 2 minutes. Beat with electric mixer about 3 minutes or until mixture is thick and starts to lose its shine. Do not overbeat. Dip by spoonfuls onto wax paper. Add a teaspoon of hot water if candy becomes too hard. *Makes 24 2½″ pralines.*

Peanut Butter Fudge

A quick microwave treat. If your mouth waters for homemade candy, make this extra-smooth treat in minutes.

1 cup creamy peanut butter
½ cup (1 stick) margarine or
    butter
1 cup semisweet chocolate chips

1 cup butterscotch chips
3 cups miniature
    marshmallows
1 cup chopped walnuts

In an 8″ × 12″ glass dish, place the peanut butter, margarine, chocolate chips, and butterscotch chips. Microwave on High for 2½ to 3 minutes. Blend well. Add the marshmallows and nuts. Stir. Place in refrigerator to set. Cut into 1″ squares. *Makes 8 dozen pieces.*

Coconut–Macadamia Nut Brittle

This delicious nut brittle is made in 7 minutes in the microwave. What could be easier?

½ cup dried coconut
½ cup light corn syrup
1 cup unroasted macadamia nuts
1 cup granulated sugar
1 tablespoon margarine or
    butter

1 teaspoon vanilla, butter,
    and nut flavoring (vanilla
    okay)
1 teaspoon baking soda

In a food processor, grind the coconut as fine as possible. Line a cookie sheet with aluminum foil and sprinkle on about ⅔ of the coconut.

In a 2-quart microwave-safe bowl, place the corn syrup, macadamia nuts, and sugar. Microwave on High for 4 minutes; stir. Microwave on High for 4 more minutes. Add margarine and flavoring. Microwave on High for 1 minute. Stir in the baking soda and spread on the prepared sheet. Top immediately with the remaining coconut. Cool.

When cool, break into pieces. *Makes 1 pound.*

PEANUT OR PECAN BRITTLE: Eliminate the coconut and use unroasted peanuts or pecans instead of the macadamia nuts.

Peanut Butter Crunch

This crispy, crunchy, no-bake peanut butter wafer is a cross between cookie and candy. It's a great take-along on hikes, or for skiing, camping, or other sports when you need a quick pickup. You can change the taste by replacing the peanut butter with almond, macadamia, or mixed nut butter.

½ cup sugar
½ cup light corn syrup
¼ teaspoon salt

1 teaspoon vanilla
1 cup peanut butter
3 cups GF cereal flakes, crushed

In a medium saucepan, heat the sugar and syrup but do not boil. Add the salt, vanilla, and peanut butter. Fold in the cereal flakes and drop by teaspoon onto wax paper. Let set until firm. *Makes 3½ dozen 2″ wafers.*

Ginger-Macadamia Chips

I discovered these tasty treats in a Hawaiian candy factory and brought the simple recipe home. To toast the nuts place them in a shallow pan in a 325° oven for 5 to 7 minutes.

12 ounces white chocolate chips
3 tablespoons chopped toasted macadamia nuts
1½ tablespoons finely chopped crystallized ginger

Place the white chocolate chips in a microwave-safe bowl. Melt on Defrost (about 3 minutes). Test. Stir in the nuts and chopped ginger. Drop by teaspoon onto wax paper. Let cool until firm. *Makes about 1 pound.*

Jeweled Squares

These white chocolate squares filled with candied fruit make a great show on the Christmas cookie tray.

½ cup minced candied
    pineapple
½ cup chopped candied cherries
½ cup chopped candied citron

½ cup chopped toasted
    almonds or macadamia nuts
One 6-ounce package white
    chocolate chips

Line an 8½″ × 4½″ bread pan with foil.

Place fruit and nuts in a bowl and mix. Melt the white chocolate chips in the microwave on Defrost. Pour over the fruit-nut mix and blend. Press into the prepared pan and allow to stand until cool. Cut into ¾″ squares. *Makes 1¼ pounds.*

Appetizers

Crackers and Toast Points

Onion Crackers
Cheese Crackers
Parmesan Toast Points

Meat or Fish Hors d'Oeuvres

Gingered Turkey Meatballs in
　　Sweet Mustard Sauce
Baked Crab Balls
Frosted Ham Mound
Chicken Liver Pâté
Happy's Quick Shrimp Dip

Dips and Spreads

Artichoke Spread
Spinach Dip
Bean Dip
Cheese Pineapple

Uncooked Mixes

Trail Mix

See also

Chicken Nuggets
Oysters Hansen Bites

Eating gluten free from a party snack table can be an exercise in frustration. In today's health-conscious climate there will probably be some vegetable sticks, but dips will be suspect, because low-fat or light sour creams often contain gluten, low-calorie cheeses might contain oats, the flavored cheeses could contain wheat, and so could the spiced meats. Potato chips, usually safe, must be viewed with suspicion now that some companies have taken to dusting their potato slices with wheat for added flavor.

All the crackers are sure to be little packets of pure toxins, and even the nut nibble mixes often have pretzel sticks or those cute little wheat cracker fishes added (hard to tell from a nut if you've left your glasses home). Not many hosts or hostesses think to add those boring little rice crackers to the shopping list when planning their snacks.

So what should we eat from an appetizer table except the fruit and vegetables?

I've learned to go to parties prepared, by taking along some of my own nibbles. I have given you a couple of crackers in this chapter and my favorite Parmesan Toast Points. These can be made ahead, for they keep well and they travel without breaking—even in an evening purse.

The other appetizers are easy to make and should certainly impress your friends when you set up your own snack table—gluten free, of course.

Onion Crackers

325°

Garbanzo bean flour and onion combine to make a flavorful appetizer cracker. Easy to make, they keep well and can be made ahead for parties. This is an adaptation from Pat Redjou's No-Gluten Solutions Children's Cookbook *(Rae Publications, 1991).*

½ cup garbanzo bean flour or
    light bean flour
¼ cup sweet rice flour
1 teaspoon baking powder
¾ teaspoon salt
¾ teaspoon paprika
½ teaspoon xanthan gum

2 teaspoons sugar
2 tablespoons margarine or
    butter
1 tablespoon vegetable oil
1 tablespoon grated onion
2 tablespoons water

Preheat oven to 325°.

In a medium bowl, blend together the garbanzo bean flour, sweet rice flour, baking powder, salt, paprika, xanthan gum, and sugar. Cut in the margarine and oil until the mixture feels like coarse crumbs. Add the onion and water and stir into a ball. If too dry, add extra water by the teaspoonful.

Place ball on oiled foil the size of a baking sheet. Roll ⅛" thick, using plastic wrap over the dough to prevent it from sticking. Slide the foil onto a baking sheet and score into 1¼" squares. Prick with a fork. Bake for 12 to 15 minutes or until lightly browned. Remove from oven and allow to cool before breaking into crackers. *Makes about 4 dozen crackers.*

Cheese Crackers

Cheese crackers so crisp they call for more, so easy to stir up you won't mind making more. My testers declared this the best cheese cracker they'd ever eaten.

Note: The cheese rolls may be formed ahead of time and frozen uncooked for later use. When frozen they can be sliced thinner. If thinner, shorten the baking time.

½ cup margarine or butter, softened
2 cups loosely packed sharp
    Cheddar cheese, grated

1 cup GF Flour Mix
1 teaspoon seasoning salt

Cream together the margarine and cheese. Add the flour and seasoning salt and mix together until the dough forms a ball. (This can be done in a food processor.) Divide the dough into 3 sections and roll each into a roll about 6″ long and 1¼″ to 1½″ in diameter. Wrap in wax paper and chill until firm.

Preheat oven to 400°. Cut dough into ⅛″ slices and place on an ungreased baking sheet. Bake for 10 minutes or until crisp and very slightly browned. *Makes about 4½ dozen crackers.*

Parmesan Toast Points

Use these as a flavorful substitute for crackers at your next party or keep them in an airtight container and have nibbles for a month or for when you travel.

Note: If I have time, I allow my bread to stand for a couple of days before slicing.

1 loaf GF bread (Dark Mock Rye, rye, or pumpernickel)	**⅓ teaspoon garlic salt**
½ cup (1 stick) margarine or butter	**⅓ cup grated Parmesan cheese**

Preheat oven to 275°.

With a sharp knife, slice the bread as thin as possible. (It will slice more easily if it is at least one day old and if the loaf is sliced lengthwise down the middle first.) Cut each half once if the loaf is square or into thirds if the loaf is round. Arrange points in a single layer on two ungreased baking sheets.

Melt the margarine. Add the garlic salt and cheese. Stir to blend well. With a pastry brush, spread the top with the mixture. Bake for 25 to 30 minutes or until crisp. Cool before storing in an airtight container until ready to use. *Makes up to 100 toast points depending on the thickness of the slices.*

Gingered Turkey Meatballs
in Sweet Mustard Sauce

A sprightly addition to your party table. Make these in the microwave in minutes to cut time and fat from frying. The meatballs can be made, cooked, and frozen up to 2 months ahead of the party, then pulled out and reheated to be served in the fresh, easy Sweet Mustard Sauce below.

MEATBALLS
1¾ pounds ground turkey
¼ cup liquid egg substitute, or
   1 egg
1 medium apple
¼ medium onion
⅓ cup crushed GF cereal flakes

1½ tablespoons grated ginger
   root
½ teaspoon salt

SAUCE
½ cup currant jelly
½ cup prepared mustard

In a large bowl, place the ground turkey. Add the egg substitute.

Peel and core the apple and cut into chunks. Place in a food processor with the onion and cereal. Chop fine. Add to the meat along with the ginger root and salt. Mix well.

Form into small cocktail-sized balls. Arrange half the meatballs on a microwave-safe pie plate so that the meatballs are around the edge with an empty space in the middle. Microwave on High 6 to 9 minutes or until the balls seem done. Drain and repeat with the remaining meatballs. Cool and freeze or serve while still hot in the following sauce.

Sweet Mustard Sauce: Heat the jelly and mustard in a small saucepan over medium heat. Stir frequently until the jelly is melted and the sauce is hot. Do not boil. *Makes one cup.*

Baked Crab Balls

Serve this tasty appetizer at your next party and hear your guests rave. These crab balls are easy to make ahead and pop into the microwave just before serving time. Serve them plain, with Double Dill Dip, or with a dip made of 1 cup of sour cream with ½ cup chopped green onion.

12 ounces cooked crabmeat or two 6-ounce cans	½ cup chopped green onions
	2 teaspoons lemon juice
2 egg whites, lightly beaten	¾ cup crushed GF cereal flakes
¼ cup yogurt or Mock Sour Cream (page 368)	or GF breadcrumbs
	1 teaspoon dried dill

Preheat oven to 375°. Spray a cookie sheet with vegetable oil spray.

In a large mixing bowl, blend crabmeat, egg whites, yogurt, green onions, and lemon juice. Form the mixture into 1″ balls and roll them in the crushed cereal combined with the dill. Place on cookie sheet. Bake 12 to 15 minutes. Serve slightly warm. *Makes 20 to 24 crab balls.* (Enough to serve 6 if these are the only appetizer served, 10 to 12 if there is a selection of appetizers.)

Frosted Ham Mound

As with other meat appetizers, this may not be as heart healthy as a spinach dip, but when the party needs an easy but hearty hors d'oeuvre, try this ham mound. To cut some fat, make it with Yogurt Cream Cheese (page 369), Light Mayonnaise, and turkey ham. Serve this with GF crackers or one of the rye breads.

2 cups ground or chopped
  cooked ham
4 ounces cream cheese, divided
⅓ cup plus 1 tablespoon
  mayonnaise, or Light
  Mayonnaise (page 366)

2 tablespoons pickle relish
3½ tablespoons sliced green
  onions
3½ tablespoons chopped
  toasted pecans

In the bowl of your food processor, combine the ham, 2 ounces of the cream cheese, 4 tablespoons of the mayonnaise, pickle relish, green onions, and chopped pecans. Process until well mixed. Chill before shaping into a small mound on your serving plate. Mix the remaining cream cheese and mayonnaise and frost the mound. Surround the mound with the crackers or bread squares. *Serves 6 to 8.*

Chicken Liver Pâté

Flavorful, smooth, and easy to make, this pâté can be varied in taste by adding olives or pickles. Make this ahead and the flavor improves. This makes a large amount; halve the recipe to serve 6 to 8.

1 pound chicken livers
½ cup (1 stick) margarine
½ cup chopped onion
1 teaspoon curry powder
1 teaspoon paprika

½ teaspoon salt
¼ teaspoon pepper
8 ounces cream cheese
¼ cup brandy
¾ cup chopped olives or
  sweet pickles (optional)

Wash chicken livers, removing any large veins, and pat dry. Melt half the margarine in a 2-quart saucepan. Add livers, onion, curry powder, paprika, salt, and pepper. Cover and simmer for about 15 minutes or until no pink shows in the livers. Remove to cool slightly. Melt the remaining margarine.

Place cooked mixture in food processor, adding the melted margarine, the cream cheese, and the brandy. Blend until smooth. Remove and stir in the olives or pickles, if using. Pack the mix into a small round bowl. Refrigerate several hours until firm or overnight.

Unmold onto a serving plate. Decorate with chopped hard-boiled eggs or parsley, if desired. Surround with either GF crackers (pages 202–3) or Dark Mock Rye Bread (page 89). *Makes 3 cups.*

Happy's Quick Shrimp Dip

The hostess at my last high school reunion gave me her favorite recipe, saying, "Everyone likes it, and it's so easy." Her measurements were casual but they worked when I tried them, so I've used them here.

One 3-ounce package cream cheese (light is fine)	2 tablespoons lemon juice
	1 to 2 green onions, cut up
2 tablespoons melted margarine	Dash Worcestershire sauce or
½ cup cooked shrimp	1 tablespoon chili sauce

Toss everything into food processor and blend. If you have time, refrigerate for an hour or so. Otherwise, serve immediately with crackers or corn chips. If the crowd is big, plan on making a second batch. *Makes about 1¼ cups.*

Artichoke Spread   325°

Keep the few ingredients needed for this quick and easy spread on your kitchen shelves for unexpected guests. Stir it up and stick it in the oven or microwave while they're removing their coats.

| One 16-ounce can artichoke hearts | ⅓ cup mayonnaise |
| 4 to 5 green onions | ½ cup Parmesan cheese |

If using the oven, preheat to 325°.

In a food processor, chop together the artichoke hearts and onions. Mix in the mayonnaise and cheese. Pour into a microwave-safe quart casserole. Microwave on High for 2 to 3 minutes or until hot, or bake for 10 to 15 minutes. Serve with GF crackers, toast points, or thin slices of one of the party breads. *Makes about 1 pint.*

Spinach Dip

Several people gave me versions of this dip but I didn't try it immediately as I am not fond of spinach. That was my mistake. Now I've added it to my appetizer table, for it makes a big hit, and I'm one of the first to have my cracker out for a spread. Using Light Mayonnaise will cut calories and cholesterol.

1½ cups plain nonfat yogurt	2 green onions, cut in 1″ pieces
½ cup mayonnaise or Light	One 10-ounce package frozen
Mayonnaise (page 366)	chopped spinach, thawed,
1 teaspoon dry mustard	drained, and patted dry with
powder	paper towels
1 teaspoon salt	One 8-ounce can water
1 teaspoon sugar	chestnuts

Place all ingredients in food processor and process 1 minute. Stir and process again until smooth and creamy. *Makes about 2½ cups.*

Note: One version of this was made without the food processor by cutting the onions, spinach, and water chestnuts fine and adding them to the first five ingredients after creaming them together.

Bean Dip

Make this delicious bean dip in seconds and eat it guilt free if it's made with Light Mayonnaise. Use as a dip for vegetables or apple slices, or spread it on GF crackers or toast points.

⅓ cup mayonnaise or Light
    Mayonnaise (page 366)
One 16-ounce can garbanzo
    beans, drained
¼ teaspoon salt

2 tablespoons fresh parsley,
    chopped
4 teaspoons lemon juice
2 green onions, using about
    5 inches

Combine all the ingredients in the small bowl of your food processor. Process 1 minute or until smooth. Stir. If too dry, add 1 extra tablespoon mayonnaise. Process again for several seconds. *Makes 1½ cups.*

Cheese Pineapple

An eye-catching way to serve a simple old favorite that can dress up the buffet table and bring compliments. I've given the most flavorful ingredients, but to save calories you can use light cream cheese (or Yogurt Cream Cheese, page 369) and water-packed pineapple. Make this ahead and freeze to save time on the day of the party. It will keep several months.

One 8-ounce package cream
    cheese
One 8-ounce can crushed
    pineapple in medium syrup,
    drained

1 teaspoon grated orange peel
¼ teaspoon cinnamon
2 tablespoons sliced almonds
Bok choy leaves for garnish
    as pineapple top

In medium bowl, combine cream cheese, pineapple, orange peel, and cinnamon. Refrigerate at least 20 minutes or until easy to mold.

Cut a piece of cardboard into a 3″ × 6″ oval the shape of a pineapple and cover with foil. Pat the cheese mixture into the shape of a half pineapple and sprinkle with the sliced almonds. Cover with plastic wrap and refrigerate or freeze until serving time. Place on oval tray or platter and use the bok choy leaves (cut and trimmed to resemble the green spears of a pineapple top) as garnish at the top of the oval. Surround the cheese with crackers from pages 202–3 or a tasty bread. The Dark Mock Rye Bread (page 89) is excellent. *Serves 8 to 12.*

Trail Mix

As a skier, I often relied on "nibbles" on the slopes to keep me going. This simple high-energy mix can be carried while hiking, backpacking, or skiing. But it also serves as an excellent snack for parties or around the fire at home. Since chocolate chips will melt in the heat, they should be added only when the mix is to be carried in cool weather, as for skiing, or served at home.

START WITH:
¼ cup sunflower seeds
¼ cup whole almonds
¼ cup coarsely chopped
   dried apricots
¼ cup dried apple bits

ADD ANY OF THESE
FOR MORE BULK:
Roasted cashews
Raisins or dried cranberries
Chopped dates, figs, or dried
   papaya
Pumpkin seeds
Chocolate chips

Mix together and store in a covered plastic container or in airtight single-serving plastic packets in the refrigerator. *Makes 1 cup or more.*

Soups

Chicken Soups

Turkey Meatball Soup with
    Noodles
Chicken and Rice Soup
Turkey Chowder
Home-style Chicken Noodle
    Soup
Mulligatawny Soup

Meat Soups

Quick Portuguese Ham and
    Bean Soup
Vegetable Soup with Meatballs

Vegetable Soups

Twenty-Minute Minestrone
Sweet Potato Soup
Vegetable Soup with Beans and
    Pasta

Fish Soup

Fish and Scallop Chowder

Dumplings

Mock Matzoh Balls
Cholesterol-free Dumplings
Fluffy Dumplings with Onion
    and Herbs

Since most canned soups contain gluten, in wheat used for thickening (modified food starch), in pasta or barley in vegetable soups, or in hydrolyzed vegetable protein in broth, the easy days of opening a can of soup for lunch or supper vanished with the diagnosis of celiac disease or a wheat allergy. I have noticed recently that there are now a few companies offering some dried soups that don't contain any toxic grains. (Remember to always read the ingredient labels.) They are great for an emergency or for traveling but certainly can't compete with the wonderful rich flavor of homemade soups.

You don't have to take a day to make soups—or even hours. I've discovered soups you can stir up quickly after work that are so filling they need only a chunk of bread and a salad to make a meal. Try one of the interesting soups here, the Turkey Meatball Soup with Noodles (or Mock Matzoh Balls), the Fish and Scallop Chowder, or the quick and spicy Mulligatawny. If your taste buds still long for some of the homey, old-fashioned soups Campbell's offered, I've added a Chicken and Rice and a Home-style Chicken Noodle that take very little time to cook.

If you've missed your fluffy dumplings or your matzoh balls, I've included three recipes tasty enough to satisfy anyone's craving.

Turkey Meatball Soup
with Noodles

This easy turkey soup takes only 15 minutes to cook, but the spices make the taste unique. For the noodles, use either purchased GF pasta or make your own (see pages 260–62). Or try the Mock Matzoh Balls (page 224) for a delicious change.

1 pound ground turkey	½ teaspoon allspice
⅓ cup GF bread crumbs	¼ teaspoon nutmeg
1 egg or 2 egg whites	½ teaspoon salt
⅓ cup chopped onion	6 cups chicken broth
1 tablespoon fresh parsley, minced,	1½ cups uncooked noodles
or 1 teaspoon dried parsley	1 cup frozen peas
½ teaspoon cinnamon	

Break the turkey into a medium-sized mixing bowl. In food processor, place the bread crumbs, egg, onion, parsley, and spices. Process about ½ minute or until ingredients are blended. Add them to the turkey and mix well.

In a large kettle or stockpot, bring chicken stock to a boil. With wet hands, form meatballs of about 1″, dropping them into the stock as they're formed. Return broth to boiling and add the pasta. When boiling again, turn turn to low and cook until pasta is not quite cooked (10 minutes for regular, 5 minutes for bean pasta). Add the peas and cook 3 minutes longer. Ladle into large soup bowls and serve immediately. *Makes 4 to 5 servings.*

Chicken and Rice Soup

While we cannot safely just open a can of soup and heat it up, this old favorite from our Campbell's soup days can be made almost as fast, but the results are far more flavorful. The recipe serves four but can easily be doubled.

5 cups chicken broth
½ cup chopped onion
½ cup cubed carrots
½ cup sliced celery
2 tablespoons chopped fresh
    parsley
¼ teaspoon dried thyme

Pinch of powdered bay leaves
¾ cup uncooked chicken, cut
    into cubes
Salt and pepper to taste
1 cup cooked rice
1 tablespoon lime juice

In a large kettle, combine the broth, onion, carrots, celery, parsley, thyme, and bay leaves. Bring to a boil and reduce heat to simmer. Cook for about 12 minutes. Add the chicken cubes and simmer until the chicken is cooked (about 6 to 10 minutes). Salt and pepper to taste. (If the stock is seasoned, you probably won't need to add more.) Stir in the rice and lime juice just before serving. *Makes 4 servings.*

Turkey Chowder

When the rainy, gray days arrive in the fall, my thoughts turn to hot soups and chowders. Try this for a new taste in thickened milk-based soups. Serve it with one of the bean breads and you'll have a full meal.

2 cups diced cooked turkey
One 16½-ounce can GF
    cream-style corn (see note)
1 cup chicken broth
1 cup diced potato
½ cup grated carrot
½ cup finely chopped onion

1 teaspoon salt (if broth is
    unsalted)
Pepper to taste
1½ cups milk or nondairy liquid
1 to 2 tablespoons instant
    potato flakes (optional)

In a large saucepan, put all the ingredients except the milk and potato flakes (if using). Bring to a boil and reduce heat to simmer. Cook for 10 minutes. Add the milk, but do not let it boil. Cook for 10 minutes more or to taste. If you prefer a thick chowder, use the potato flakes and add them when you add the milk. *Makes 6 servings.*

Note: There are some brands of canned cream-style corn that are gluten free, but always read the labels.

Home-style Chicken Noodle Soup

A quick and easy soup filled with chunks of chicken and your own homemade noodles.

Note: There are several GF soup bases on the market. (Always read the label.) Some are salted, others are not. Season to taste if unsalted.

1 recipe Cholesterol-free
   Pasta (page 261) or Bean
   Flour Pasta (page 262)
7 cups chicken stock, or 7
   cups water plus 6 tea-
   spoons granular chicken
   soup base (see note above)
1½ teaspoons dried minced
   onion

One 12½-ounce can chunk
   chicken or two 5-ounce cans
   or 2 cups diced cooked
   chicken
1 teaspoon parsley flakes
Salt and pepper (optional, see
   note above)

Make up the pasta and cut into thick noodles.

In a large kettle, place chicken stock, onion, chicken, and parsley. Bring to a boil, turn to simmer, and cook 15 minutes. Drop in the fresh noodles. Allow the kettle to return to a boil. Turn to simmer and cook for approximately 15 minutes for regular pasta, or 7 to 10 minutes for bean pasta. *Makes 6 to 8 servings.*

Mulligatawny Soup

There are as many recipes for this soup as there are states in India, but this adaptation of my aunt's is my favorite. Although chicken thighs are more flavorful than white meat, you can lower the cholesterol by using breasts. The apple may be chopped in the food processor or by hand.

1 tablespoon margarine or butter
1 large chopped onion
2 to 3 teaspoons curry powder (to taste)
1 teaspoon grated ginger root
2 cloves garlic, minced
1 pound skinned, boned chicken, chopped into small bits
2¾ cups chicken broth

⅓ cup GF Flour Mix
2 cups milk (can be low-fat) or nondairy liquid, thinned
4 tart cooking apples, peeled, cored, and chopped very fine
Salt and pepper to taste
¼ cup chopped parsley
1 tablespoon lemon juice (optional)

In a large heavy saucepan, melt the margarine. Add the onion, curry powder, ginger root, and garlic. Sauté on medium heat until the onion is translucent. Add chicken and sauté 5 minutes more. Add the broth and simmer 10 minutes.

Mix flour with a small amount of the milk. Add the rest and stir into the soup. Cook 10 minutes or until thickened, stirring constantly. Stir in apples and cook 5 minutes more. Salt and pepper to taste. Remove from heat and stir in parsley and lemon juice (if used). *Makes 8 servings.*

Quick Portuguese Ham and Bean Soup

This delicious ham and bean soup can be made in minutes if you have a small pressure cooker. Otherwise it takes about 20 minutes. One cup of ham stock can replace that amount of water to add more flavor.

Note: If you don't have a pressure cooker, brown ham in large saucepan, then add the liquids and vegetables. Cook until tender (15 to 20 minutes). Add beans and cook until heated.

¼ cup cooked ham
One 14½-ounce can red kidney
   beans
Juice from beans and enough
   water to make 3 cups
1¼ cups frozen mixed vegetables

One 8-ounce can V-8 juice
½ cup chopped cabbage
1 tablespoon chopped fresh
   parsley
Salt and pepper to taste

Mince the ham and brown in the bottom of the pressure cooker. Drain the beans, reserving the juice. Add water to make 3 cups liquid and pour over the ham. Add the vegetables, V-8 juice, cabbage, and parsley. Cover, set the control on the pressure cooker at 15, and cook for 3 minutes after the control jiggles. Remove from heat and let stand 5 minutes. Then reduce pressure by letting cold water run over cooker.

Return the cooker to the stove and add the beans. Cook until the beans are heated through. Usually no extra seasoning is needed, but if it is, salt and pepper to taste. *Makes 4 servings.*

Vegetable Soup with Meatballs

This quick soup can be a full meal with the addition of a hearty bread. Serve fruit for a low-calorie dessert or splurge on a richer one. Like most soups, this is even better the second day, or it can be frozen for later meals.

SOUP	MEATBALLS FOR SOUP
6 cups chicken broth or meat stock	1 pound extra-lean ground beef
One 5.5-ounce can V-8 juice	⅓ cup grated Parmesan cheese
1½ cups uncooked GF pasta	½ teaspoon minced fresh garlic
1½ cups frozen mixed vegetables	
Salt and pepper to taste (or use salt-free seasoning)	

In a large pot, bring the broth and V-8 juice to a boil. Add the pasta and cook about 4 minutes. Mix together the ingredients for the meatballs.

Add the vegetables and seasoning to broth and turn heat to simmer. Form the meat mixture into about ¾″ balls and drop into the bubbling soup. Simmer about 7 minutes longer, until the meat, pasta, and vegetables are all cooked. *Makes 6 to 8 servings.*

Twenty-Minute Minestrone

If you use canned and frozen vegetables, you can put this soup on the table in minutes.

5 cups beef or chicken or vegetable broth	1 teaspoon sugar (optional)
One 14½-ounce can diced tomatoes	1 cup GF pasta (macaroni or spirals)
One 8-ounce can tomato sauce	2 cups frozen mixed vegetables
1 teaspoon dried crushed basil	One 15½-ounce can cannellini (white kidney) or Great Northern beans, drained
1 teaspoon dried crushed thyme	Grated Parmesan cheese for topping (optional)
¼ teaspoon black pepper	

In a large kettle or saucepan, combine broth, tomatoes, tomato sauce, herbs, pepper, and sugar (if used). Bring to a boil. Add the remaining ingredients. Simmer uncovered until the pasta and vegetables are cooked, about 15 to 20 minutes. Serve in soup bowls with a sprinkle of Parmesan cheese for accent and taste. *Makes 6 servings.*

Sweet Potato Soup

Wonderfully quick and delightfully delicious. You can use either leftover sweet potato or a large fresh sweet potato microwaved approximately 7 minutes on High.

1 cup cooked, peeled sweet potato	¾ cup milk or nondairy liquid
1½ cups chicken stock	Salt and pepper to taste
	Dab of butter or margarine (optional)

Combine sweet potato, chicken stock, and milk in food processor or blender. Pulse until smooth. Season to taste and pour into a saucepan to cook until hot. Serve in bowls with a dab of butter or margarine if desired. *Makes 2 to 3 servings.*

Vegetable Soup with Beans and Pasta

This hearty, homey favorite is so easy to put together and so quick to cook that it may become a standby. Serve this with fresh bread or biscuits (made from the Buttermilk Biscuit Mix, page 55) and end the meal with your favorite dessert. For the pasta, use any of the purchased GF small pastas.

2 tablespoons vegetable oil

1 large carrot, diced

1 clove garlic, minced

2 celery stalks, sliced

1 medium onion, chopped

One 5.5-ounce can V-8 juice

4 cups vegetable or beef stock

One 15-ounce can kidney
  beans, drained

¾ cup frozen peas

1 cup GF small pasta

Salt to taste

In a large kettle or saucepan, heat the oil. Add the carrot, garlic, celery, and onion and sauté until the onion is translucent, about 5 minutes.

Add the V-8 juice, beef stock, and kidney beans. Bring to a boil, reduce heat, and simmer for 10 minutes. Add the pasta, and when the pasta has about 5 minutes left to cook, add the peas. (Some of the new corn pastas will cook in 5 minutes or less. If using one of these, add the peas with the pasta.) Cook until the pasta is done. Taste. If the stock was unsalted, add more salt, if necessary. *Makes 4 to 5 servings.*

Fish and Scallop Chowder

The flavors of Hawaii blend delicately in this slightly sweet and absolutely delicious seafood chowder. Halve the recipe to serve 2 or double it to serve 7 to 8.

⅔ cup scallops

⅔ cup mild white fish
  (halibut, snapper, mahi
  mahi, or other)

3 tablespoons margarine or
  butter

6 green onions, sliced thin

2 cups water

2 tablespoons fresh parsley,
  chopped

2 large potatoes, peeled and
  diced into ¾″ cubes

Salt and pepper to taste

1 cup evaporated milk or
  nondairy liquid, unthinned

½ cup coconut milk

2 to 3 tablespoons potato starch

Wash the scallops and fish and cut into bite-sized pieces. Set aside.

In a large saucepan or kettle, heat the margarine. Sauté the onions slightly and add the water and parsley. Tumble in the potato cubes, and salt and pepper lightly. (Add more, if needed, after the chowder is done.) Bring the water to a boil, lower heat, and cook until the potatoes are tender, about 15 minutes.

Add the fish and scallops and cook until the fish is opaque, about 4 to 5 minutes. Pour in the evaporated milk and coconut milk. Make a paste of the potato starch and a little cold water and add to the chowder. Cook until the chowder thickens slightly. *Makes 4 servings.*

Mock Matzoh Balls

Beth Hillson of the Gluten Free Pantry sent this tasty adaptation of her grandmother's matzoh ball recipe, replacing matzoh meal (crushed, unleavened but gluten-filled crackers) with potato starch and almond meal. Add these to Turkey Meatball Soup (page 216) or your favorite chicken soup recipe.

Note: NutQuik is an almond meal (containing xanthan gum) packaged by Ener-G-Foods; it can be purchased through them or in health food stores.

2 eggs
¾ teaspoon salt
A few grinds of pepper
¼ teaspoon cinnamon
2 tablespoons vegetable oil
   or chicken fat

⅓ cup plus 2 tablespoons finely
   ground blanched almonds or
   NutQuik (see note above)
⅛ teaspoon xanthan gum (if
   using almonds)
⅓ cup plus 1 tablespoon potato
   starch

Separate the eggs, placing yolks in a medium mixing bowl and the whites in a small bowl suitable for beating.

To the yolks, add salt, pepper, cinnamon, and oil. Mix.

Beat the whites until stiff but not dry and fold into yolks. Add the almond meal and xanthan gum (or NutQuik, ground finer in food processor) and potato starch in thirds, folding carefully into the egg mix. Refrigerate for 2 hours.

When your soup is within 15 minutes of being fully cooked, bring to a boil and lower heat to medium. Mix the matzoh ball batter lightly. Drop by heaping teaspoons into boiling soup. Cover and turn heat to simmer. Cook 15 minutes. Serve immediately. *Makes 4 servings.*

Cholesterol-free Dumplings

These are a more chewy dumpling than the matzoh balls and easily replace noodles or pasta in a meal. The trick to success is adding just the right amount of flour, but if you do add too much, they can be saved by adding a teaspoon or two of water or cold soup stock.

⅓ cup plus 1 tablespoon rice flour

⅓ cup plus 1 tablespoon potato starch flour

½ teaspoon salt

⅛ teaspoon onion salt

Pinch parsley flakes (optional)

¾ teaspoon powdered chicken or beef soup base

2 tablespoons vegetable oil

2 large egg whites

Whisk together the two flours. Set aside. In a medium mixing bowl, place salt, onion salt, parsley flakes (if used), powdered soup base, and oil. Whisk together.

Beat the egg whites until thick but not dry. Fold into the seasoning and oil mix. Add the flour, folding in a third at a time until the consistency of drop cookie dough. If too thick, add water or cold soup stock 1 teaspoon at a time.

Drop by rounded teaspoon into boiling chicken or beef stock. Turn heat to simmer, cover, and cook 15 minutes. (No peeking!) *Makes 4 servings.*

Fluffy Dumplings
with Onion and Herbs

A wonderful dumpling for topping stews or for chicken and dumplings. See page 321 for a Poached Chicken with Vegetables that takes this topping perfectly. These contain no fat except that in the egg and the milk; don't use nonfat milk or your dumplings will be tough.

Note: You may replace the liquid egg substitute with 1 extra-large egg.

½ cup rice flour	⅓ cup milk or nondairy substitute
⅓ cup potato starch flour	½ teaspoon dried basil
2 teaspoons baking powder	1 tablespoon fresh parsley,
½ teaspoon salt	chopped
½ teaspoon sugar	2 tablespoons finely chopped
⅓ cup liquid egg substitute	green onion

In a mixing bowl, whisk together the rice flour, potato starch flour, baking powder, salt, and sugar. Set aside.

Beat the egg and add the milk. Make a well in the dry ingredients and quickly stir in the liquids. Fold in the herbs and onion.

Drop by tablespoon into simmering broth. The dumplings can be close together. Cover tightly and reduce heat to simmer. Cook about 15 minutes or until tender. *Makes 4 to 6 servings.*

Luncheon and Supper Dishes

Quiches

Spinach Quiche
Crustless Hamburger Quiche
Quick Zucchini Quiche

Crêpes

Bean Flour Crêpes with
    Chicken and Spinach
    Filling
Seafood Crêpes with Shrimp
    Sauce

Burritos, Enchiladas, and Fajitas

GF Flour Tortillas
Bean Flour Tortillas
Enchiladas
    Cheese Enchiladas
    Meat Enchiladas
    Chicken Enchiladas

Burritos and Fajitas
    Beef Burritos
    Shredded Pork Burritos
    Seafood Burritos
    Chicken Fajitas
    Burritos for a Party

Casseroles

Potato-Sausage Casserole
Cheeseburger Casserole

Sandwiches and Pizza

Hot Pockets
    Tuna Salad Pockets
    Ham and Cheese Pockets
Easy Pizza
Bean Flour Pizza Crust
Fresh Vegetable Pizza

Potatoes

Meat-Stuffed Potatoes
   Chicken Topping
   Chicken Dijon Topping
   Cheese and Broccoli
     Topping

Luncheon Salads

Chicken Luncheon Salad with
   Curried Dressing
Easy Rice Salad
   Garlic Mayonnaise Dressing
   Ginger Vinaigrette

Quick supper dishes often rely on eggs or cheese, and some of the following are no exception. But in all cases, I've given ways to lower the cholesterol and fat so the end result is a healthier meal with the same wonderful taste.

Here you'll find a wide range of dishes from quiches to quick-to-fix casseroles made from the versatile Buttermilk Biscuit Mix on page 55. There are baked potatoes stuffed with a variety of toppings and a bean flour crêpe with filling that will make your guests beg for the recipe. I've also added two recipes for making tortillas so you can have a burrito party.

A word of warning, though. Buying "light" can be hazardous to the celiac diet, because many cheeses and sour creams called "light," "low fat," or "no fat" contain gluten in the form of oats or wheat.

Spinach Quiche

350°

In this tasty crustless quiche I lowered the cholesterol but saved the flavor. Reduced-fat cheeses will lower the cholesterol count even more, but be sure to check for gluten! Serve this with a few slices of fruit and you have a full luncheon or supper. For a vegetarian quiche, replace the bacon with 2 tablespoons mock bacon bits.

5 slices turkey bacon
One 9-ounce package frozen
    chopped spinach, squeezed
    to drain
2 tablespoons GF Flour Mix
¾ cup liquid egg substitute
¾ cup 2% milk or nondairy
    liquid, thinned

¼ cup Light Mayonnaise
    (page 366)
1 cup sliced mushrooms
1 cup grated Cheddar cheese
½ cup grated Swiss cheese
½ cup sliced green onions

Preheat oven to 350°. Spray a 9″ pie pan with vegetable oil spray. Cook the bacon until crisp, then crumble.

In a small bowl, toss the spinach and flour until well mixed. Set aside. In a large bowl, combine the liquid egg substitute, milk, and mayonnaise. Stir in the mushrooms, cheeses, spinach mixture, onions, and bacon. Pour into the prepared pan. Bake for 1 hour or until knife inserted near the center comes out clean. Let stand a few minutes before serving. *Makes 6 to 8 servings.*

Crustless Hamburger Quiche 350°

For an easy supper, toss together this quick quiche and while it's baking, prepare some fruit slices or a tossed salad to serve beside it.

½ pound extra-lean ground beef
½ cup mayonnaise or Light
   Mayonnaise (page 366)
½ cup milk or nondairy liquid
2 eggs or ½ cup liquid egg
   substitute

1 tablespoon cornstarch
1½ cups grated Swiss cheese
½ cup thinly sliced green
   onions
Salt and pepper to taste

Preheat oven to 350°. Spray a 9″ pie tin with vegetable oil spray.

Brown the meat over medium heat. Drain and set aside. Blend together the mayonnaise, milk, eggs, and cornstarch until smooth. Stir in the meat, cheese, onions, and seasoning. Pour into the prepared pan and bake for 35 to 40 minutes or until golden brown on top and a knife inserted in the center comes out clean. *Makes 6 servings.*

VARIATION: For a change of flavor, use ½ cup chopped broccoli flowerets in place of the green onions.

Quick Zucchini Quiche 350°

This quick and delicious quiche uses the Buttermilk Biscuit Mix in place of a crust. Whip it up in minutes and then relax for the hour it takes to bake.

½ cup chopped onion
3 tablespoons vegetable oil
¾ cup liquid egg substitute or
   3 eggs, beaten lightly

3 cups grated zucchini
1½ cups Buttermilk Biscuit Mix
   (page 55)
1 cup grated Cheddar cheese

Preheat oven to 350°.

In a large frying pan, sauté the onion in the oil. Stir in the rest of the ingredients and spoon into a deep 9″ pie pan. Bake for 55 minutes. Remove from oven and let set 5 minutes to finish cooking before serving. *Makes 6 servings.*

Bean Flour Crêpes with Chicken and Spinach Filling

375°

Any make-ahead dish is perfect for the working hostess. The bean flour mix makes extra-tasty crêpes that are so good, your family will love them, as will your guests. You can make up the crêpes ahead and store them in the refrigerator (for several days) or freezer to pull out anytime for stuffing.

Note: This filling can also be used to stuff the pasta as used in the manicotti recipe (page 266).

CRÊPES
⅔ cup Light Bean Flour Mix (page 32)
½ teaspoon salt
¾ cup liquid egg substitute or 3 eggs
1½ cup milk or nondairy liquid
2 tablespoons melted butter or margarine (not oil, or crêpes may stick)

FILLING
2 cups cooked chicken, diced

One 10-ounce package chopped frozen spinach, defrosted and drained
One 4-ounce can mushroom pieces, drained
1 teaspoon paprika
¼ cup liquid egg substitute or 1 egg

SAUCE
1 recipe Cream of Chicken Soup (page 62), equivalent to one 10-ounce can
¼ cup grated Parmesan cheese

Crêpes: Place flour, salt, and liquid egg in a medium bowl. Whisk together or mix with hand eggbeater until smooth. Slowly beat in the milk and melted butter. Refrigerate to rest for 1 to 2 hours.

Using a 7″ skillet or crêpe pan, heat a small amount of oil and pour in

¼ cup batter, or spoon in approximately 3 tablespoons or enough for a very thin covering. You may have to tilt the pan to coat the entire bottom. Cook until the bottom of the crêpe is golden brown and the top seems dry, then turn, barely cooking the reverse side. Slip the crêpe onto wax paper. Repeat the process until all the batter is used. (If you have a Teflon pan, oil only for the first crêpe.) *Makes about 1 dozen 7″ crêpes.*

Filling: Combine the chicken, spinach, mushrooms, paprika, and egg. Place ½ of the filling in each crêpe and roll up. Place seam side down in a 9″ × 12″ baking dish.

Sauce: Preheat oven to 375°. Make up the chicken soup, adding the Parmesan cheese when you remove soup from the stove. Pour the sauce over the crêpes. Bake for 20 minutes. *Makes 6 servings.*

Seafood Crêpes with Shrimp Sauce

350°

Delicious made with either rice flour or bean flour crêpes. You will need 1 batch of about 10 to 12 crêpes. For the cooked seafood use two or more of these: fresh cooked or imitation crab or lobster, shrimp, white fish, and scallops.

Note: The crêpes can be prepared ahead and refrigerated to bake just before serving time.

1 batch Bean Flour Crêpes
 (page 232) (or Crêpes from
 The Gluten-free Gourmet)
2 tablespoons margarine
 or butter
¾ cup celery, thinly sliced
½ cup green onions, thinly
 sliced

2 cups cooked diced seafood
½ cup mayonnaise or Light
 Mayonnaise (page 366)
1 teaspoon curry powder
1 teaspoon lemon juice
1 recipe Shrimp Sauce
 (page 63)

Preheat the oven to 350°. Spray a 9″ × 11″ baking dish or casserole with vegetable oil spray.

In a small skillet, melt the margarine. Add the celery and onions and sauté until tender-crisp. Combine the seafood, mayonnaise, curry powder, and lemon juice in a bowl, then add the celery and onion mixture. Fill each crêpe across the center with 1 to 2 heaping tablespoons of the filling. Roll and place, seam side down, in the prepared dish. Top with the Shrimp Sauce and bake 15 to 20 minutes until hot. *Makes 6 servings.*

GF Flour Tortillas

These tortillas are made in the traditional way by flattening and rolling and then cooking on a hot griddle. They may be a bit of trouble to make but they keep well in the refrigerator or freezer. Use them for enchiladas, burritos, or fajitas.

2 cups GF Flour Mix (page 33)	2 teaspoons non-instant milk
1½ teaspoons xanthan gum	powder or nondairy
2 teaspoons sugar	substitute
1 teaspoon salt	1 cup warm water

In bowl of your electric mixer, place flour mix, xanthan gum, sugar, salt, and milk powder. Whisk together. Add the water and beat on Medium speed for about 1 minute.

Remove dough from mixer and form a ball. Divide the ball into 6 or 8 parts and, working on cornstarch-dusted plastic wrap, roll out each piece very thin until it forms a 10″ to 12″ round. Roll all the pieces, separating them with plastic wrap before cooking.

Heat a griddle to medium-hot or hot and cook each tortilla about 1 minute per side. *Makes 6 large or 8 smaller tortillas.*

Bean Flour Tortillas

Wonderfully easy! These take no rolling but are simply poured into a hot skillet and cooked like a pancake or crêpe. Their delicate flavor blends well with any filling.

⅓ cup light bean flour

½ cup cornstarch

2 tablespoons tapioca flour

½ teaspoon salt

½ cup liquid egg substitute,
    or 2 eggs, or 3 egg whites

1½ cups water

Oil for brushing skillet

In a medium bowl, place the bean flour, cornstarch, tapioca flour, and salt. Whisk together. Add the egg substitute and beat together until smooth. Slowly beat in the water. Let rest in the refrigerator for at least 20 minutes.

Heat a 9″ skillet or frypan over high heat, brushing the pan lightly with oil. Be sure it is hot enough for water to dance on the surface before starting to cook the tortillas. Spoon in about 4 tablespoons of batter or enough to just cover the bottom of the skillet. Cook until the bottom of the tortilla is golden brown and the edges curl and the top seems dry. Turn and barely cook the other side. Slip onto wax paper. Repeat the process.

Store, separated by wax paper, in a plastic bag in the refrigerator or freezer until ready for use. Reheat in microwave before filling. *Makes about 8 tortillas.*

Using the the Bean Flour Tortillas (page 235), or purchased GF corn tortillas, you can make several kinds of enchiladas.

These all call for one 9″ × 13″ baking dish and one recipe of the Enchilada Sauce on page 360.

CHEESE ENCHILADAS: Dip 12 purchased corn tortillas or homemade bean flour tortillas into the Enchilada Sauce, one at a time, and fill with grated Cheddar cheese and diced onions. Roll them and pack into your baking dish. Pour any remaining sauce over them and bake uncovered at 325° for about 15 minutes. *Makes 12 enchiladas.*

MEAT ENCHILADAS: Using about 1 pound of lean ground meat, brown in a frying pan, breaking it up as it cooks. Season with garlic salt or salt and pepper. Add 3 tablespoons of chopped onion and sauté until onion is translucent. Pour about ½ cup Enchilada Sauce into the meat mix. Dip corn or bean flour tortillas into sauce, fill with the meat mix, roll, and place in the baking dish. Pour remaining sauce over and top with about ½ cup grated Cheddar cheese. Bake at 325° for about 15 minutes. *Makes 12 enchiladas.*

CHICKEN ENCHILADAS: Cut 1 whole skinned chicken breast into ¼″ slices and cook in a frying pan in about 1 tablespoon vegetable oil or 2 tablespoons chicken stock. Season with garlic salt or salt and pepper to taste. Add about 2 tablespoons chopped onion and cook until translucent. Dip tortillas into Enchilada Sauce, fill with the chicken mix, roll, and place in the baking dish. Pour remaining sauce over them and top with about ½ cup grated Cheddar cheese. Bake at 325° for about 15 minutes. *Makes 12 enchiladas.*

Burritos and Fajitas

We can't eat these at the fast food places, but now we can have them at home. Pull a batch of the GF Flour Tortillas or the Bean Flour Tortillas out of the freezer and reheat in the microwave for any one of the following.

BEEF BURRITOS: In a skillet, cook 1 pound lean ground beef with ½ cup chopped onion and one package GF dry taco seasoning mix. Moisten with a few tablespoons V-8 juice, tomato juice, or thinned ketchup. Spread on your tortillas and top with some grated cheese and some of the Enchilada Sauce (page 360), if desired. Roll and eat. *Makes 8 to 10 burritos.*

SHREDDED PORK BURRITOS: Use cooked pork and shred about 3 cups. In a frying pan, cook 1 cup chopped onion and a clove of minced garlic in 2 teaspoons vegetable oil. Add about 1 to 3 tablespoons diced jalapeño pepper and the pork. Cook until heated. Place in tortillas with shredded lettuce, diced tomatoes, and grated cheese. Use salsa if desired. Roll and eat. *Makes 8 to 10 burritos.*

SEAFOOD BURRITOS: It may not be authentic, but a restaurant in Hawaii serves a mix of cooked crab, fish, and shrimp in a mayonnaise sauce, rolled in a flour tortilla. Absolutely wonderful, my companions said. I came home and tried this with my own GF tortillas. Excellent!

To make the mayonnaise sauce, thin mayonnaise with a bit of milk and add a squirt of lime or lemon juice and a touch of curry or mustard.

CHICKEN FAJITAS: Heat about 1 tablespoon oil in a large skillet or wok. Cook 4 chicken breast halves that have been sliced into strips. Add 1 sliced onion and 1 bell pepper, seeded and cut into strips. Cook and stir until chicken is no longer pink and the juices run clear, about 8 to 10 minutes. Stir in 1 teaspoon chili powder and ¼ cup lime juice. Use about ½ cup of the mixture for each tortilla. Top with sour cream or guacamole, add chopped tomato, and fold for eating. *Makes 8 fajitas.*

Burritos for a Party

To throw a burrito party, all it takes is a stack of GF Flour Tortillas or Bean Flour Tortillas plus bowls of the following:

Shredded lettuce
Grated cheese
Chopped tomatoes
Refried beans or mashed cooked pinto beans seasoned
   with the Enchilada Sauce (page 360) if desired
Salsa
Green onions, chopped
Yogurt, sour cream, guacamole
Enchilada Sauce (optional)

Let the guests pick their fillings. Roll the burritos and eat with your hands.

Potato-Sausage Casserole 350°

This delicious blending of potato and sausage is one of the family favorites. I like it because it's so easy. Serve it with a tossed salad or coleslaw and finish the meal with fruit. To lower cholesterol, use turkey sausage.

¾ to 1 pound bulk sausage
   (pork or turkey)
¾ cup crumbled GF bread
1 cup milk or nondairy liquid
½ teaspoon salt

⅛ teaspoon dried thyme
Italian seasoning to taste (if
   sausage flavor is mild)
3 medium potatoes, peeled and
   grated
1 medium onion, chopped

Preheat oven to 350°. Spray a 2½-quart casserole with vegetable oil spray.

Crumble the sausage into a skillet and brown.

Crumble the bread into the prepared casserole and pour the milk over it. Add the salt, thyme, and added Italian seasoning if needed. Put in the grated potatoes and onion. Drain the fat from the sausage and add to the casserole. Mix together gently. Bake, covered, from 45 to 60 minutes or until the potato tests done. *Makes 4 to 5 servings.*

Cheeseburger Casserole   400°

Use the Buttermilk Biscuit Mix for this quick and easy supper dish. The recipe calls for beef, but you can lower the cholesterol by using ground turkey breast.

1 pound low-fat ground beef (or turkey)	1½ cups milk or nondairy liquid, thinned
1 large onion, chopped	¾ cup Buttermilk Biscuit Mix (page 55)
½ teaspoon salt	
¼ teaspoon pepper	¾ cup liquid egg substitute or
1 cup Cheddar cheese, grated	3 eggs

Preheat oven to 400°. Spray an 8″ square casserole with vegetable oil spray.

In a large frying pan, cook the meat and onion until the meat is browned and the onion translucent. Add salt and pepper and spread in the bottom of the prepared casserole. Sprinkle with the grated cheese.

Beat the milk, biscuit mix, and egg substitute until smooth. Pour over the meat and cheese. Bake 35 minutes or until brown and a knife inserted in the center comes out clean. Let set 5 minutes before cutting. *Makes 4 servings.*

These wonderfully versatile meals-in-a-bun can be eaten hot from the oven or (better yet) carried to work to make a hot sandwich fresh from the lunchroom microwave. The fillings suggested below do not need cooking. This is a revised version of my ever-popular Crumpet recipe from More from the Gluten-free Gourmet; *you can also use the Salem Crumpets recipe (page 95).*

1½ cups GF Flour Mix	1 tablespoon dry yeast
1½ teaspoons baking powder	¼ cup liquid egg substitute or
1 teaspoon xanthan gum	1 egg
½ teaspoon salt	½ teaspoon vinegar
1½ tablespoons sugar (divided)	1½ tablespoons vegetable oil,
1 cup lukewarm water	melted margarine, or butter

Mix together the flour, baking powder, xanthan gum, and salt. Set aside.

Add 1 teaspoon of the sugar to the water and stir in the yeast. Set aside.

Place 6 English muffin rings on a baking sheet and spray them with vegetable oil spray.

In a mixing bowl, with the mixer at low speed, blend together the remaining sugar, liquid egg substitute, vinegar, oil, and yeast water. Beat in half the flour mixture. With a spoon, stir in the remaining flour and beat until smooth.

Using only half the dough, divide among the 6 rings, spreading evenly over the bottom of each. Divide any of the following fillings and place on the center of each bun. Spread, but don't let the filling touch the edges of the rings. Divide the remaining dough and spread gently over the filling. Cover and let rise until doubled in bulk, 40 to 45 minutes for regular yeast or 20 to 25 minutes for rapid-rising yeast.

Bake in a preheated 375° oven for 20 to 25 minutes. Serve hot, refrigerate, or freeze. *Makes 6 buns.* (This recipe can be doubled, but the following fillings will have to be doubled also.)

TUNA SALAD POCKETS: In a food processor blend until well mixed:

One 6-ounce can tuna, drained
1 tablespoon chopped green
onions
2½ tablespoons mayonnaise

¼ teaspoon celery salt (or to
taste)
1 tablespoon sweet pickle
relish (optional)

HAM AND CHEESE POCKETS: Mix together or chop in a food processor:

¼ cup ham, chopped fine
½ cup grated cheese

2 tablespoons mayonnaise
1 tablespoon sweet pickle relish
(optional)

Use your imagination for other tasty fillings: chopped cooked chicken, turkey, beef, or pork combined with mayonnaise and seasonings.

Easy Pizza   425°

No cookbook would be complete without an easy pizza. This quick yeast crust can be stirred up in minutes. Spread with a purchased GF pizza sauce, some grated mozzarella, and whatever else you like on your pizza (ham bits, pineapple, anchovies, sausage, or tomatoes and other vegetables).

1½ cups GF Flour Mix (page 33)
1½ teaspoons baking powder
1 teaspoon xanthan gum
½ teaspoon salt
1 teaspoon sugar

⅞ cup lukewarm water
1 tablespoon rapid-rising yeast
1 egg or ¼ cup liquid egg
substitute
1 tablespoon vegetable oil

Preheat oven to 425°.

Spray a baking sheet or 15″ round pizza pan with vegetable oil spray.

Blend together the flour, baking powder, xanthan gum, and salt. Set aside. Add sugar to the water and stir in the yeast. Let bubble slightly.

In a mixing bowl, beat with hand mixer at low speed the egg, oil, and the yeast water. Beat in half the flour mixture. With a spoon stir in the rest.

Pour the batter onto the prepared baking sheet and spread with a spatula to a 12½″ circle with slightly raised edges. Allow to rise about 10 minutes and then spread on the sauce, cheese, and other toppings. Bake for 25 to 30 minutes. *Serves 6.*

Bean Flour Pizza Crust 400°

(Yeast, Rice, and Egg Free)

This crispy-thin pizza crust stirs up in minutes and tastes super. Partially bake it, spread on a bit of pizza sauce and cheese, and finish baking. Or, if you prefer, top the unbaked pizza shell with sauce, meat, cheese, olives, green peppers, etc., and bake all at one time.

1½ cups **Light Bean Flour Mix** (page 32)	¼ teaspoon salt
	¾ cup milk or nondairy liquid
1 teaspoon baking powder	¼ cup vegetable oil

Preheat the oven to 400°.

In a medium bowl, combine flour mix, baking powder, and salt.

Measure the milk and stir in the vegetable oil until blended. Stir this liquid into the dry ingredients. Spread in a 10″ circle on a cookie sheet, making the edges slightly thicker.

Bake for about 10 minutes. Spread on a pizza sauce and your favorite pizza toppings and return to the oven for about 9 to 10 minutes. If you prefer, spread the sauce and your toppings on the unbaked crust and bake for about 20 to 25 minutes.

Fresh Vegetable Pizza

Try this healthy change from the cheese-and-pizza-sauce-based hot pizzas. This calls for one cooked pizza shell. You can use either the Easy Pizza crust (page 241) or follow directions for the Salem Crumpets on page 95 for pizza, but don't spread on the filling. Instead, bake at 400° for 12 to 14 minutes and cool before filling as directed below.

1 baked pizza crust	Approximately 4 cups of mixed
4 ounces cream cheese	chopped vegetables from the
¼ cup mayonnaise	following: mushrooms, broccoli
½ teaspoon dill weed	flowerets, green and red bell
⅛ teaspoon onion powder	peppers, zucchini, cauliflower,
⅛ teaspoon garlic powder	tomatoes, green onions

In a small bowl, blend the cream cheese and mayonnaise. Add the dill weed, onion powder, and garlic powder. Spread over the cooled pizza crust. Top with your choice of the chopped or diced vegetables. Serve immediately or seal with plastic wrap and refrigerate for up to several hours. *Makes one 12½″ pizza.*

Meat-Stuffed Potatoes

A full meal in a baked potato is one of my quick and easy standbys when I don't feel like cooking—or have already spent too many hours in the kitchen. The recipes below serve 4. Adjust to your own needs.

1 pound extra-lean ground beef	4 tablespoons margarine or sour cream
Onion salt	½ to ¾ cup grated Cheddar cheese
4 fist-sized baking potatoes	2 to 3 green onions, sliced thin
Salt and pepper to taste	

In a skillet, brown the meat. Season with onion salt. Turn heat to low.

Scrub the potatoes and puncture with a knife. Microwave on High for approximately 4 to 5 minutes per potato. Remove from microwave and let sit for 4 minutes to continue cooking.

To serve, cut an x on the tops of the potatoes and squeeze open. Salt and pepper to taste. Add the margarine or sour cream. Spoon in the hot meat sauce and sprinkle on the cheese. Return to the microwave for 25 seconds or until the cheese melts slightly. Top with the green onions. *Makes 4 servings.*

CHICKEN TOPPING: Microwave 4 potatoes as above, and combine the following:

> One 11½-ounce can chunk chicken, drained, or
>   1½ cups cooked diced chicken (see note, page 245)
> 3 green onions, sliced thin
> ⅓ cup mayonnaise or Light Mayonnaise (page 366)
> Topping: 4 tablespoons grated Parmesan cheese

Divide the mixture among the 4 baked potatoes and top each with 1 tablespoon grated Parmesan cheese. Place potatoes in a flat pan and bake in a 400° oven for about 6 minutes.

CHICKEN DIJON TOPPING: Microwave 4 potatoes as above and combine the following:

> One 11½-ounce can chunk chicken, drained, or
>   1½ cups cooked diced chicken (see note, page 245)
> ¾ cup broccoli flowerets, chopped
> ¼ cup mayonnaise or Light Mayonnaise (page 366)
> 1 tablespoon Dijon mustard
> Topping: 4 tablespoons grated Cheddar cheese

Divide the mixture among the 4 baked potatoes and top each with 1 tablespoon grated Cheddar cheese. Bake as above.

Note: Ground turkey may be substituted for the chicken in these recipes by cooking it as the ground beef above and then stirring in the remaining ingredients. Since the topping will be hot, the stuffed potatoes can be microwaved for about 25 seconds or until the cheese is melted.

CHEESE AND BROCCOLI TOPPING: Microwave 4 potatoes and combine the following:

> 1 recipe Cream of Chicken Soup (page 62), the equivalent of one
>   10-ounce can
> ½ cup grated Cheddar cheese (or to taste)
> 1 cup cooked broccoli flowerets
> ½ teaspoon prepared mustard

Heat thoroughly and serve over the split potatoes. Garnish with a dash of paprika, if desired. *Makes 4 servings.*

Chicken Luncheon Salad with Curried Dressing

My favorite luncheon salad! This was once served in the old open-air Honolulu air terminal restaurant. The old terminal is gone now but I've put the flavors together from memory. This was made with mahi mahi in Hawaii, but I've substituted chicken. You can prepare this ahead and toss together just before serving.

DRESSING
¼ cup pineapple juice, or ¼ cup chicken broth plus 2 teaspoons brown sugar
1½ to 2½ teaspoons curry powder
⅔ cup mayonnaise or Light Mayonnaise (page 366)
1 tablespoon lemon juice

SALAD
2 cups cooked chicken or mahi mahi

One 11-ounce can pineapple and mandarin orange segments
1 cup sliced celery
One 8-ounce can sliced water chestnuts
4 green onions, sliced thin
1 cup sweetened shredded coconut or ½ cup chopped macadamia nuts
1 cup thawed baby peas (optional)

In a small saucepan, heat the pineapple juice with the curry powder. Simmer for 2 minutes. Cool and add to mayonnaise and lemon juice. Blend well. Fold in the chicken or fish and refrigerate until ready to toss with other ingredients.

Serve in a large lettuce-lined bowl or in individual lettuce cups. *Makes 4 to 6 servings.*

Easy Rice Salad

This filling salad can change flavor every time you make it, since I've given a choice of cooked chicken, pork, or ham and a variety of dressings. Use up leftover rice or cook it fresh for the salad; use either the bell pepper or raisins, depending on your preference. This recipe serves 6 to 8, but you can cut the ingredients to your taste for fewer servings. No need for exact measurements.

3 cups cooked brown rice	½ cup diced celery
1½ cups cooked chicken, pork or ham, cut into cubes or slivers	¼ cup diced red or green bell peppers, or mixed (optional)
½ cup sliced green onions	½ cup slivered almonds or cashews
1 cup frozen peas, thawed	1 cup raisins (optional)

In a large bowl, combine all the ingredients. Toss with your favorite GF Italian dressing or either of the following dressings. Remove to a serving bowl. Serve immediately or, for more flavor, cover and chill before serving. *Makes 6 to 8 servings.*

GARLIC MAYONNAISE DRESSING: Combine ½ cup mayonnaise (Light Mayonnaise, page 366, is fine), 1 teaspoon fresh lemon juice, ¼ cup water, and 2 garlic cloves, mashed. Blend well and toss with the salad.

GINGER VINAIGRETTE: (My favorite when I use the almonds and raisins in the salad.) In a jar with a lid, combine 2 tablespoons sherry, 3 tablespoons vegetable oil, ¼ cup cider vinegar, ¼ teaspoon fresh grated ginger root, 1 clove minced garlic, and 1 tablespoon honey mustard. Cover and shake well. Toss with the salad.

Rice, Beans, and Pasta

Rice Dishes

Mock Rice-A-Roni
Spiced Pilaf with Apricots and
    Raisins
Microwaved Rice with
    Vegetables
Risotto with Shrimp and
    Asparagus

Rice and Bean Dishes

Quick Rice and Beans
Rice and Lentil Seafood Salad

Bean Dishes

Twenty-Minute Chili
Country Bean Pot

Pasta

Toni's Terrific Pasta Machine
    Mix
Cholesterol-free Pasta
    Chestnut Fettuccine
Bean Flour Pasta
Top-of-the-Stove Lasagne
Fettuccine with Lamb and Pine
    Nuts
Stove-Top Chicken Tetrazzini
Turkey Manicotti

Corn Dish

Mealie

See also

Chicken-Rice Casserole with
    Fruit
Mary's Party Casserole
Chicken Rice Plus
White Clam Sauce with
    Fettuccine

Pork Cutlets with Fruit and
    Rice
Quick Lamb Stroganoff
Barbecued Beef and Noodles

This is a short chapter because I gave you a wide variety of bean, rice, and pasta casserole dishes in my second book, *More from the Gluten-free Gourmet,* and because you will find some recipes of this sort in the Meat, Poultry, and Seafood chapters.

What is here are some quick dishes for that night when you have to put a meal on the table in a hurry, a corn dish to substitute for rice, and three pasta recipes.

The first is a terrific new pasta mix for those electric pasta machines; the second is a cholesterol-free variation of my original pasta; and the third is a whole new (and tasty) pasta made from a bean flour mix. Use these in any of the pasta dishes in this book or in my other two books. Or pull out your own favorite and try it using GF homemade noodles.

I'm always amazed when I demonstrate pasta making that many in the audience are hesitant to try making their own pasta. If you keep some of the Pasta Base Mix from page 60 made up, it takes only a few minutes to stir up, roll out, and cut a batch of homemade spaghetti or noodles to serve three or four. Toss this fresh from the cutting board into boiling water, and pasta can be the evening meal in less time than it takes to cook rice. With the new machine mix you can make four batches at a time in a few minutes and freeze enough to have pasta for 8 to 12 servings.

Of course, you can always buy GF pasta from the suppliers listed on pages 376–81, although the best brand, Drei Pauley, has unfortunately been discontinued at this time. There is a brown rice pasta, Pastariso, that holds its shape better than most rice ones; it's available in some large markets and health food stores. To me, it still tastes like rice, so I cook it in water flavored with beef, chicken, or vegetable soup base. I should mention that some of the corn or corn-and-rice pastas are also improving in taste and texture.

Mock Rice-A-Roni 400°

A "Rice-A-Roni" pilaf may not be gourmet, but it is quick, easy, and tasty. This can be baked for about 40 minutes or stirred up on top of the stove in half that time.

1 tablespoon vegetable oil	2½ cups chicken stock
½ cup chopped onion	2 tablespoons GF soy sauce
1½ cups Mock Rice-A-Roni	3 tablespoons slivered almonds
Mix (page 61)	(optional)
1 teaspoon dried thyme	

STOVE-TOP COOKING: In a large skillet, heat the oil. Sauté the onion until translucent. Add the Mock Rice-A-Roni Mix and thyme. Stir until the rice is coated. Pour in the chicken stock mixed with the soy sauce. Add the almonds (if used). Bring to boil, reduce heat, cover, and allow to simmer for 20 minutes or until the liquid is absorbed.

BAKED PILAF: Preheat oven to 400°. Follow recipe above, but after the stock is added to the rice, transfer to a 1½-quart casserole with a tight-fitting lid. Place in the oven and bake for 40 minutes. Remove and let stand about 10 minutes to finish cooking before removing lid. *Makes 6 to 8 servings.*

Spiced Pilaf with
Apricots and Raisins

This quick pilaf, slightly sweet with fruit, should add a tasty choice to your rice dishes. Serve it with roast poultry, ham, or other meats that don't have gravies or sauces. It goes together in minutes, takes only 20 minutes to cook, and is wonderful reheated the next day—or the next.

2 to 3 tablespoons vegetable oil	3 cups chicken stock
	½ cup dried apricots, sliced
1 medium onion, chopped	¼ cup golden raisins
⅛ teaspoon turmeric	½ cup slivered almonds
¼ teaspoon ground cloves	(optional)
1½ cups white rice	Salt to taste

Heat the oil in a medium saucepan. Add the chopped onion, turmeric, and cloves. Sauté about 5 minutes or until the onion is translucent. Pour in the rice and stir to coat the grains.

Add the chicken stock, apricots, and raisins and bring to a boil. Reduce the heat to low. Cover and cook about 20 minutes or until the rice is tender and the liquid is absorbed. Fluff with a fork and add the almonds, if used. Salt to taste (you probably won't need the salt if the chicken stock is salted). *Makes 6 to 8 servings.*

Microwaved Rice with
Vegetables

Make this rice side dish for your dinner in minutes. Serve it with leftover meat and a salad to make the full meal.

Note: If you have no meat or want to make a main dish, add ¾ cup peeled and deveined uncooked baby shrimp for the last 2 minutes of cooking time.

1½ cups hot vegetable broth or water

1½ cups instant rice, uncooked

½ cup grated carrot

3 green onions, sliced thin

2 tablespoons GF soy sauce

2 teaspoons vegetable oil

½ teaspoon garlic salt

¼ cup sliced almonds

¾ cup raw shrimp, peeled and deveined (optional)

Set the broth to heat.

In a microwave-safe 2-quart casserole, place the rice, carrot, onions, soy sauce, oil, and garlic salt. Mix well and pour on the hot broth. Cover with glass lid or cooking wrap and microwave on High for approximately 6 minutes or until the liquid is absorbed and the rice is tender.

Let stand 5 minutes before fluffing with a fork and sprinkling with the nuts. *Makes 4 servings.*

Risotto with Shrimp and Asparagus

A top-of-the-stove "quickie" that makes a full meal with a slice or two of fresh fruit on the side.

4 cups chicken broth

1 cup water

1 tablespoon margarine or butter

1 tablespoon olive or vegetable oil

2 cloves garlic, minced

½ medium onion, chopped

1½ cups arborio rice

½ cup dry white wine (or water)

¼ teaspoon crushed saffron (optional)

½ pound asparagus (cut in 1" pieces)

½ pound raw shrimp, peeled and deveined

⅓ cup grated Parmesan cheese

In a saucepan, bring broth and water to a simmer. Leave on low heat.

In a large frypan or saucepan, heat margarine and oil over medium heat. Stir in garlic and onion. Cook until onion is translucent, stirring often. Add the rice and stir until completely coated. Add the wine and cook, stirring, until the liquid is almost absorbed.

While this is cooking, mix ½ cup of the hot broth and the saffron until the mixture is bright yellow. Stir this into the rice. Then add the asparagus.

Continue adding hot broth ½ cup at a time, while stirring gently until the liquid is almost absorbed (about 20 minutes).

When half the broth is used, add the shrimp. Continue adding the liquid until only ¼ cup remains. At this point, the shrimp should be opaque at the center, the asparagus should be tender, and the rice should be firm but tender. Remove from the stove and stir in the last bit of broth and the Parmesan cheese. Serve immediately. *Makes 4 to 5 servings.*

Quick Rice and Beans

This Caribbean-style rice dish contains some fat in the coconut milk but is cholesterol free. It can be stirred up in minutes and tastes delicious. Serve it with baked or grilled chicken or fish and tropical fruit slices.

⅔ cup canned coconut milk	½ teaspoon sugar
1⅓ cups water	2 cups instant white rice
4 green onions, sliced thin	(uncooked)
1 teaspoon dried thyme	One 15-ounce can kidney beans,
1 clove garlic, minced	drained and rinsed
½ teaspoon salt	

Put the coconut milk and water in a medium saucepan. Add the onion, thyme, garlic, salt, and sugar. Bring to a boil and then add the rice. Cover and simmer until the rice absorbs all the liquid. Stir in the beans and cook until they are heated through. Serve immediately. *Makes 5 to 6 servings.*

Rice and Lentil Seafood Salad

This party salad won raves from those watching their cholesterol and those who praised the taste. I like it because I can make it a day ahead and have time to relax before a party. If desired, decorate the top with a few strips of pimiento or some slices of red pepper just before serving.

½ cup white rice
½ cup green lentils
1¾ cups water
½ teaspoon salt
¼ teaspoon dried thyme or
    parsley
¼ teaspoon onion salt

Dash garlic powder
¼ cup Italian dressing
1 cup frozen green peas
3 green onions, sliced thin
1 cup chopped celery
1 cup cooked shrimp, broken

Wash the rice and lentils. Place in a medium saucepan and add the water, salt, thyme (or parsley), onion salt, and garlic powder. Cover and bring to a boil. Reduce heat and simmer until the liquid is absorbed (approximately 15 to 20 minutes). Remove from the stove and stir in the dressing while still hot.

Chill before adding the frozen peas, onions, celery, and shrimp. Pour into a salad bowl and refrigerate for at least 6 hours. Overnight is better. *Makes 8 servings if it is the only main dish. Serves 10 to 12 at a buffet.*

Twenty-Minute Chili

Perfect for that night you're too tired to cook. You can have this chili on the table in twenty minutes if you have a packet of Basic Beef Quartet in the freezer and the cans of beans and tomatoes on your kitchen shelf.

1 quart packet Basic Beef Quartet
(page 300)
One 14½-ounce can stewed
tomatoes
2 to 3 teaspoons chili powder (or
to taste)

One 27-ounce can kidney
beans, drained
1 cup shredded Cheddar
cheese
¼ cup chopped onion

Thaw the beef and empty the packet (with liquid) into a 2- to 3-quart saucepan. Add the stewed tomatoes and chili powder. Bring to a boil, cover, reduce heat, and simmer 10 minutes. Add the beans and cook until heated through. Serve in bowls topped with the cheese and onion. *Makes 6 servings.*

Country Bean Pot   350°

This combination of four beans with a sweet and sour taste makes an easy casserole for picnic, potluck, party, or family dinner. I suggest a turkey sausage, but if you use pork, be sure to pour off the fat. This can be put together ahead of time and baked hours later.

1 pound turkey or pork sausage
1½ cups chopped onions
One 15-ounce can pork and
beans
One 15-ounce can butter beans
One 15-ounce can lima beans

One 15-ounce can pinto
beans
½ cup apple cider vinegar
¾ cup brown sugar
½ teaspoon garlic salt
¼ teaspoon dry mustard

In a large frypan, cook the sausage, breaking it up into small bits. Remove to Dutch oven or large kettle. In the drippings, sauté the onion until clear. If there isn't enough fat, add a small amount of chicken stock or water to keep the onions from burning. Add to the pot.

Open the cans of beans and drain off about 2 tablespoons of the liquid in each can. Pour beans into the pot. Add the vinegar, brown sugar, garlic salt, and mustard. Stir well. Cook over high heat, bringing to a boil. Turn to simmer and cook for 10 minutes. Remove from stove top to oven and bake uncovered at 350° for about 1 hour. *Makes 8 to 10 servings.*

Toni's Terrific Pasta Machine Mix

If you've been waiting for the perfect mix for your electric extrusion pasta machine, wait no more. When Toni offered me her recipe for this book, I didn't hesitate a second. With this mix you can feed the whole family wonderful homemade gluten-free pasta. This one mix will make 4 batches (over a dozen servings). Or it can be frozen in one- or two-portion packets and the celiac can have pasta for weeks.

Toni wisely suggests running the 4 batches one after the other to save time and labor. She keeps the face of the die moist with vegetable oil spray while pouring the next measured batch into the machine. By doing this you recover what would normally be left in the mechanism and wasted, which amounts to almost a whole additional batch. If you wish to change dies, do so at any time by following directions for your machine.

This recipe was developed specifically for the Pasta Express, the machine both Toni and I use, but it will also work in the Simac. So far, other machines have not been tested with this recipe, but for other extrusion machines, the only change necessary should be to add a small amount of water if the mix is too dry or more of the dry mix if too moist.

Note: Granulated lecithin is liquid lecithin adsorbed onto defatted soy flour. Those with a severe sensitivity to soy may replace it with 2 teaspoons of liquid lecithin added to the liquid ingredients in each batch and eliminate the granulated lecithin in the master recipe.

Basic Mix

2 cups white rice flour	4 teaspoons salt
2 cups sweet rice flour	1 cup dry egg whites (packed)
2 cups cornstarch	6 tablespoons granulated
2 cups potato starch flour	lecithin (see note above)
2 cups tapioca starch	¼ cup xanthan gum

Mix well and store in tightly covered canister. It will keep for several months at room temperature.

For each batch of pasta combine:

> 1 large egg, beaten
> 1 tablespoon vegetable oil
> ½ cup water
> 2¾ cups basic mix

For the 4 batches I run in tandem, I put each measure of basic mix in a plastic bag to have ready for the next batch and whip the next set of liquids while watching the former batch turn in the mixer.

Place in machine according to directions and tumble until the correct texture is reached. (This will take about 8 minutes in the Pasta Express.) Extrude the pasta, cutting off at the die with a spatula when the strands reach the desired length. Gently coil them into a nest and wait for the next length. (Toni suggests starting with the linguine die, for the strands are easy to handle and the pasta holds sauce well.)

The fresh pasta may be cooked immediately in boiling salted water to which a little oil has been added. Test for doneness, as it cooks very quickly (start testing at 3 minutes). Drain and mix immediately with sauce, or if waiting for another step (as in making a casserole), mix with a little oil to prevent sticking.

To pack for freezing, I use new plastic meat trays from my butcher and lay a length of plastic wrap on them. I place on enough coils for a family serving and wrap tightly in the plastic, then seal in a freezer-weight Ziploc bag.

Cholesterol-free Pasta

(Rice Free)

In keeping with the theme of this book (and on my doctor's orders) I reworked my original Egg Pasta recipe into this lighter version. It tastes just as great! Note that because egg substitutes contain gums, I was able to cut down on the xanthan gum. This makes a very small batch and can easily be doubled and worked in two balls. (You may use egg whites rather than the egg substitutes, but the resulting pasta is gray and not as tasty.)

⅓ cup tapioca flour
⅓ cup cornstarch
2 tablespoons potato starch
   flour
2 teaspoons xanthan gum

½ teaspoon salt
½ cup liquid egg substitute
1 tablespoon vegetable oil
Extra cornstarch for kneading
   and rolling

Combine the tapioca flour, cornstarch, potato starch flour, xanthan gum, and salt. Beat the egg substitute slightly and add the oil. Pour this mix into the flours and stir until a ball forms. Knead a minute or two, working in extra cornstarch until the dough will not accept any more and is firm enough to roll.

Place the ball on the breadboard, and roll as *thin as possible*. This dough is tough and even if almost transparent will still handle well. Slice into very narrow strips for spaghetti, wider ones for noodles. If using for lasagne, cut into 2″ × 6″ rectangles. The pasta is now ready to cook immediately or to freeze uncooked for later use.

To cook, drop into boiling salted water to which a few drops of vegetable oil have been added. This will take about 12 to 15 minutes to cook, depending on the thickness and size of your pieces. You will have to test for doneness. *Makes 2 to 3 servings for spaghetti, fettuccine, or the Top-of-the-Stove Lasagne (page 263); serves 5 to 6 in a noodle casserole.* Use it also for the manicotti (page 266).

CHESTNUT FETTUCCINE: The following pasta, with its sweet, nutty flavor, is well worth your seeking out the chestnut flour in a health food store or fine grocery.

Replace the potato starch flour with chestnut flour. Cook as above. Serve hot with a dab of butter or margarine and some grated mild cheese that doesn't overpower the wonderful flavor of the chestnut noodles.

Bean Flour Pasta

Don't miss this! The flavor is absolutely wonderful, with a faint nutty taste. Use this as fettuccine, in any of your favorite pasta casseroles, or with your choice of pasta sauces. It also makes wonderful lasagne noodles and manicotti rectangles.

Note: I find this even easier to knead, roll out, and handle than my other pasta. It cooks faster than other pastas, so be careful not to overcook it.

1 cup Light Bean Flour Mix (page 32)	1 tablespoon oil (vegetable or olive)
2 teaspoons xanthan gum	½ cup liquid egg substitute, or 2 eggs
½ teaspoon salt	Cornstarch for kneading

In a medium bowl, combine the Light Bean Flour Mix, xanthan gum, and salt. Whisk together the oil and the eggs (or substitute). Pour into the flours and stir until a ball forms. Knead a minute or two, adding more cornstarch if necessary, and work it in until the dough will not accept any more and is firm enough to roll.

Place the ball on a cutting board dusted with cornstarch and roll as thin as possible. This dough is not as tough as the other pasta, so it will roll easily but still handle well. Slice into very narrow strips for spaghetti, wider ones for noodles or fettuccine. If using for lasagne, cut into 2" × 6" rectangles. The pasta is ready to cook immediately or to freeze uncooked for later use.

If you have a hand-crank (Atlas or other make) machine, the dough can be flattened and cut in that.

To cook, drop into boiling salted water to which a few drops of vegetable oil have been added. The cooking will take from 5 to 7 minutes, depending on whether it is to be used for a casserole (leave very *al dente*) or eaten with cheese or sauce. You will have to test for doneness. *Makes 3 to 4 servings for fettuccine or Top-of-the-Stove Lasagne below; serves 5 to 6 in a noodle casserole.*

Top-of-the-Stove Lasagne

Hungry for lasagne and no time to fuss? Then this easy method using noodles is for you. Because the flavor of the pasta will be stronger than in baked lasagne, I suggest using homemade pasta, either wide-cut noodles or, as I prefer, small 1½" squares of pasta. I serve this with a tossed salad and one of the homemade light breads cut thick, buttered, sprinkled with garlic salt, and then toasted on a baking sheet under the broiler.

A double recipe of fresh homemade
    pasta (pages 261–63)
1 pound extra-lean ground beef
One 14½-ounce jar GF pasta sauce
1 cup ricotta cheese

1 cup grated mozzarella
    cheese
2 tablespoons grated
    Parmesan cheese
    (optional)

Prepare the pasta and start it cooking in a large saucepan in boiling salted water with a few drops of vegetable oil added.

In a skillet, brown the meat and add the pasta sauce to heat.

When the pasta is cooked to taste, drain. Return it to the saucepan and stir in the ricotta and mozzarella cheese until they are melted. Spoon onto serving plates and top with the meat sauce. Sprinkle with grated Parmesan cheese if desired. *Makes 4 to 5 servings.*

Fettuccine with Lamb and Pine Nuts

This new and delightful pairing of lamb and fettuccine can be on the table in minutes. This is best with homemade noodles but a good GF spiral may be substituted.

Double recipe fresh homemade
   pasta (pages 261–63)
1 pound lean lamb
   (shoulder or other cut)
¼ cup olive oil
3 cloves garlic, minced
½ cup finely chopped onion

½ teaspoon dried rosemary
¼ teaspoon nutmeg
1 teaspoon salt
¼ teaspoon pepper
2 tablespoons margarine or
   butter, melted
½ cup pine nuts, for topping

Prepare the pasta and set water to boil. Wash the lamb, remove any fat, and slice into thin strips. Start the pasta cooking.

In a wok or large, deep skillet, heat the oil. Add the garlic and onions and sauté until soft (about 2 minutes). Add the lamb and sauté over medium-high heat until cooked, about 5 minutes. Sprinkle on the rosemary, nutmeg, salt, and pepper. Stir in and cook another 2 minutes. Reduce heat and pour in the margarine.

Drain the fettuccine when done, add it to the meat, and toss well. Serve on warm plates and top each serving with the pine nuts. *Makes 4 to 5 servings.*

Stove-Top Chicken Tetrazzini

If you have the Creamed Soup Base, you can make the sauce for this tasty creamed chicken dish in about the time it takes to cook the pasta.

Note: If you don't have the Creamed Soup Base, use the sauce recipe on page 266.

1 recipe fresh homemade pasta (pages 261–63) or 7 ounces GF spaghetti	1 cup chicken broth
	½ cup milk or nondairy liquid
1 tablespoon margarine or butter	2 cups cooked chicken, cubed
	2 tablespoons dry sherry
½ cup sliced green onions	¼ cup grated Parmesan cheese
2½ cups fresh mushrooms, sliced	Extra Parmesan cheese or chopped parsley, for topping (optional)
¼ cup Creamed Soup Base (page 62)	

Prepare the pasta and start it cooking in boiling salted water to which a few drops of oil have been added. Test for doneness, as pasta cooking times vary. When done, drain and set aside.

Meanwhile, melt margarine in large saucepan. Add onions and mushrooms and cook, stirring, until mushrooms are tender.

In a small bowl, combine the soup base, chicken broth, and milk and blend. Add to the saucepan and cook until the mixture boils and thickens, stirring constantly. Add chicken and sherry and cook until heated. Stir in cheese and when melted add cooked fettuccine (or spaghetti) and toss gently. Serve on plates and garnish with the additional topping, if desired. *Makes 4 servings.*

SAUCE: To replace the soup base, combine ¼ cup rice flour, ¼ teaspoon garlic powder, and ⅛ teaspoon pepper. Continue as above.

Turkey Manicotti   350°

I've lowered the cholesterol in this crowd-pleasing pasta casserole. Make this ahead for a potluck or buffet or just make it up and freeze for a quick supper on a busy day.

1 recipe fresh homemade pasta (pages 261–63), cut into 12 oblongs approximately 4″ × 5″	1 teaspoon Italian seasoning
	¼ cup liquid egg substitute
	½ cup shredded mozzarella cheese
1 pound ground fat-free turkey breast	2 tablespoons Parmesan cheese
3 tablespoons finely chopped onion	One 14½-ounce jar GF spaghetti sauce

Prepare the pasta and start it cooking in boiling salted water to which a few drops of vegetable oil have been added.

In a frypan, cook the turkey over medium-high heat, stirring to break into small bits. When almost cooked, add the onion and sauté until clear. Remove from heat and stir in the seasoning, egg substitute, mozzarella and Parmesan cheeses, and about 3 tablespoons of the spaghetti sauce.

Preheat oven to 350°. Pour 1 cup of the spaghetti sauce into a 9″ × 12″ flat baking dish. Fill the pasta by spooning a couple of tablespoons of the mixture into each of the pasta rectangles, working one at a time. Roll the manicotti and place it seam side down in the sauce. Repeat with the others, packing them tightly so the stuffing will not escape the ends.

Pour the remaining sauce over the top. Cook immediately, refrigerate for later in the day, or freeze. Bake for about 30 minutes. *Makes 6 servings.*

Mealie

For those allergic to rice or desiring to rotate grains in their diet, use this corn dish as an alternative, topped with a spicy or flavorful sauce.

1 cup white cornmeal	½ teaspoon salt
¾ cup cold water	2½ cups boiling water

Spray the inside of a heavy 1½- to 2-quart saucepan with vegetable oil spray.

In the saucepan, stir together the cornmeal, cold water, and salt. Gradually stir in the boiling water. Cook on high, stirring constantly until the mixture boils. Reduce heat and cook, stirring, about 15 minutes or until the mealie pulls away from the sides of the pan.

Spoon immediately into bowl, or stop stirring and return heat to high for about half a minute, then invert pan over a low serving bowl or platter to form a round, firm shape. *Makes 6 to 8 servings.*

Vegetables and Salads

Potatoes

Oven-Roasted Potatoes
Quick Potatoes au Gratin

Vegetables

Spiced Winter Squash
Scandinavian Red Cabbage
Cauliflower Cakes

Salads

Summer Bean Salad
Sweet and Sour Coleslaw
Cabbage Slaw with Variations
Soufflé Salad with Tofu
    Mayonnaise
Tofu Salad with Shrimp

Vegetables are a basic in our celiac diet. We don't need a recipe for boiling potatoes or steaming broccoli, but in this section I've offered some variations for our taste excitement. Most of these are quick to prepare and cook. A few are salads or casseroles that can be prepared ahead. All of them will give the busy cook the luxury of serving a more interesting vegetable dish that's still gluten free.

Oven-Roasted Potatoes 350°

Simple and delicious, these roasted potatoes need no extra seasoning, butter, or gravy. Leaving the skin on preserves vitamins.

3 fist-sized potatoes
2 tablespoons oil
1 tablespoon Onion Soup Mix (page 63)

Preheat oven to 350°.

Scrub potatoes well and cut each one into 6 chunks. Toss in a plastic bag with the oil and Onion Soup Mix. Place in small covered casserole and bake for about 1 hour. *Makes 3 to 4 servings.*

Quick Potatoes au Gratin 350°

Put this casserole together in minutes, as a side dish to meatloaf, baked chicken, or fish.

1 recipe cream of chicken soup from Creamed Soup Base
(page 62)
1 cup GF ranch style salad dressing
2 cups grated Cheddar cheese
½ cup chopped onion
⅛ teaspoon pepper
One 16-ounce package frozen Southern-style hash brown
potatoes

Preheat oven to 350°.

Make the soup as described on page 62. Mix this with the salad dressing, cheese, onion, and pepper. Stir in the potatoes. Spoon into a 2½-quart casserole or an 8″ × 12″ baking dish. Bake 45 to 55 minutes or until thoroughly cooked. *Makes 6 servings.*

Spiced Winter Squash

The hint of spice and lime makes this our family's favorite squash dish. It's quick, too, because this flavorful casserole can be microwaved to serve in 15 minutes. Or, if you have the time you can bake it in the oven.

4 cups winter squash (peeled
  and diced ¼″ × ¾″)
3 tablespoons margarine or
  butter, melted

2 tablespoons brown sugar
1 tablespoon lime juice
1 teaspoon pumpkin pie spice
Salt to taste

Salt the squash lightly and place in a 2-quart microwave-safe casserole. Mix the butter, sugar, lime juice, and pumpkin pie spice. Pour over the squash pieces. Microwave on High for approximately 15 minutes or until the squash is tender, stirring several times during cooking. If using a conventional oven, bake at 350° for about 1 hour, until tender. *Makes 4 to 5 servings.*

Scandinavian Red Cabbage

Scandinavian Red Cabbage is often offered as a side dish at holiday meals in my Scandinavian neighborhood, but I've found it popular with guests anytime. It can be served either hot or room temperature and can be prepared ahead and reheated.

3 tablespoons margarine
3 tart apples, peeled, cored, and chopped
1 cup sliced onion
1 small head red cabbage, shredded
¼ cup brown sugar
2 tablespoons fruit vinegar (raspberry, cranberry, or apple cider)
1 teaspoon salt
¼ teaspoon allspice
¼ teaspoon cloves
2 tablespoons currant jelly
¼ cup red wine

In a large, heavy Dutch oven, melt the margarine. Add the apples and onion and sauté until the onion is translucent. Stir in the cabbage and cook about 7 minutes or until wilted. Add the sugar, vinegar, salt, allspice, and cloves. Cover and cook until the cabbage is tender but still crisp. Add the jelly and wine and cook uncovered for about 5 minutes longer. This may be served immediately or refrigerated and reheated, or served at room temperature. *Makes 6 to 8 servings.*

Cauliflower Cakes

A new shape for an old vegetable. You might even tempt the children to eat cauliflower in this pancake form.

2 cups broken cauliflower
    flowerets
½ cup liquid egg substitute or
    2 whole eggs
2 tablespoons chopped onion
1 teaspoon baking powder
1 tablespoon bean flour (or
    soy flour)

½ teaspoon salt or to taste
2 teaspoons oil for frying

OPTIONAL TOPPINGS:
Sour cream, mayonnaise,
    ketchup, grated cheese

Place all ingredients in a food processor or blender. Blend until the dough looks like pancake batter.

Heat a griddle or frypan and add oil. When hot, drop the cakes onto the griddle in 4″ to 6″ rounds. Turn heat to medium high and brown on one side, then turn. Serve immediately with a dab of sour cream mixed with a touch of mustard for flavor, Light Mayonnaise (page 366), a dash of ketchup, or a sprinkling of grated Cheddar cheese. *Makes 4 to 6 servings.*

Summer Bean Salad

This is one of my favorite salads for a crowd. It's simple to put together, can be made the day before, and keeps for several days. You can cut the sugar to ⅔ cup or you can use a sugar substitute. Always taste when using a diet sugar, for there is a difference among the various brands in quantity needed.

½ cup wine vinegar
½ cup vegetable oil
¾ cup sugar or sugar
    substitute
1 large red onion, sliced thin
1 green pepper, cut into
    rings or strips

One 15-ounce can cut green
    beans
One 15-ounce can cut wax beans
One 15-ounce can kidney beans
One 15-ounce can garbanzo
    beans

In a small bowl, blend together the vinegar, oil, and sugar. Set aside.

Drain the juice from the 4 cans of beans and empty them into a large bowl. Slice the onion and the green pepper, after discarding the seeds, and add to the beans. Stir the dressing and pour over the vegetables. Toss lightly.

Refrigerate several hours or overnight and toss again. *Makes 10 to 12 servings.*

Sweet and Sour Coleslaw

Great for barbecues and picnics, this coleslaw is wonderful for a party when you want to cook ahead. Make this the day before. Keep leftovers refrigerated and eat for several days.

1 large head cabbage (3 pounds)	¾ teaspoon salt
2 large mild onions, sliced thin	4 teaspoons dry mustard
⅔ cup sugar plus 1 tablespoon, divided	1 teaspoon celery seeds
¾ cup apple cider vinegar	¾ cup vegetable oil

Shred the cabbage. Place in a large plastic container and top with the onions. Sprinkle on the ⅔ cup sugar.

In a small pan, combine the remaining tablespoon of sugar, vinegar, salt, mustard, and celery seeds and bring to a boil. Add the salad oil and pour over the cabbage while still hot. Cover and refrigerate for 8 hours or overnight. Toss before serving. *Makes 12 servings.*

Cabbage Slaw with Variations

Salads of fresh greens often take the place of a cooked vegetable side dish in our house, since they pair so satisfactorily with casseroles and pastas. In this day of trying to find more fiber in our diet, a cabbage slaw is the perfect answer. Use chopped napa cabbage, sliced red or green cabbage, or pick up an easy prepackaged slaw mix from the produce section of the grocery store, and top it with your favorite dressing.

A simple and tasty slaw can be merely the cabbage with dressing, or with the following variations to add variety so the family will never tire of coleslaw. Or, if everyone has a different taste, put some of the additions in side dishes and let each person make his or her own version.

Use one or more of the following:

FRUIT: Chopped apple, raisins, or pineapple tidbits or canned mandarin orange sections.

VEGETABLES: Purchased broccoli slaw, grated carrots, sliced raw cauliflower, broccoli flowerets, grated raw zucchini, slivered jicama, or turnip.

BEANS: Kidney or garbanzo beans.

CHEESE: Small blocks of Cheddar or crumbled feta cheese.

SHELLFISH: Cooked shrimp dresses up slaw for company.

Soufflé Salad with Tofu Mayonnaise

Fat is cut and protein added in my favorite molded vegetable salad. This has a crisp crunch and tastes cool for a summer meal. Double the recipe for a large (12-cup) mold for party or potluck.

One 3-ounce package lemon
   gelatin
1 cup hot water
⅓ cup cold water
½ cup (5 ounces) medium tofu
2 tablespoons mayonnaise or
   Light Mayonnaise (page 366)
2 tablespoons vinegar

½ teaspoon salt
1½ cups shredded cabbage
½ cup diced celery
½ cup sliced radishes
2 tablespoons chopped onion
2 tablespoons minced green
   pepper

Dissolve gelatin in the hot water. Blend together the cold water, tofu, mayonnaise, vinegar, and salt. Stir into the gelatin and refrigerate until not quite jelled.

Remove from refrigerator and beat with handheld mixer until frothy. Add the cabbage, celery, radishes, onion, and green pepper. Pour into a 6-cup mold and refrigerate from 3 hours to overnight. I use a 5″ × 8″ loaf pan and unmold onto a platter to garnish with radish roses. *Serves 6 to 8.*

TOFU SALAD WITH SHRIMP: Eliminate the radishes and replace with ½ to ¾ cup whole shrimp. (If you buy uncooked shrimp, use some of the cooking water to replace the hot water in the recipe.)

Strictly Vegetarian

Casseroles

Vegetable Potpie
Vegetarian Lasagne
Broccoli Casserole
Rice and Vegetable Casserole

Crêpes

Mushroom Enchiladas in
    Bean Flour Crêpes

Stove-Top Dishes

Mushroom Stroganoff
Vegetable Pasta with Cheese
    Sauce

Biryani (Indian Pilaf)
Garbanzo Beans with
    Vegetables

Salads

Pasta Salad with Summer
    Vegetables

Vegetarian Burgers

Veggieburger
Mock Chickenburger
Riceburger
Beanburger

E ven if you aren't a vegetarian, these recipes are tasty enough to please any palate.

This section came from reader demand for purely vegetarian recipes, and I started with a lot of apprehension. To my surprise, I really enjoyed the vegetarian main dishes I created and now use them for variety in my own menu planning.

The meat-free burgers were the most difficult because there were so many recipes, and at first I thought everything I made tasted the same. I certainly couldn't buy one to taste, because all the burgers on the market contain gluten. Gradually, through experimentation, I discovered what I liked in the burgers and what would make each one different. The four I offer here are all new recipes, and each has a distinctly different taste.

Since eating vegetarian *and* gluten free (especially if one is also lactose intolerant) is most difficult, I don't offer any nutritional advice on this diet; these recipes are just offered as an addition to the menu.

Vegetable Potpie 400°

This wonderful-tasting potpie is not a "quickie" dish, but the time spent putting it together is well worth it. If you are not strictly vegetarian, try the Quick Soup Mix variation below instead of the White Sauce.

1 fist-sized potato, peeled and cubed
1 cup sliced carrots
1 cup uncooked lima beans
1 tablespoon margarine
2 cups sliced mushrooms
1 cup celery in ½" slices
1 medium onion, chopped
Italian seasoning to taste
Salt and pepper to taste

WHITE SAUCE
3 tablespoons margarine or butter
5 tablespoons GF Flour Mix

2 cups low-fat milk, or 1 cup nondairy liquid plus 1 cup water
Water to moisten
1 teaspoon Worcestershire sauce

TOPPING
1¼ cups Buttermilk Biscuit Mix (page 55)
½ cup grated sharp Cheddar cheese
1 egg, or ¼ cup liquid egg substitute
⅓ cup water

In a 2½-quart microwave-safe casserole, place diced potato, carrots, and lima beans. Add 1 teaspoon water and microwave on High for 8 minutes. Remove and let stand until ready to mix into pie.

In a large frying pan, melt the margarine and sauté the mushrooms, celery, and onion until the onion is translucent. Sprinkle on the seasonings. Combine these with the microwaved vegetables in the casserole.

White Sauce: Melt the 3 tablespoons margarine in a saucepan over medium heat. Stir in half the flour. Add half the milk, stirring slowly to keep it from lumping. Mix the other half of the flour with a couple of tablespoons water and stir into the sauce, then add the rest of the milk.

Cook until it thickens slightly. (It will thicken more in baking.) Pour sauce over the vegetables and add the Worcestershire sauce.

Topping: Make 1 batch of drop biscuits from the biscuit mix according to the directions (Plain Biscuits, page 55), adding the cheese before stirring in the egg and water. Drop onto the top of the vegetables and sauce and bake at 400° for 20 to 25 minutes or until the biscuits are browned. *Makes 5 to 6 servings.*

QUICK SOUP MIX SAUCE: Melt 1 tablespoon margarine in saucepan. Thin 5 tablespoons Creamed Soup Base (page 62) with ½ cup water and add to pan. Add ½ cup more water and 1 cup milk or nondairy substitute and cook until thickened.

Vegetarian Lasagne 375°

So flavorful you'll never miss the meat. I use the fresh pasta or the exciting new Bean Flour Pasta cut into lasagne strips, but there are GF lasagne pastas available. There is also a pasta made of lentils for those who like the strong lentil flavor. You may top this with the Cheddar cheese or leave it off to avoid the added cholesterol. For a spicier taste, sprinkle each layer with Italian seasoning and a dash of basil.

1 recipe Cholesterol-free Pasta (page 261) or Bean Flour Pasta (page 262), or 8 ounces GF lasagne noodles
One 28-ounce jar meatless spaghetti sauce
2 cups sliced or chopped fresh mushrooms
¾ cup chopped broccoli slaw or 1 grated zucchini
1 carrot, grated (optional)
1 large onion, chopped
2 cups ricotta cheese
1 cup grated Cheddar cheese (optional)

Cook pasta and let cool while preparing vegetables. Preheat oven to 375°.

Spray a 9″ × 13″ baking pan with vegetable oil spray. Pour in a few tablespoons of the spaghetti sauce. Layer in a third of the pasta, half the vegetables, half the ricotta cheese, and a third of the remaining sauce. Add another layer of pasta. Put in remaining vegetables and ricotta cheese and another third of the sauce. Top with the remaining pasta. Pour on the remaining sauce and top with the grated cheese, if used. Cover and bake about 1 hour, removing cover halfway through cooking. *Makes 6 servings.*

Broccoli Casserole   350°

This can be a main luncheon or supper dish when served with slices of fruit and some bread or crackers, or it can be a side dish for a large dinner. This tastes almost better the second day, so it can be made ahead and reheated if desired.

1½ cups crumbled GF bread	¼ cup (½ stick) melted
1½ cups chopped broccoli	margarine or butter
3 eggs, beaten lightly	1 teaspoon salt
¾ cup milk or nondairy liquid	3 tablespoons sugar
1 cup grated Cheddar cheese	

Preheat oven to 350°. Spray an 8″ square baking dish with vegetable oil spray.

Cover the bottom of the dish with the bread. Lay the broccoli on next. Mix together the beaten eggs, milk, cheese, margarine, salt, and sugar. Pour over the broccoli and bread. Cover with foil and bake 35 minutes. *Makes 9 servings.*

Rice and Vegetable Casserole 350°

This dish looks as good as it tastes, with its colorful vegetables and bright beans in the rice base. Use it as a main dish for a family dinner or a side dish for company. For variety, substitute roasted kasha (buckwheat) kernels for the rice. (Buckwheat is from the rhubarb family, not the wheat family.)

¾ cup rice (brown or white)
½ teaspoon salt or to taste
1 cup button mushrooms, quartered
1 cup carrots, in half slices
One 15½-ounce can kidney beans, drained and rinsed
½ cup cashews

3 tablespoons chopped fresh parsley
¼ cup chopped onion
½ teaspoon garlic salt
One 14½-ounce can vegetable broth, or 1½ cups vegetable stock
½ cup Cheddar cheese, grated

Preheat oven to 350°.

Pour rice in the bottom of a 2-quart casserole and sprinkle with salt. Add the mushrooms, carrots, beans, cashews, parsley, onion, and garlic salt. Tumble together and add the vegetable broth. Cover and bake for about 1 hour, stirring once at 30 minutes. Remove, sprinkle on the cheese, and let stand 5 minutes for the cheese to melt. *Makes 6 to 8 servings.*

Note: This can be made ahead, cooked, and frozen. Do not add the cheese until the casserole is thawed and reheated by microwaving, or by baking for about 55 minutes.

Mushroom Enchiladas
in Bean Flour Crêpes

400°

A great make-ahead dish! This filling entree needs only a salad or fruit slices to complete the meal. I've used all button mushrooms, but it's more flavorful if you add other fresh mushrooms to the buttons. The enchiladas can be made ahead and stored for up to a day or frozen for later baking. A topping is optional.

One recipe Bean Flour
   Crêpes (page 232)
1 recipe Cream of Mushroom
   Soup or Cheese Sauce
   (pages 62–63), optional
2 tablespoons margarine or
   butter
1 cup red onion, finely
   chopped

2 cloves garlic, minced
2 cups sliced mushrooms
¾ cup grated Monterey Jack
   cheese
¾ cup cream cheese
1 tablespoon chopped chives
2 tablespoons chopped parsley
1 teaspoon dried rosemary (or
   2 teaspoons fresh)
Salt and pepper to taste

Prepare crêpes. Spray a 9″ × 13″ baking dish with vegetable oil spray.

Prepare the mushroom soup or cheese sauce (if used). Let cool.

In a medium saucepan, melt the margarine. Sauté the onion and garlic until translucent. Add the mushrooms and sauté for about 4 minutes. Remove pan from heat and cool. Mix in the two cheeses and the seasonings.

Fill each crêpe with 3 tablespoons of the mix and roll into a cylinder. Arrange with seam side down in the baking dish. Repeat until all the crêpes are filled. Top with mushroom soup or cheese sauce if desired. Cover with foil and bake in a preheated 400° oven for about 20 minutes.

If these are to be stored before baking, cover with plastic wrap and refrigerate or seal well and freeze for up to 3 months. Be sure to remove plastic wrap and replace with foil before baking. If frozen, these will take slightly longer to bake. *Makes 4 to 6 servings.*

Mushroom Stroganoff

Stir up this quick stroganoff, serve over pasta or rice, add a green or fruit salad, and you'll never miss the meat in your meal. I used fresh button mushrooms but you can add more flavor by including some shiitake or chanterelle mushrooms.

1½ recipes fresh homemade pasta (pages 261–63), or 12 ounces GF dried pasta, or 1½ cups white rice

4 cups sliced mushrooms (about 1¼ pounds)

½ cup diced onion

2 tablespoons olive oil

Pinch each of dried thyme and oregano

Salt and pepper to taste

1 cup light sour cream or nonfat nondairy substitute

1 cup vegetable stock

2 tablespoons GF flour mix

2 tablespoons cold water

Grated Parmesan cheese for garnish

Set the pasta or rice to cooking.

In a large frying pan over medium-high heat, sauté the mushrooms and onion in hot olive oil. Add the thyme, oregano, salt, and pepper. Cook until the mushrooms are tender.

Add the sour cream and stir until melted. Add the vegetable stock. Mix flour with the water and add to the pan, stirring constantly until the sauce thickens. If necessary, add more seasoning. Lower heat until the pasta or rice is ready to serve. Spoon this onto separate plates, add the stroganoff, and top with Parmesan cheese. *Makes 4 servings.*

Vegetable Pasta
with Cheese Sauce

Make this meatless but high-energy meal in minutes. Put your pasta to boil (either homemade or your favorite GF pasta), stir up the cheese sauce, and set the table. This calls for a package of your favorite frozen vegetables, but you may prefer to cut your own for a fresher taste. Use about 4 cups overall of a mix of any of these: sliced mushrooms, diced carrots, sliced celery, broccoli flowerets, cauliflower flowerets, sliced green or red bell peppers, zucchini, and frozen peas or lima beans. Have several colors and shapes.

One recipe fresh homemade
    pasta (pages 261–63), or
    8 ounces GF dry pasta
One 16-ounce package of
    favorite frozen vegetable
    mix

CHEESE SAUCE
¼ cup GF Flour Mix
Dash of pepper
⅛ teaspoon nutmeg
½ teaspoon salt
One 12-ounce can evaporated
    milk or 1½ cups nondairy
    liquid
¾ cup grated Swiss cheese
Sliced almonds for topping
    (optional)

Put the pasta to boil in salted water. Add vegetables the last 5 minutes of cooking time.

Prepare the Cheese Sauce: In a jar with a lid, shake together the flour, pepper, nutmeg, salt, and milk. Cook in a saucepan over medium heat until bubbly. Stirring, cook for 1 minute more. Stir in the cheese.

Drain pasta and gently stir in the cheese sauce. Divide onto serving plates and top with the almonds, if used. *Makes 4 generous servings.*

Biryani

(Indian Pilaf)

Biryani, from the northern part of India, may be prepared with lamb or chicken, but for the many Indians who are vegetarians, this recipe would be their choice. The list of ingredients seems long, but much of it is the variety of seasonings.

3 tablespoons olive or
   vegetable oil
1 clove garlic, minced
1 onion, chopped
½ red or green pepper, seeded
   and cut into 1″ squares
2 cups uncooked white
   basmati rice (or brown
   rice)
¼ teaspoon cloves
¼ teaspoon cumin
¾ teaspoon cinnamon

1 teaspoon fresh ginger root,
   grated
4 cups vegetable stock (or water),
   heated to boiling
1 cup green beans (fresh or
   frozen), cut in 1″ pieces
1 cup carrots or sweet potatoes,
   cut in 1″ chunks
1 cup cauliflower flowerets
¾ cup fresh or frozen green peas
½ cup cashews or peanuts

In a large Dutch oven or heavy saucepan, heat the oil on medium heat. Sauté the garlic, onion, and pepper until the onion is translucent. Add the rice and stir until coated with oil. Add the cloves, cumin, cinnamon, and ginger root and cook for about 2 minutes, stirring.

Pour in the stock and stir until it boils again. Add the green beans, carrots, and cauliflower. Cover and simmer for about 40 minutes, then add the peas and finish cooking, about 5 minutes longer.

Before serving, toast the nuts in a 350° oven for about 12 minutes. Spoon the biryani into a serving bowl or in separate servings on plates and top with the toasted nuts. For a taste contrast, serve this with sliced tomatoes and cucumbers. *Makes 4 to 5 servings.*

Garbanzo Beans with Vegetables

This spiced vegetable sauce is a real winner when served with hot rice.

2 tablespoons vegetable oil
1 clove garlic, minced
1 large onion, chopped
1 cup winter squash in ¾″
  pieces
1 cup vegetable broth
Salt to taste if broth is
  unsalted

1 teaspoon sugar (optional)
¼ cup raisins
1 teaspoon cinnamon
1 teaspoon turmeric
¼ teaspoon powdered ginger
One 15-ounce can garbanzo
  beans, drained
1 teaspoon lime juice

In a large saucepan or frypan, heat the oil and sauté the garlic and onion until the onions are translucent. Stir in the squash, broth, raisins, sugar (if used), cinnamon, turmeric, and ginger. Cover and simmer about 8 minutes or until the squash is tender.

Add the garbanzo beans and simmer another 5 minutes. Add the lime juice and serve hot with white rice. *Makes 4 to 5 servings.*

Pasta Salad
with Summer Vegetables

Marinated fresh vegetables team with pasta and cheese for a delightful hot-day lunch or dinner. Remember to put the vegetables and spices to marinate for at least 2 hours before tossing with the pasta. The Bean Flour Pasta is wonderful in this dish.

1 cup green onions, sliced thin
1 cup celery, diced
1 cup green pepper, chopped
  fine
1 cup zucchini, diced
3 small tomatoes, peeled and
  chopped, or 1½ cups cherry
  tomatoes, halved
2 cloves garlic, minced
3 tablespoons cider or fruit
  vinegar

1 tablespoon sugar
⅓ cup chopped fresh parsley
1 teaspoon fresh rosemary or
  ½ teaspoon dried
Pinch of dried oregano
Salt and pepper to taste
1 recipe fresh homemade
  pasta (pages 261–63), or
  8 ounces GF fettuccine
½ cup grated Parmesan cheese

In a large bowl with lid, combine the onions, celery, green pepper, zucchini, tomatoes, garlic, vinegar, sugar, parsley, and rosemary. Mix lightly and season to taste with the oregano, salt, and pepper. Cover and refrigerate for 2 to 6 hours.

Shortly before the meal, cook the pasta in boiling salted water. Drain and rinse with cold water. Pour into a serving bowl and gently tumble in the marinated mixture. Sprinkle with some of the cheese, reserving the rest to serve as each portion is dished up. *Makes 8 servings.*

Four Vegetarian Burgers

I was almost stumped when the wife of a fellow celiac asked me to create a vegetarian burger her husband could have when she ate hers, bought from the local market. I started by reading the ingredient list on vegetarian burgers in my local market's freezer section. This wasn't a lot of help, because they all contained unpronounceable things like autolyzed yeast extract, tripolyphosphate, thiamine mononitrite, disodium guanylate, and succinic acid.

Then I remembered that when I was young on the farm, we often added cooked rice, bread crumbs, or ground nuts (I can pronounce these) to extend hamburger in meatloaves and patties. (You do that when there are nine around the table, most of them teenagers with healthy appetites.) By experimenting and reading a lot of recipes, I've come up with four meat-free patties that are so tasty I've added them to our regular diet.

Veggieburger

This "burger" is crusty and light. It makes a great pattie to serve plain or topped with yogurt or ketchup. It's a little soft to go into a hamburger bun, so I serve it as a replacement for meat along with a rice or potato dish. All I need beside this is a slice of fruit for a full meal.

1½ cups grated zucchini
1 cup chopped mushrooms
½ cup grated Monterey Jack
   cheese
⅓ cup rice bran
3 tablespoons minced onions
3 tablespoons GF Flour Mix
   (page 33)
1 tablespoon GF steak sauce
   (optional)

½ teaspoon dried thyme
½ teaspoon dried rosemary
Salt and pepper to taste
2 eggs, or ½ cup liquid egg
   substitute, beaten slightly
1 tablespoon vegetable oil
   for frying

In a bowl place the zucchini, mushrooms, cheese, rice bran, onions, flour mix, steak sauce (if used), thyme, rosemary, and salt and pepper. Mix well. Stir in the eggs.

Heat the oil in a large frying pan and drop in the burgers, shaped into 4 or 5 rounds about ¾″ thick. Cook on medium heat for about 4 to 5 minutes each side or until they are a deep golden. Serve them on buns with condiments as you would a hamburger, or serve them as meat patties to accompany a potato or pasta salad. *Makes 4 to 5 patties.*

Mock Chickenburger

Nuts and ricotta cheese combine with the other ingredients to give this the flavor of chicken or turkey. It's firm, tasty, and can be used in a sandwich or served as a pattie. I usually just throw everything into the food processor and let it run a bit, but I've given directions for hand mixing, which gives more chew and texture to the pattie.

Note: If you don't have the Italian seasoning, replace with ¾ teaspoon dried basil and ¾ teaspoon oregano plus a dash of garlic salt, and salt and pepper to taste.

2 eggs or ½ cup liquid egg
   substitute
½ cup chopped nuts (walnuts,
   pecans, cashews)
½ cup ricotta cheese
1 cup fresh GF bread crumbs
4 green onions, sliced thin

¼ cup rice bran
2 tablespoons chopped fresh
   parsley
1½ teaspoons Italian seasoning
Salt to taste
1 tablespoon vegetable oil

Beat the eggs slightly. Stir in the nuts, ricotta cheese, bread crumbs, onions, rice bran, parsley, and seasoning.

Heat the oil in a skillet. Spoon in 4 patties, making them about ½″ thick. Cook over medium-high heat about 4 minutes each side or until each side is crusty and brown. *Makes 4 servings.*

Riceburger

Delicious and firm, these can be sandwiched with a slice of cheese and tomato for a burger or they may be eaten as a pattie. The pattie is delicious topped with guacamole or mayonnaise spiced with a dash of mustard. The recipe calls for brown rice, with the rice bran optional. If you use white rice, be sure to add the rice bran.

2 cups cooked brown rice
2 tablespoons rice bran
   (optional)
3 tablespoons dry roasted
   sunflower seeds
2 tablespoons dry milk powder
2 tablespoons soy or bean flour
½ cup chopped onion
½ teaspoon garlic salt

1 teaspoon GF soy or steak
   sauce
¼ teaspoon powdered ginger
1 teaspoon dried parsley or
   2 teaspoons chopped fresh
2 eggs, or ½ cup liquid
   substitute
Salt to taste
1 tablespoon vegetable oil for
   frying

Place all ingredients except the salt and vegetable oil in a food processor. Pulse until well mixed and the rice is chopped fine.

Heat the oil on a large griddle or frying pan. Drop the patties in 6 rounds and smooth to about ½″ thick. Cook on medium heat 2 to 4 minutes on each side or until brown. *Makes 6 burgers.*

Beanburger

With a flavor all its own, this burger can be served as a pattie, or it can be sandwiched with condiments and lettuce to be eaten like any burger. Mustard, mayonnaise, onion, tomato, and avocado all complement this very different pattie.

Note: For an egg-free pattie, add ½ teaspoon xanthan gum and ¾ teaspoon baking powder to the bean flour before adding to the mix. Omit the egg and add 2 to 3 tablespoons vegetable stock or water.

½ cup diced carrot
1 cup chopped broccoli or
   sliced zucchini
1 stick celery
3 tablespoons onion
1 cup light bean flour
   (garbanzo bean flour may
   be substituted)

2 tablespoons vegetable oil
2 teaspoons Italian seasoning
Salt to taste (if seasoning doesn't
   contain salt)
⅓ cup liquid egg substitute, or
   1 egg plus 1 egg white (see
   note above)
1 tablespoon oil for frying

Place the carrot, broccoli, celery, and onion in a food processor and chop fine. Add the bean flour, oil, seasoning, and egg substitute. Pulse until the ingredients form a smooth batter.

Heat the oil in a large frying pan. Drop the batter by large spoonfuls to form six to eight 4″ patties about ½″ thick. Turn the heat to medium and cook slowly, about 4 minutes each side. Serve warm. *Makes 6 to 8 patties* (most people like 2 patties).

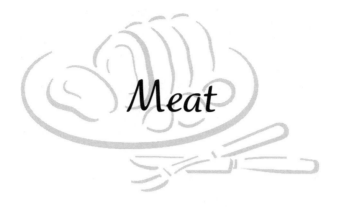

Meat

Make Ahead to Freeze

Basic Beef Quartet

Stove-Top Dishes

Twenty-Minute Beef Stew
Quick Hungarian Goulash
Barbecued Beef and Noodles
Quick Lamb Stroganoff

Casseroles

Sweet and Sour Cabbage with
    Hot Dogs
Pork Cutlets with Fruit and
    Rice

Baked Dish

Short Ribs with Cola Sauce

Microwave Dishes

Meatloaf for the Microwave
    Cheese-filled Meatloaf

See also

Beef-Asparagus Stir-Fry
Pork with Apple Slices
Stir-Fry Beef with Chinese
    Cabbage
Stir-Fry Beef with Orange
    Sauce
Sweet and Sour Pork
Twenty-Minute Chili

With today's emphasis on cutting fats and cholesterol, many of us are searching for ways to stretch the meat in a dish or to use leaner meats. Casseroles are often the answer.

As celiacs, we've already learned that when we order meat in a restaurant, it must be in its simplest form, never marinated, breaded, or in a sauce or casserole. Boring, isn't it?

At home, we can let our imaginations go and combine lean meat in exciting new dishes for the whole family in casseroles and stove-top preparation.

One of the recipes I use a lot, and which is very popular with my testers, is Basic Beef Quartet, with the meat cooked ahead and then frozen to pull out later to create four different time-saving dinners.

Basic Beef Quartet

To make a casserole or stew in minutes, make up this large batch of cooked beef on a spare evening or weekend to keep in the freezer as a handy helper. From this one recipe you can make four casseroles: Twenty-Minute Chili (page 258), Twenty-Minute Beef Stew, Hungarian Goulash, or Barbecued Beef and Noodles.

5 pounds inexpensive boneless
   beef roast
3 tablespoons vegetable oil
5 cloves garlic, minced
2 cups chopped onions

1½ teaspoons salt
½ teaspoon pepper
One 5.5-ounce can V-8 juice
   plus enough water to make
   2½ cups

Wash beef and cut into ¾″ pieces, discarding gristle and fat.

In a large Dutch oven, heat 1 tablespoon of oil. Brown the meat, a quarter of the batch at a time, adding extra oil as needed. Cook the garlic and onion in the same juices until the onion is clear. Return the beef to the pan. Add the salt and pepper, V-8 juice, and water. Bring to a boil, cover, and simmer 1½ to 2 hours until the meat is tender. Cool.

Spoon the mixture into four 1-quart Ziploc freezer bags. Remove air by rolling the bags before sealing. Freeze flat for easy thawing. *Makes approximately 8 cups of beef with liquid.*

Twenty-Minute Beef Stew

Have the full-bodied flavor of beef stew in just a few minutes. For this you can prepare the vegetables as shown below or use one 24-ounce package of frozen stew vegetables. One tablespoon lemon juice may be substituted for the wine. Serve this with chunks of fresh bread and a green salad or slaw.

⅔ cup water or beef broth
½ teaspoon salt
2 medium potatoes, peeled and cut into 1" chunks
1 cup carrots, cut in ¾" pieces

1 packet Basic Beef Quartet (page 300), thawed
1 cup fresh mushrooms, quartered
2 tablespoons red wine
2 tablespoons rice flour

In large saucepan or Dutch oven, bring water and salt to boiling. Add the potatoes and carrots. Bring to boil and reduce to simmer. Cook for 15 minutes or until the vegetables are beginning to become tender. Add the thawed meat and juices. Bring back to simmer. Add the mushrooms and wine. Cook 2 to 3 minutes longer (the mushrooms should remain firm). Thicken by making a paste of rice flour or GF Flour Mix and a couple tablespoons of water. Add some of the hot liquid and then stir into the stew. Cook a minute or two. *Makes 4 to 5 servings.*

Quick Hungarian Goulash

A meal in minutes. You can make the goulash in the same time it takes to cook the rice or noodles to serve with it. All this needs is a salad or fresh fruit for a full meal.

1 packet Basic Beef Quartet (page 300), thawed
1 cup carrots, julienned
½ cup water or beef broth
½ teaspoon pepper
1 teaspoon paprika

¼ teaspoon ground cloves
1 teaspoon brown sugar
2 tablespoons rice flour
¼ cup water
¼ cup sour cream or nondairy substitute

In a large saucepan, place the beef with its juices, the carrots, water or broth, and season with the pepper, paprika, cloves, and brown sugar.

Bring to boil and add the rice flour, made into a paste with the water. Stir in. Simmer until the carrots are tender.

Just before serving, stir in the sour cream and heat through. Remove from heat and serve over cooked rice or noodles. *Makes 4 to 5 servings.*

Barbecued Beef and Noodles

Quick and easy. I like this best with homemade pasta (pages 261 and 262) but if you don't want to fuss, any GF dry noodles will soak up the spicy barbecue flavor. This needs only a salad to complete the meal.

1 packet Basic Beef Quartet (page 300), thawed	1 tablespoon Worcestershire sauce
½ cup tomato sauce	2 tablespoons vinegar
1 cup water	¼ teaspoon dry mustard
2 tablespoons brown sugar	1½ cups dry GF noodles or 1 recipe fresh pasta

Place the beef and juices in a large saucepan. Add the tomato sauce, water, brown sugar, Worcestershire sauce, vinegar, and mustard. Bring to a boil. Turn to simmer and cook about 10 minutes.

Add the pasta and cook as directed. The fresh Cholesterol-free Pasta will take about 12 minutes (7 minutes for the Bean Flour Pasta) or until it tests done. *Makes 3 to 4 servings.*

Quick Lamb Stroganoff

Stir this low-calorie stroganoff together in less than twenty minutes, just the time to cook the pasta or rice to serve with it. Add a few slices of fruit or a small tossed salad for a full meal. If lamb is not available, substitute ground turkey.

1 recipe Cream of Mushroom
   Soup (page 62)
1 pound ground lamb
½ medium onion, chopped
2 cloves garlic, minced

2 cups sliced mushrooms
Salt and pepper to taste
½ cup low-fat sour cream or
   nondairy substitute

Prepare the mushroom soup. Set aside.

Into a large skillet, crumble the ground lamb. Cook over medium-high heat until the meat begins to brown. Remove drippings. Add the onion and garlic and cook until the onion is translucent. Add the mushrooms and stir in the mushroom soup. Turn heat to low and cook, stirring often, for about 10 minutes. Season, if desired, with salt and pepper. Stir in the sour cream and cook only until heated through. Serve over hot buttered noodles or rice. *Makes 4 servings.*

Sweet and Sour Cabbage with Hot Dogs

350°

A tasty vegetable, fruit, and meat dish to spice up the winter diet. This can be put together in minutes and baked for an hour while the busy cook relaxes. Small red potatoes make a great accompaniment. Add one of the home-baked breads and you have a meal.

3 cups finely sliced cabbage
2 apples, peeled, cored, and
  chopped
5 hot dogs, cut into 1" lengths

SAUCE
2 tablespoons margarine or
  butter
¼ cup brown sugar
½ cup water, divided
¼ cup cider vinegar
½ teaspoon salt
1 tablespoon cornstarch

Preheat oven to 350°.

In a microwave-safe 2-quart casserole, place washed and sliced cabbage. Microwave on High for approximately 3 minutes or until the cabbage is tender-crisp. Remove from the microwave and add a layer of apples, then the hot dogs.

In a small saucepan, melt margarine, stir in the sugar, ¼ cup water, vinegar, and salt. Dissolve the cornstarch in the remaining ¼ cup water and add to the hot mixture, stirring until thick and clear. Pour over the casserole. Cover and bake at 350° for 1 hour. *Makes 4 to 5 servings.*

Pork Cutlets
with Fruit and Rice

350°

The old-fashioned taste of this full-meal casserole belies the few minutes it takes to put together. Stir up a slaw or toss a salad and you'll have dinner on the table with little fuss.

8 lean pork cutlets (about
    1½ pounds)
1 tablespoon oil (optional)
Salt and pepper to taste
2 tablespoons margarine
½ large onion, chopped
1½ cup instant rice, uncooked
1 apple, peeled, cored, and
    diced

1 cup dried pitted prunes,
    chopped
1 teaspoon salt
Dash of pepper
Pinch poultry seasoning or
    coriander
1½ cups chicken stock

Preheat oven to 350°. Spray a 2½-quart casserole with vegetable oil spray.

Wash the meat and trim off any fat. In a large skillet, heat the oil (if used) and brown the cutlets quickly, adding salt and pepper to taste. Place on platter and drain any drippings from pan.

Melt the margarine in same skillet and sauté the onions until translucent. Pour into the prepared casserole. Add the rice, apple, prunes, salt, pepper, and poultry seasoning. Mix, and pour on the chicken stock. Top with the browned cutlets. Cover and bake for 35 to 45 minutes or until the cutlets are tender. *Makes 5 to 6 servings.*

Short Ribs with Cola Sauce 325°

Many barbecue sauces contain vinegar, which may not be gluten free, so to enjoy an all-American barbecue taste, you can make your own. You can prepare the sauce ahead and marinate the ribs in it, or you can bake the ribs in the sauce immediately. Have your butcher cut the ribs to approximately 3 inches and trim the fat. I like to serve these with a rice pilaf or buttered noodles.

4 to 5 pounds beef short ribs
Salt, pepper, and garlic powder
   to taste
1½ cups carbonated cola drink
   (may be diet or decaffeinated)

1 cup chili sauce
3 tablespoons
   Worcestershire sauce
6 to 10 drops Tabasco
   sauce, or to taste

Preheat oven to 325°. Spray a skillet or Dutch oven with vegetable oil spray.

Brown the meat on all sides. Drain any excess fat. If you are using a skillet, remove the ribs to a large casserole. If you are using the Duch oven, leave ribs in it.

Sprinkle the ribs with the salt, pepper, and garlic powder, turning the ribs to season all sides.

Mix the cola, chili sauce, Worcestershire sauce, and Tabasco sauce and pour over the ribs. Cover with a tight-fitting lid and either marinate for up to 12 hours or bake immediately. Bake for 1½ to 2 hours or until tender. *Makes 8 to 10 servings.*

Meatloaf for the Microwave

Have a hankering for meatloaf but not the hour it takes to bake? Then this recipe is for you. I've given directions for a plain meatloaf or one stuffed with cheese. Both can become family standbys. If you have time, either meatloaf may be baked in a conventional oven at 350° for 1 hour. See page 361 for a topping sauce.

1 pound extra-lean ground beef
2 tablespoons Onion Soup Mix
 (page 63)
1 egg or ¼ cup liquid egg
 substitute

¼ cup GF barbecue sauce or
 Cranberry Barbecue Sauce
 (page 360)
¼ cup dried GF bread crumbs
 or crushed GF cereal
4 slices American cheese
 (optional)

PLAIN MEATLOAF: In a large bowl, combine all the ingredients except the cheese. Form a round mound and place in a round microwave pan. Cover with wax paper and microwave on High for 12 minutes. Let it rest 5 minutes before cutting to serve. (If you have more time, you will get a slightly moister meatloaf if you microwave at 50 percent power for 25 minutes. Again, let it rest 5 minutes before serving.) *Makes 3 to 4 servings.*

CHEESE-FILLED MEATLOAF: Mix as above but divide the mixture in half, placing half in a microwave ring mold. Layer on the cheese slices and top with the remaining mixture. Cook as above. *Makes 3 to 4 servings.*

Poultry

Poultry Prepared Ahead

Anytime Cooked Poultry for
　　Casseroles and Salads

Casseroles

Chicken-Rice Casserole with
　　Fruit
Hurry-Up Chicken Potpie
Swiss Chicken Bake
Light Chicken Fricassee
Scalloped Chicken
Easy Chicken Divan
Mary's Party Casserole
Chicken Rice Plus

Stove-Top and Oven Chicken

Gingered Turkeyburgers
　　Gingered Turkey Loaf

Poached Chicken with
　　Vegetables and
　　Dumplings
Rosemary Chicken Poached in
　　Orange Juice
Quick Curried Chicken Pieces
Chicken Breasts Parmesan
　　Chicken Nuggets

Microwave Chicken

Chicken with Pineapple Sauce

Crockpot Chicken

Sauce

Creamy Curry Sauce for
　　Poultry, Pork, or Shrimp

See also

Chicken with Cranberries and
　　Cashews
Ginger Chicken

Stir-Fry Turkey Breast with
　　Asparagus
Sweet and Sour Chicken

*W*hen I picked up a package of fresh ground fat-free turkey from my favorite meat market, the woman standing next to me said, "I always wondered if anybody bought that. What in the world can you do with it?"

"Lots of things. Gingered Turkeyburgers, make a turkey loaf, stuff manicotti. Make fresh turkey sausage by adding sausage seasoning from your butcher."

Since I've been working to lower the cholesterol and cut unnecessary fat in my recipes, I've found a lot of uses for poultry and, as I love variety, I've used it in many different ways—from lightening favorite casseroles to finding new combinations that please the whole family and guests.

Most of these are aimed to reduce the cook's time in the kitchen as well as the fat. But again I've included a few party-type dishes that take more time to prepare but can be made ahead to save the cook's time on the day of the party.

Anytime Cooked Poultry for Casseroles and Salads

For those recipes for casseroles and salads that call for cooked chicken or turkey, here's an easy microwave solution so that you can have chicken in 15 minutes or keep it frozen for use anytime.

Use a glass-lidded, microwave-safe casserole large enough to hold 4 whole chicken breasts or one turkey breast without crowding the meat together or squeezing it against the sides of the dish. Wash the meat carefully and place in one layer. Sprinkle lightly with salt and pepper, if desired.

Cover and cook at 75 percent power or on 7 (Roast) for approximately 15 minutes. Test for doneness. The meat should be tender when pricked with a fork and the juices should run clear. Be sure the meat is fully cooked. A large turkey breast may require more time. Remember that microwaves differ in power.

Use immediately or let cool and cut from the bones into pieces you usually use. Store in the refrigerator up to 2 days or package in freezer bags in the amounts used in your favorite recipes. It will keep well in the freezer for about 2 months.

Thaw chicken overnight in the refrigerator in its freezer package. For quick thawing, place chicken pieces in a microwave-safe covered casserole and heat at Defrost just until the chicken is thawed but not hot. Usually this takes 4 to 6 minutes.

Chicken-Rice Casserole with Fruit

350°

Wonderfully tasty! This one-dish meal takes only a tossed salad to complete. It goes together in minutes. Then you can relax for the time it takes to bake.

1 cut-up frying chicken or 8 pieces of chicken	1½ cups chicken stock
1 tablespoon vegetable oil	1 apple, peeled, cored, and diced
Salt and pepper to taste	1 cup chopped dried apricots
2 tablespoons margarine	1 teaspoon salt (if stock is unsalted)
½ cup chopped onions	¼ teaspoon dried rosemary or about 1 teaspoon crushed fresh
1½ cups instant rice, uncooked	

Preheat oven to 350°. Spray a 2½-quart casserole with vegetable oil spray. Wash the chicken pieces and pat dry. Skin if desired.

In a large skillet, heat the oil and brown the chicken pieces, adding salt and pepper to taste. Place on platter and drain any drippings from pan.

Melt margarine in same skillet and sauté the onions until translucent. Pour into the prepared casserole. Add the rice, apple, apricots, salt, and rosemary. Mix these together and pour on the chicken stock. Top with the browned chicken. Cover and bake for 35 to 45 minutes or until the chicken is done. *Makes 4 to 5 servings.*

Hurry-Up Chicken Potpie   375°/400°

This main dish casserole can be stirred up quickly and popped into the oven while you relax. Make it in one large dish or 6 small ones.

3 cups cooked chicken or
   turkey
One 10-ounce package frozen
   mixed vegetables
1 recipe Cream of Chicken
   Soup (page 62), the
   equivalent of one
   10-ounce can
⅔ cup evaporated milk or
   nondairy liquid

3 tablespoons chopped fresh
   parsley or 1 tablespoon dried
½ teaspoon dried rosemary

CRUST:

¾ cup rice flour
¾ cup instant potato flakes
¼ cup grated Parmesan cheese
⅓ cup margarine or butter
Cold water to moisten

Preheat the oven to either 375° or 400°.

Spray a 2½-quart casserole (or six ¾-cup ones) with vegetable oil spray. Cube the chicken or turkey and place in casserole. Top with the frozen vegetables. Make up 1 recipe of the chicken soup from the powdered mix and add the milk or nondairy liquid to it. Stir into the chicken and vegetables along with the parsley and rosemary.

Crust: Stir together the rice flour, potato flakes, and Parmesan cheese. Cut in the margarine until the mixture resembles coarse crumbs. Stir in cold water, 1 tablespoon at a time, until the dough forms a ball. Roll or pat out on rice-floured board until it fits the casserole or can be cut to fit the small casseroles. Lay the crust on top of the chicken mixture, sealing the edges. Bake for 45 to 50 minutes in the 375° oven or 25 to 30 minutes in the 400° oven until the pastry is golden brown. *Makes 6 servings.*

Note: If you prefer, instead of the potato-cheese crust above, top with biscuits made from Buttermilk Biscuit Mix (page 55).

Swiss Chicken Bake 350°

It's easy to prepare this wonderfully moist, lightly seasoned chicken dish, which needs only a vegetable or salad for a full meal. If you don't use the buttered crumb topping, try serving this with tiny red potatoes garnished with butter (or Molly McButter) and parsley. Use any amount of chicken desired but pick a pan the right size to hold the chicken in one layer.

1½ pounds boneless chicken breasts or thighs
1 to 1½ teaspoons honey mustard
One 4½-ounce can sliced mushrooms (optional)
½ pound Swiss cheese, grated
1 recipe Cream of Mushroom Soup (page 62), the equivalent of one 10-ounce can
1½ cups GF dried bread crumbs plus 2 tablespoons melted butter or margarine (optional)

Preheat oven to 350°.

In a 9″ square baking dish, place the chicken in one layer to cover the bottom. Spread on the honey mustard. Drain the mushrooms (if used), reserving the liquid to make the soup. Sprinkle the mushrooms over the chicken. Cover with the Swiss cheese.

Make the soup and pour over the cheese. Toss the bread crumbs in a plastic bag with the melted butter and top the casserole. Bake for 1 hour. *Makes 3 to 4 servings.*

Light Chicken Fricassee

350°

In this very different fricassee the sweet potatoes add to both looks and flavor. Toss the ingredients in a casserole, pop it into the oven, and relax until it's time to add the peas just before serving. The crunch of a Waldorf or apple salad goes nicely with this.

1 recipe Cream of Mushroom
 Soup (page 62), the
 equivalent of one
 10-ounce can
8 pieces of chicken, skinned
 but not deboned
1½ teaspoons dried thyme

½ teaspoon salt (or to taste)
3 medium sweet potatoes,
 peeled and cut into 2-inch
 chunks
One 16-ounce package frozen
 peas

Preheat oven to 350°.

Make the soup according to the directions on page 62. Pour it into a large casserole or 4-quart Dutch oven. Place the chicken in the soup, turning to coat it. Sprinkle with the thyme and salt and add the sweet potato chunks. Cover and bake 50 minutes.

Add the peas, cover, and bake another 10 minutes or until the chicken is done and the sweet potatoes are tender. *Makes 4 servings.*

Scalloped Chicken

350°

Use up any of your GF dry bread in this chicken casserole, a far lighter version of Mayonnaise Chicken from The Gluten-free Gourmet. *For the cracker crumbs there are at least three GF rice crackers on the grocery shelves: Weight Watchers Harvest Rice crackers or two varieties of Hol-Grain rice crackers.*

Note: For a different taste, substitute ½ cup coarsely chopped cashews for the mushrooms.

3 cups GF bread, cubed

1 cup GF cracker crumbs

3 cups chicken broth

¾ cups liquid egg substitute
  or 3 eggs, lightly beaten

1 teaspoon poultry seasoning

¾ cup diced celery

¼ cup chopped onion

3 cups cooked chicken, cubed

1 cup fresh mushrooms, sliced,
  or one 8-ounce can, drained

½ cup buttered GF bread
  crumbs (optional)

Preheat oven to 350°. Butter a 2- or 2½-quart casserole.

In a large mixing bowl, combine bread cubes and cracker crumbs. Stir in the broth, egg substitute, poultry seasoning, celery, onion, chicken, and mushrooms. Spoon into the prepared casserole. Top with bread crumbs if desired. Bake for 1 hour. *Makes 6 to 8 servings.*

Easy Chicken Divan   450°

Chicken and broccoli in cheese sauce makes a great dish for company or family. And so easy! Serve this with white rice or quartered red potatoes and either a green salad or fruit slices. If you have cooked leftover chicken, use about 1½ cups.

2 cups (1 pound) broccoli cut
  into spears, or one 10-ounce
  package frozen broccoli

One 12½-ounce can chunk
  chicken or two 5-ounce
  cans, drained

1 recipe Cream of Chicken
  Soup (page 62), the
  equivalent of one
  10-ounce can

¾ cup grated Cheddar cheese

⅓ cup milk or nondairy
  substitute

3 tablespoons dried GF bread
  crumbs

1 tablespoon melted margarine

Preheat oven to 450°.

Wash broccoli and place in a 2½-quart casserole. Cover and microwave for 3 minutes on High. Remove and tumble in the chicken.

Meanwhile make the soup. When thickened, stir in the cheese until melted. Stir in the milk. Pour over the chicken and broccoli. Toss the bread crumbs with the margarine and sprinkle on the casserole. Bake for 20 minutes or until hot and bubbling. *Makes 4 to 5 servings.*

Mary's Party Casserole   350°

This chicken dish may be a bit fussy to make but it is well worth the trouble, because the work is all done the day before the party. And it will bring raves from the guests. You can also divide the casserole and freeze it for three meals.

3 whole chicken breasts or 1 whole chicken	1¼ cups uncooked basmati rice (or brown rice)
1 cup water	One 4½-ounce can sliced mushrooms
¾ teaspoon curry powder	1 cup sour cream or nondairy substitute
¾ cup cooking sherry	1 recipe Cream of Mushroom Soup (page 62), the equivalent of one 10-ounce can
1 teaspoon salt	
½ cup celery, sliced	
½ cup onion, diced	

In a large kettle, combine chicken, water, curry, sherry, salt, celery, and onion. Bring to a boil and reduce heat to simmer. Cook 1 hour. Remove from heat and drain, reserving the liquid to cook rice. When cool, remove chicken from bones and cut into bite-size pieces.

In a 3-quart saucepan place reserved liquid plus enough water to make 3 cups. Bring to boil and add the rice. Reduce heat to low, cover, and cook 45 minutes.

Mix cooked rice, chicken, mushrooms, sour cream, and mushroom soup. Place in greased 3-quart casserole. Cover and refrigerate 8 hours or overnight.

Still covered, bake in a preheated 350° oven for 1 hour. *Makes 8 to 10 servings.*

Chicken Rice Plus　　　　350°

For a full-meal casserole, try this easy-to-make broccoli-stuffed dish. Just add a salad and you have dinner prepared in minutes. One cup fresh broccoli flowerets may be substituted for the frozen package.

4 boneless, skinless chicken breast halves
1 recipe Cream of Chicken Soup (page 62), the equivalent of one 10-ounce can
½ cup cold water
½ cup mayonnaise

½ teaspoon curry powder
½ cup grated Parmesan cheese
⅔ cup uncooked brown or white rice
One 10-ounce package frozen broccoli
¼ cup sliced almonds (optional)

Preheat oven to 350°. Spray a 9″ × 11″ baking dish with vegetable oil spray.

Wash the chicken and set aside. Prepare the soup as directed on page 62 and add the cold water, mayonnaise, curry, and cheese.

Sprinkle the rice over the bottom of the baking dish. Layer the broccoli over the rice. Pour on half the sauce. Top with the chicken pieces and add the remaining sauce. If desired, sprinkle on the sliced almonds. Cover with foil and bake for 1 hour. *Makes 4 servings.*

Gingered Turkeyburgers

*Mix ground turkey or chicken with apple, onion, and fresh ginger for a won-
derfully different burger. Grill, broil, or fry the patties and eat them stuffed in
Onion Buns or Sesame Seed Buns (page 96).*

1½ pounds ground turkey or chicken	⅓ cup GF bread crumbs
¼ cup liquid egg substitute or 1 egg white	1½ tablespoons grated ginger root
1 medium apple	Salt and pepper to taste
¼ medium onion	¼ cup ketchup (optional)

Place the ground turkey or chicken in a large bowl. Add the egg substitute.

Peel and core the apple and cut into chunks. Place it in a food processor with the onion and bread crumbs. Chop all ingredients fine. Add to
the meat along with the ginger root. Salt and pepper to the family's taste.
One tester added ¼ cup ketchup.

Mix thoroughly and shape into 4″ patties about ¾″ thick. Grill on barbecue (not too hot) for about 15 to 20 minutes. If you prefer, broil in oven
with meat 7 inches from heat, or fry for 10 to 15 minutes in an oiled pan.
Makes 6 servings.

GINGERED TURKEY LOAF: This mixture may also be baked as a loaf
by patting into a round shape. Bake for 1 hour in a 350° oven. Cool 5
minutes before slicing. *Makes 6 servings.*

Poached Chicken with Vegetables and Dumplings

This modernized cold-weather chicken dish pairs perfectly with the Fluffy Dumplings on page 226. Skinning the chicken but leaving the bones cuts the fat but still gives the dish great flavor. All this needs is a salad or some slices of fruit to complete the meal.

8 pieces of chicken, skinned
if desired
1 large onion cut into 8
pieces, or several very small
whole onions
2 stalks celery sliced in ½"
pieces
4 carrots cut in 1" sections
1 teaspoon thyme

½ teaspoon powdered bay
leaves
2 teaspoons Creamed Soup Base
(page 62)
Pinch red pepper flakes
Salt and pepper to taste
Water to cover
¾ cup frozen lima beans to be
added just before dumplings
One recipe Fluffy Dumplings
(page 226)

Wash the chicken. Skin if desired and remove fat. Place in a large pot. Add the remaining ingredients. Bring to a boil on high and turn immediately to simmer. Cook 17 minutes. Add lima beans and cook 3 minutes more.

Top with the dumplings, spooning on small tablespoonfuls. Bring stock back to a boil. Reduce heat to simmer and cover (no peeking). Cook for about 15 minutes. *Makes 4 servings.*

Rosemary Chicken Poached
in Orange Juice

This very light chicken is still delicious. Make it in about 15 minutes while some white rice is cooking. Thicken the sauce with a tablespoon or two of GF Flour Mix to serve over the rice for a main dish. Or serve the chicken in its sauce with red potatoes and a salad.

3 chicken breasts, halved and skinned or 6 thighs (leave bone in for more flavor)	Salt and pepper to taste
	1 cup orange juice
	1 to 2 tablespoons GF Flour Mix (optional)
1 tablespoon fresh rosemary leaves or 1 teaspoon dried	2 oranges sliced (for garnish)
	Parsley for garnish (optional)

Wash the chicken and remove any fat. Place in a large skillet and salt and pepper to taste. Sprinkle on the rosemary and add the orange juice. Bring to a boil, then lower heat to simmer. Cover and cook about 15 minutes or until the chicken is done. If desired, thicken the sauce with GF Flour Mix dissolved in a little water. Serve the chicken garnished with the orange slices and parsley, if desired. *Makes 3 to 5 servings.*

Quick Curried Chicken Pieces

Unlike my other chicken curries, this recipe takes fresh chicken and quick-cooks it with a light curry flavor. The thin sauce may be used over white rice or little red potatoes. Just add a salad or fruit to complete the meal. You may use either chicken breasts or thighs in this recipe. The thighs are more flavorful but the breast contains less fat.

1 pound boneless, skinless chicken	1 teaspoon sugar (optional)
1 tablespoon vegetable oil	½ teaspoon salt
¼ cup chopped onion	Dash ground ginger
1 tablespoon GF Flour Mix	⅓ cup water
1 teaspoon curry powder	½ cup sour cream or nondairy substitute

Wash chicken and cut into about 2½″ sections (the thighs into 2 parts and the breasts into 4).

In a large skillet, heat the oil. Cook the chicken over medium-high heat until brown on all sides. Add the onion, the flour mixed with the curry, sugar (if used), salt, and ginger. Tumble lightly. Add the water and simmer, covered, for about 10 minutes or until the chicken is thoroughly cooked. Stir in the sour cream and remove from the heat. Serve immediately. *Makes 4 servings.*

Chicken Breasts Parmesan 350°

If you like a thick, crunchy crust and tender, moist chicken, this recipe is for you. It's quick to prepare and takes only 35 minutes to bake.

2 whole chicken breasts, skinned and boned	2 tablespoons lemon juice
1 egg	¾ cup GF bread crumbs
¾ cup plain yogurt	¾ cup grated Parmesan cheese
	1 teaspoon seasoning salt

Preheat oven to 350°. Spray a baking pan with vegetable oil spray.

Wash chicken and cut each side of the breast lengthwise into 2 pieces. (This makes 8 pieces.)

In a shallow bowl, beat the egg. Mix in the yogurt and lemon juice.

In a shallow pan, mix bread crumbs, cheese, and seasoning salt.

Dip the chicken pieces into the yogurt mix, then into the crumbs. Roll to cover completely. Place slightly apart on the baking sheet. Bake for 35 minutes. *Makes 4 servings.*

CHICKEN NUGGETS: For appetizer-sized pieces, cut the meat into 1½″ squares. Follow the directions above but cut the baking time to 20 to 25 minutes. Test for doneness.

Chicken with Pineapple Sauce

(Microwave or Oven)

A flavorful chicken bake that takes about as long as cooking the white rice to accompany it—if you use the microwave. If you have more time, bake in the oven for an hour. Save preparation time by buying chicken parts already skinned but with the bone in for more flavor. For an added taste treat, toss in ¼ cup dried cranberries before cooking.

8 to 10 pieces of chicken or 1 whole chicken cut up, skin removed

2 tablespoons Onion Soup Mix (page 63)

One 8-ounce can pineapple tidbits

1½ cups chicken broth

THICKENING

3 tablespoons cornstarch

¼ cup cold water

Place chicken pieces in an 8″ × 12″ microwave-safe baking dish. Scatter on the Onion Soup Mix. Drain the pineapple, reserving the juice. Tumble the fruit over the chicken. To the juice, add the chicken broth and pour over the casserole.

Cover with wax paper and microwave on High for 18 to 22 minutes, rearranging the pieces halfway through cooking. Mix the cornstarch and water. Stir into the liquid around the chicken and microwave on High 1 minute longer. Stir and repeat until thickened. Serve with rice. *Makes 4 to 5 servings.*

OVEN METHOD: Prepare chicken as above but cover casserole with lid or aluminum foil. Bake 1 hour at 350°. Then add the thickening and bake about 5 minutes longer.

Crockpot Chicken

Chinese flavored and easy! Set the crockpot to cooking in the morning and the chicken will be cooked when you get home from work. Serve the chicken with rice, red potatoes, or pasta. If desired, pour the sauce into a saucepan and cook with two tablespoons GF Flour Mix until it thickens slightly. Chellie's Chutney (page 364) is excellent with this dish.

8 pieces of chicken	1 tablespoon brown sugar
¾ cup chopped onions	1 clove garlic, minced
1 cup chicken stock	Salt and pepper to taste
1 tablespoon grated ginger root	

Wash chicken and pat dry.

Place about half the onions and the chicken in a slow cooker. In a bowl, combine the chicken stock, ginger root, brown sugar, and garlic. Pour over the chicken. Top with the remaining onion. Cover and cook on Low for 6 to 8 hours. If necessary, season with salt and pepper. *Makes 4 servings.*

Creamy Curry Sauce
for Poultry, Pork, or Shrimp

This easy-to-make curry sauce creates a new meal from leftover cooked chicken, pork, or shrimp. The flavor is creamy rich and the amount of curry can be adjusted to any taste. Curry powder comes in a variety of strengths—start with 1 tablespoon and add more to taste.

2 tablespoons margarine or
    vegetable oil
1 cup minced onion (1
    medium onion)
1 apple, pared and diced
½ cup thinly sliced celery
½ cup sliced mushrooms
    (eliminate if using shrimp)
3 tablespoons sweet rice flour
1 to 2 tablespoons curry
    powder

4 teaspoons sugar
1 tablespoon fresh grated
    ginger root
2 cups chicken broth
1 cup low-fat milk or nondairy
    liquid, thinned
⅓ cup coconut flakes or ¼
    cup coconut milk (optional)
1 teaspoon salt (or to taste)
2 cups cooked chicken, pork,
    or shrimp

In a large heavy kettle or Dutch oven, melt margarine. Add onion, apple, and celery. Turn heat to low, cover and cook 8 minutes, stirring occasionally. Add mushrooms (if used) and cook 2 minutes longer.

Blend flour, curry powder, sugar, and ginger root. Add to the pan, and stir until smooth. Add chicken broth and cook until thickening starts. Add the milk, coconut (if used), and salt. Turn heat to low and cook 20 minutes.

Add the chicken, pork, or shrimp and allow to stay on burner until the meat is heated through. Serve with white rice and one of the chutneys on pages 363–64. *Makes 6 servings.*

Seafood

Fish

Fish in Foil Packets
Poached Salmon
Poached Bottomfish
Salmon Baked with Sweet
    Ginger Sauce
White Fish Baked in Milk

Shellfish

Seafood Newburg
Crab Cakes
   Salmon Cakes
White Clam Sauce with
    Fettuccine
Oysters Hansen
   Oysters Hansen Bites
Shrimp and Pea Salad

See also

Baked Crab Balls
Fish and Scallop Chowder
Ginger Scallops
Happy's Quick Shrimp Dip
Hot Tuna Salad Pockets
Rice and Lentil Seafood Salad
Risotto with Shrimp and
    Asparagus
Seafood Burritos
Seafood Crêpes with Shrimp
   Sauce
Shrimp and Tofu in Lemon
   Sauce
Tofu Salad with Shrimp

Seafood is a healthy alternative to red meats, so when my doctor suggested (rather forcefully) that I cut my cholesterol and fat intake, I turned to seafood as the alternative. But I soon discovered that I liked my fish rolled in batter and deep fried (more fat) or baked in a crust rich with Parmesan cheese (more cholesterol).

In a frantic search for new recipes, I found many that satisfied both my doctor's demands and my own palate. In this section you'll find a wide variety to suit all tastes, from simple poached fish (in wonderfully flavored liquids) to White Clam Sauce with Fettuccine (GF, of course).

The real secret to having the best-tasting fish dish is the same as with vegetables—the fresher the better. But with today's processing, flash-frozen fish can be as tasty as fresh, for it is frozen on processor boats anchored right on the fishing grounds. If you buy frozen fish, be sure to ask at your fish market (or meat counter) how the fish was processed. If it is thawed when you buy it, ask how long it has been out of the freezer.

Fish in Foil Packets

This tasty fish and vegetable combination is easy to make for any family meal but showy enough for company. Prepare the packets ahead of time and refrigerate to save time. I've served this with small red potatoes, boiled, or sweet potatoes, boiled and sliced with a dash of Molly McButter. Add a salad for a full meal.

For each packet serving you will need:

> ¼ to ⅓ pound white bottomfish (bass, rockfish, halibut, etc.)
> Dash of lemon pepper
> Squeeze of lemon juice
> ⅓ to ¼ carrot, julienned
> 2 to 3 mushrooms, quartered
> 6 or so thick half-slices of zucchini (1 zucchini to make 6 packets)
> Salt to taste (optional)

Preheat oven to 400°.

Wash fish and cut it into single portions. Place on aluminum foil rectangles about 12″ by the width of the roll. Top with the lemon pepper and lemon and then the vegetables. Salt if desired. Seal by pulling up the sides of the foil and folding together in several ½″ folds. Repeat with the ends of the foil.

Bake for 20 minutes. Serve in the packets and let guests or family open them on their plates so none of the juices are lost.

Poached Salmon

Salmon is so flavorful that it can be—and is—served either cold or hot. This recipe lets you prepare your fish early in the day to be refrigerated for serving cold, but is so easy that you can cook it at the last minute for serving hot.

Serve this plain or with a garnish of twisted orange slices, lemon wedges, mayonnaise, tartar sauce, or hollandaise sauce. Top the mayonnaise or sauces with a dash of dill, if desired.

1½ pounds salmon, filleted   ½ medium onion, sliced thin
1 lemon, sliced   6 to 7 cups water
1 cup white wine

Cut the salmon into 6 even servings.

In a pan large enough to hold the fillets in one layer, place the lemon, wine, onion, and water and bring to a boil. Slip the fillets gently into the water and poach at a low simmer for 10 minutes. Remove to the serving plates or place on a platter and refrigerate until serving time. *Makes 6 servings.*

Poached Bottomfish

To lower the fat but give flavor to simple bottomfish like perch, bass, or rock cod steaks or fillets, try this poaching liquid. Then if you wish, thicken the liquid to form a sauce to serve over rice or pasta. Serve with a colorful vegetable like carrots, broccoli, or a mixture of vegetables such as the frozen mixed Oriental vegetables.

1⅓ pounds perch, bass, or
    other bottomfish
1 tablespoon margarine
1 tablespoon vegetable oil
1 tablespoon real maple syrup
⅛ teaspoon dry mustard
1 tablespoon GF soy sauce

1 cup water
¼ cup dry sherry

SAUCE
1 tablespoon GF Flour Mix
    blended with 2 tablespoons
    water

In a pan large enough to hold the fish in one layer, put margarine, oil, syrup, mustard, soy sauce, water, and sherry. Bring to a boil. Lower temperature to simmer and cook a few minutes to blend the flavors.

Gently lower fish into hot water and poach until the fish is opaque and flakes easily, about 5 minutes. Remove fish either to plates or serving platter and make the sauce by adding the flour mixture and stirring constantly until it thickens. Serve the sauce on the side and let your guests pour it over both fish and rice or pasta. *Makes 4 to 5 servings.*

Salmon Baked with Sweet Ginger Sauce

450°

Quick, easy, and delicious, because the sauce is baked right on the salmon steaks or fillets. The time is about 12 minutes from preparation to table, and it may be prepared several hours ahead of time and refrigerated. Use a plain honey mustard or try one of the more exotic ones with fruit or macadamia nuts added. Serve this with coleslaw and parsleyed red potatoes.

6 salmon steaks about 1 inch thick, or fillets cut into 6 servings
1½ tablespoons grated ginger root
1 tablespoon sweet honey mustard
1½ tablespoons honey

1 teaspoon lemon juice
¼ teaspoon salt
¼ cup chopped macadamia nuts or cashews (optional)

Preheat the oven to 450°. Wash salmon and arrange in a shallow foil-lined pan big enough to hold the fish in one layer.

Combine the ginger root, mustard, honey, lemon juice, and salt. Add the nuts, if used. Spread over the top of fish and bake for approximately 10 minutes or until the fish turns from translucent to opaque. Remove from oven and turn on broiler. Broil about 1 minute or until the glaze sizzles. Watch carefully for burning. *Makes 6 servings.*

White Fish Baked in Milk

When my doctor suggested I eat more fish in order to lower my cholesterol, I tried many ways to cook it. This is my all-time favorite. The milk (or milk substitute) and the parsley seem to cut down the fishy smell and taste. If you're like me, you'll learn to cook more than you need for just one meal. Although the fish is good hot from the oven, it tastes even better in casseroles or cold in sandwiches and salads.

1½ to 2 pounds firm white fish (ling cod, rockfish, halibut, or red snapper)
4 tablespoons margarine or butter
One 12-ounce can evaporated milk, or 1½ cups nondairy liquid

1 tablespoon dried parsley or 2 tablespoons chopped fresh
1 teaspoon paprika
½ teaspoon lemon pepper
2 tablespoons GF soy sauce

Preheat oven to 350°. Wash the fish and pat dry. In a 9″ × 13″ pan, melt the butter on the stovetop. Turn off the heat and add the milk, parsley, paprika, lemon pepper, and soy sauce. Remove from the stove. While the mixture is still warm, add the fish pieces, placing them in a layer covering the bottom of the pan. Turn once so each side is coated and allow to set for 10 minutes. Bake for 20 to 25 minutes or until the fish flakes easily and is not translucent. Do not overbake. Remove fish from milk and drain to serve. *Makes 6 to 8 servings.*

Seafood Newburg

Take only minutes in the microwave to create this gourmet dish. Use skim milk and egg substitute to keep down the fat and cholesterol. For more flavor, buy shrimp uncooked (in the shell or shelled) and simmer for a few minutes to turn them opaque or pink. Save the cooking water to use in the Newburg. For the seafood mixture use shrimp and crab (or lobster), or shrimp and scallops. GF imitation crab or lobster tastes wonderful in this dish.

2 tablespoons margarine or butter

2 tablespoons sweet rice flour

½ teaspoon salt

¼ teaspoon paprika

½ teaspoon mustard powder

Grind of black pepper

1 cup evaporated skim milk or nondairy liquid, thinned

½ cup shrimp water or low-fat milk

3 tablespoons sherry

½ cup liquid egg substitute, or 2 eggs

2 tablespoons lemon juice

1 pound mixed shellfish, cooked

2 green onions, sliced thin, for garnish

In a microwave-safe bowl, place margarine or butter. Microwave on High for 30 seconds or until melted.

Stir in the rice flour, salt, paprika, mustard, and pepper. Add the evaporated skim milk, shrimp water (or milk), and sherry. Microwave on Medium-High 4 to 7 minutes or until thickened, stirring two or three times.

Stir some of the hot mixture into the liquid egg substitute, and add it to the sauce with the lemon juice. Microwave on Medium-High for 1 to 3 minutes or until thickened, stirring once. Stir in the seafood.

Serve in gratin dishes over Parmesan Toast Points (page 204) or buttered cubes of oven-toasted GF bread. Or, if you prefer, serve with rice or GF noodles. *Makes 4 servings.*

Crab Cakes

A flavorful way of stretching crab. These patties can be made up ahead of time and refrigerated so there's little work at mealtime. These go well with flavored rice or with small red new potatoes and a side of sliced fruit.

½ pound fresh crabmeat or imitation crab or lobster	1 green onion, minced
½ cup GF bread, crumbled	1 tablespoon minced green or red bell pepper
2 tablespoons mayonnaise or Light Mayonnaise (page 366)	Dash Worcestershire sauce
2 tablespoons fresh parsley, chopped	¼ cup liquid egg substitute, or 1 egg, beaten
1 tablespoon prepared mustard	Salt and pepper to taste
	1 tablespoon oil for frying

Combine the crab, bread, mayonnaise, parsley, mustard, green onion, green pepper, and Worcestershire sauce. Add the egg substitute and blend well. (I use the food processor.) Season to taste with salt and pepper. Form into 8 small patties or 4 large ones.

Heat 1 tablespoon of oil in a large skillet. Turn heat to medium and fry the cakes until golden brown, about 2 to 3 minutes each side. *Makes 4 servings.*

SALMON CAKES: Replace the crabmeat with fresh uncooked salmon. Replace the pepper with lemon pepper.

White Clam Sauce with Fettuccine

Absolutely delicious! The sauce takes only minutes to stir up so you can start your pasta cooking while you make it. This has a delicate taste, so use a good-quality store-bought GF pasta or, better yet, make your own. The Bean Flour Pasta goes well with this.

Two 6½-ounce cans minced clams
3 tablespoons margarine or butter
3 tablespoons olive oil
2 garlic cloves, minced
⅓ cup fresh parsley, chopped fine
½ teaspoon black pepper

2 teaspoons GF Flour Mix
½ cup grated Parmesan cheese
1 recipe of fresh home-made pasta (pages 261–62), or 6½ ounces dry pasta

Drain clams, reserving the liquid in a measuring cup. Set aside.

In a large skillet, over medium heat, melt the margarine. Add the oil, garlic, and parsley. Cook, stirring occasionally, for about 3 minutes. Add the clams and cook 5 minutes more.

Blend the pepper and flour. Add to the ingredients in skillet. Cook 2 minutes. Discard all clam liquid but ½ cup. Add this (including the sediment) to the hot pan. Bring to a boil and cook 1 minute.

Tumble the sauce and the Parmesan cheese gently with the hot, drained pasta. Serve immediately. *Makes 4 to 5 servings.*

Oysters Hansen

Gourmet oysters without heavy breading or deep frying. A neighbor on the island where we summer introduced me to these fresh from the water. When I altered the recipe for the gluten intolerant and she tasted them, she switched to this recipe. Oysters (like all seafood) change taste with age, so ask for very fresh oysters at your fish market. For a wonderfully different appetizer see the Oysters Hansen Bites below.

1 pint fresh small oysters	¼ cup soy flour (or use all rice flour)
2 to 3 tablespoons margarine or butter	2 tablespoons fresh parsley, minced
½ cup rice flour	Seafood seasoning, lemon pepper, or salt and pepper to taste

Drain the oysters. In a shallow pan, mix the flours, minced parsley, and seasoning. Dredge the oysters thoroughly with the flour mix.

In a skillet, heat the margarine on medium-high heat. Fry the oysters, turning them often and keeping them separate from each other. Keep turning and frying until the coating is a toasty brown. The oysters should come out oval-shaped and crusty. Serve immediately. *Makes 4 servings.*

OYSTERS HANSEN BITES: Cut each oyster into 1″ sections. Dredge each section as above and, when cooking, be sure to keep shaking the skillet so they turn out round little nibbles. Serve hot from the pan (an electric skillet is great for this) and let the guests pick up their bites with toothpicks or appetizer forks. *Serves 6 to 8.*

Shrimp and Pea Salad

This very easy seafood salad can be prepared ahead and refrigerated to be stirred together at the last minute.

Note: Make this with the yogurt as suggested or, for the lactose intolerant, substitute ½ cup of Light Mayonnaise.

1 cup cooked shrimp, peeled and deveined	3 tablespoons mayonnaise or Light Mayonnaise (page 366)
One 16-ounce package frozen peas	⅓ cup plain yogurt (see note above)
1 teaspoon dill weed	1 tablespoon ketchup
½ cup onion, minced	Lettuce leaves (optional)

About half an hour to an hour before serving, mix together the shrimp, peas, dill weed, and onion in a large bowl.

Blend mayonnaise, yogurt (if used), and ketchup. Mix into the salad.

Line a salad bowl with lettuce leaves and spoon salad into the bowl. Keep refrigerated until served. *Makes 6 to 8 servings.*

Stir-Fries

Chicken or Turkey Stir-Fries

Sweet and Sour Chicken
Stir-Fry Turkey Breast with
  Asparagus
Ginger Chicken
Chicken with Cranberries and
  Cashews

Beef or Pork Stir-Fries

Sweet and Sour Pork
Stir-Fry Beef with Chinese
  Cabbage
Beef-Asparagus Stir-Fry

Stir-Fry Beef with Orange
  Sauce
Pork with Apple Slices

Seafood Stir-Fries

Ginger Scallops
Shrimp and Tofu in Lemon
  Sauce

Sauces

Sweet and Sour Sauce
Stir-Fry Sauce
Citrus Stir-Fry Sauce

A true stir-fry is not merely food for the body—it should be a feast for the eyes.

The art of Asian stir-frying is an ancient one, making the best use of little fuel, a small amount of meat, and a variety of compatible vegetables in a sauce where the flavors mingle agreeably. Sadly, the modern versions we encounter in restaurants flout all the rules, using vegetables that do not go well together and too much meat, and often tasting only of the soy-flavored sauce.

In this section, I've tried to balance the Asian versions with some of the more tempting American dishes. I have Americanized some dishes and found that some are just as delicious with the soy sauce omitted.

For a good stir-fry, the vegetables and meat should be cut into shapes that are alike or the same size. All the preparation should be completed before the wok or deep skillet is placed on the stove. The table should be set, the rice cooking, and the family close by—stir-fried food is best straight from the pan to the plate.

Almost all the recipes have their own sauce, but I've also given recipes for sauces you can make ahead: a simple basic stir-fry sauce, a citrus sauce without soy sauce, and a sweet and sour sauce. These will save a lot of time if stir-frying is one of your favorite ways of cooking.

If you haven't cooked this way before, here are some tips for the very best stir-fry:

1. Prepare all ingredients ahead of time, including the sauce.
2. Cut the meat into uniform strips or cubes to ensure even cooking. Slightly freezing the meat makes it easier to produce uniform slices. When possible, cut meat across the grain for tenderness.
3. Be sure your wok or skillet is large enough for the ingredients.
4. Never cover the pan unless the recipe calls for it. Vegetables will steam instead of fry. Some longer-cooking vegetables, such as carrots or broccoli, are often precooked slightly before being added to the wok.
5. Group vegetables according to the time it takes them to cook. Begin with those requiring the longest time, then add others.
6. While stir-frying, turn the food continuously.
7. You can replace the oil in stir-frying with broth or water.

Sweet and Sour Chicken

You can't get a meal much faster or better than this old favorite served with plain white rice. Although there are sweet and sour sauces on the grocery shelves, those I checked contained some form of gluten, so I've included an easy sauce you can stir up in minutes (see page 355).

Note: For a taste change, omit the water chestnuts and add almonds, peanuts, or cashews. For a spicier flavor, add ½ teaspoon crushed red pepper flakes.

¾ pound chicken breast, boned and skinned

2 tablespoons cornstarch

2 tablespoons vegetable oil

1 red bell pepper, seeded and cut in ¼″ slices

½ pound Chinese peapods or one 9-ounce box frozen peapods

One 8-ounce can sliced water chestnuts, drained

¾ cup Sweet and Sour Sauce (page 355)

4 green onions, sliced

Wash chicken and pat dry. Slice into ½″ strips. Place cornstarch in a plastic bag and tumble the chicken to coat well.

In a large, deep skillet or wok, heat the oil. With heat at medium-high, cook the chicken, stirring with a wooden spoon until brown on all sides (about 3 to 4 minutes). Remove to a bowl.

To the juices left in the pan, add the pepper, peapods, and water chestnuts. Stir-fry for 2 to 3 minutes or until vegetables are tender-crisp. Pour in the sauce and return the chicken to the pan. Stir until the sauce coats chicken and vegetables. Remove to a bowl and top with the sliced green onions. *Makes 4 servings.*

Stir-Fry Turkey Breast
with Asparagus

A very different stir-fry that because of the asparagus brings a taste of spring. This can be accompanied by buttered fresh pasta or small red potatoes. If you can't find the sliced fresh turkey breast, substitute skinned, boneless chicken breast.

½ pound sliced turkey breast	½ cup chicken broth
1½ teaspoons ground coriander	2 tablespoons lemon juice
1 tablespoon vegetable oil	Salt and pepper to taste
1 cup fresh asparagus cut into	6 to 8 green onions, sliced thin
1½″ pieces	1 teaspoon grated lemon peel

Wash turkey slices and place between two pieces of foil. Pound to flatten and tenderize. Slice crosswise into ¼″ strips. Tumble with the coriander. (Use immediately or refrigerate in a plastic bag for up to 3 hours.)

Heat the oil in a wok or heavy skillet. Add the turkey and stir-fry until just cooked (about 3 minutes). Transfer to a bowl. To the drippings in the pan add asparagus and chicken broth. Cook until asparagus is tender and the broth is reduced (about 4 minutes). Return the meat to the pan, mix in the lemon juice, and season to taste with salt and pepper. When warm, add the green onion and lemon peel and toss to blend. Serve immediately. *Makes 3 to 4 servings.*

Ginger Chicken

This full-meal stir-fry uses half a chicken breast to serve two. Set your rice to cooking, then start the chicken. You'll have the meal on the table in 20 minutes. Serve this with slices of fruit or a tossed salad. That will save room for a dessert.

Note: You may substitute your own mix of fresh vegetables for the frozen vegetables. Be sure to cut them small enough to cook in a short time.

½ boneless chicken breast, skinned
1 tablespoon cornstarch
1 tablespoon GF soy sauce
1 teaspoon grated ginger root
1 tablespoon oil

4 green onions, sliced thin
1½ cups frozen mix of broccoli, carrots, and water chestnuts
½ cup chicken broth
1 tablespoon chopped macadamia or cashew nuts

Wash chicken and cut into thin strips and place in a bowl. Combine the cornstarch, soy sauce, and ginger root. Tumble with the chicken until well coated.

Heat the oil in a wok or deep skillet and cook the chicken until lightly browned. Stir in the onions, frozen vegetable mix, and broth. Cook, stirring once or twice, from 3 to 5 minutes or until the vegetables are done to taste. Serve over rice. Sprinkle with the nuts. *Makes 2 servings.*

Chicken with Cranberries and Cashews

This is one of the hottest items in a popular Asian take-out place near my home. When I asked for it to be made with no soy sauce, the battery of seven cooks looked up from their long stove top, probably wondering who the crazy woman was. But one of the cooks did make this to my order, and it was delicious. Make it as written below or add some GF soy sauce.

¾ pound chicken breast, boned and skinned

1 teaspoon orange zest

⅔ cup orange juice

2 tablespoons dry white wine

1 tablespoon cornstarch

½ teaspoon chicken bouillon granules

2 tablespoons vegetable oil

One 8-ounce can sliced water chestnuts, drained

6 to 8 snow peas, bias-cut to 1½ inches

½ cup dried cranberries

½ cup cashews (or peanuts)

Wash chicken and pat dry. Slice into ½″ strips. Set aside.

Combine the orange zest, orange juice, wine, cornstarch, and chicken bouillon granules. Set aside.

In a wok or deep skillet, heat the oil. Cook chicken at Medium-High, stirring, until brown on all sides, about 3 minutes. Remove to a bowl. To the pan juices, add the water chestnuts and snow peas. Stir-fry for 2 to 3 minutes or until vegetables are crisp-tender. Add the cranberries and cashews and pour in the orange mixture. Cook until thickened. Add chicken and serve as soon as it is heated. *Makes 4 servings.*

Sweet and Sour Pork

Pork and pineapple are perfect partners in this stir-fry. Serve it with white rice and a salad for a quick and easy dinner. This uses a sweet and sour sauce that you can stir up in minutes.

¾ pound pork loin or prepared stir-fry pork strips
2 tablespoons cornstarch
2 tablespoons vegetable oil
1 red or green pepper, seeded and cut into ¼″ slices

One 8-ounce can sliced water chestnuts, drained
One 8½-ounce can pineapple chunks, drained
¾ cup Sweet and Sour Sauce (page 355)
4 green onions, sliced thin

Wash pork loin and slice across grain into thin slices. Place cornstarch in a plastic bag and tumble the meat to coat well.

In a large, deep skillet or wok, heat the oil. With heat at medium-high, cook the pork, stirring with a wooden spoon until brown on all sides (about 3 to 4 minutes). Remove to a bowl.

To the juices left in the pan, add the pepper, water chestnuts, and pineapple. Stir-fry for 2 to 3 minutes or until vegetables are crisp-tender. Pour in the sauce and return the pork to the pan. Stir until the sauce coats the meat and vegetables. Remove to a serving bowl and garnish with the sliced green onions. *Makes 4 servings.*

Stir-Fry Beef with
Chinese Cabbage

The list of ingredients looks long, but this quick and colorful meal can be put on the table in less than 30 minutes. You can save time if you have Stir-Fry Sauce (page 356) in your refrigerator. Start the meat on its 10-minute marinade and then prepare the rest of the ingredients. Serve this with white rice and a slice or two of fruit for a full meal.

½ pound beef steak cut into ⅛″ strips

1 tablespoon dry sherry
1 tablespoon soy sauce

MARINADE
1 teaspoon cornstarch
1 tablespoon GF soy sauce
½ teaspoon fresh grated ginger root

OTHER INGREDIENTS
½ small head napa cabbage
3 tablespoons oil (less if wok or skillet is Teflon coated)
1 clove garlic, minced
1 red bell pepper, seeded and cut in strips
2 green onions, sliced thin

SAUCE
1 tablespoon cornstarch
1 tablespoon sugar
½ cup beef broth

In a small bowl, place meat and add cornstarch, soy sauce, and ginger root. Tumble and let marinate for 10 minutes.

Mix sauce ingredients. Set by stove. Cut cabbage across the head into about ¾″ slices.

Heat wok (or skillet) over high heat. Add half the oil. When oil is hot, add meat. Stir-fry until browned (about 2 minutes). Remove to bowl. If necessary, add the remaining oil, the garlic, and bell pepper. Cook about half a minute. Add the cabbage and stir-fry for about 2 minutes. The cabbage should be crisp-tender. Return meat to pan, add the cooking sauce, and cook until it boils and thickens. Mix in the onions and serve immediately. *Makes 2 or 3 servings.*

Beef-Asparagus Stir-Fry

A crunchy stir-fry to be tossed together in minutes. Set the rice to cook and then tumble together these few ingredients.

¾ pound top round steak
1 pound fresh asparagus or
    one 9-ounce package
    frozen
One 8-ounce can sliced water
    chestnuts
½ cup green onions, sliced thin
2 teaspoons olive oil

SAUCE
½ cup beef broth
3 tablespoons GF soy sauce
½ teaspoon garlic salt
1 tablespoon cornstarch
    (alternately, use ¼ cup Stir-
    Fry Sauce [page 356] plus
    ½ cup beef broth)

Wash and slice the steak into ¼" strips about 2" long. Cut asparagus into 1" pieces. Drain the water chestnuts.

In a small bowl, mix together the beef broth, soy sauce, garlic salt, and cornstarch (if you are making your own sauce). Set aside.

In a wok or large, deep skillet, heat the oil over medium-high heat. Add the steak. Cook about 2 minutes. Add the asparagus, water chestnuts, and onions and cook another 4 to 5 minutes or until the vegetables are crisp-tender. Stir in the sauce and cook, stirring gently until thickened and clear. Serve immediately over hot rice. *Makes 4 servings.*

Stir-Fry Beef with Orange Sauce

With this tangy sauce, you can enjoy the leanest cuts of beef. Serve this over plain white rice to enjoy the flavor of the beef in sauce.

1 pound lean bottom round steak or 1 pound stir-fry beef
1 orange
2 tablespoons vegetable oil
4 green onions, cut in 1″ slices
1 clove garlic, minced

2 tablespoons apple cider vinegar
1 tablespoon GF soy sauce
10 drops sesame oil
1½ teaspoons orange zest
1 tablespoon honey
2 teaspoons cornstarch dissolved in ¼ cup water

Wash steak and cut across the grain into ¼″ strips. After grating the rind to make zest, cut the orange and extract the juice until you have ¼ cup.

In a wok or large frypan, heat 1 tablespoon oil. Add beef and stir-fry until the meat is browned, about 2 minutes. Remove to bowl.

Add the last tablespoon oil, heat, and add the onions, stir-frying for about 1 minute, or until softened slightly. Add garlic and cook another minute. Return the meat to the wok.

Add the orange juice, vinegar, soy sauce, sesame oil, orange zest, and honey. Cook about 2 minutes longer. Stir in the cornstarch dissolved in the water and cook until the sauce boils and thickens. Serve over beds of white rice on individual plates. *Makes 4 servings.*

Pork with Apple Slices

Pork teams perfectly with apple and cranberries (or raisins) in this easy, soy sauce–free stir-fry. Serve this with white rice and a green salad for taste and texture contrast.

1 pound lean boneless pork	1 tablespoon vegetable oil
¾ cup apple juice	2 apples, cored and sliced
1 teaspoon powdered	lengthwise
chicken bouillon	1 bunch green onions cut in
½ teaspoon apple pie spice	1″ pieces
1 tablespoon cornstarch	¼ cup dried cranberries or raisins

If serving with rice, be sure it is almost done before starting the stir-fry.

Rinse the meat and cut it into bite-sized pieces.

For the sauce, combine the apple juice, chicken bouillon, spice, and cornstarch. Set aside.

In a wok or large frying pan, heat the oil and stir-fry half the pork at a time, about 2 to 3 minutes for each batch, or until cooked through. Combine in the wok, stir in the sauce, and cook until thickened. Add the apple slices, onion, and cranberries. Cook for about 1 minute in the sauce. Serve immediately. *Makes 4 servings.*

Ginger Scallops

Scallops in a ginger sauce make a wonderful change from breaded seafood. If you are going to serve this with rice or buttered new potatoes, start them first, as the cooking time for the scallops is very short. As with all stir-fry recipes, be sure to have all the ingredients prepared ahead before you heat the frypan or wok.

12 ounces fresh scallops	1½ tablespoons dry sherry
⅛ teaspoon Chinese-style	1½ tablespoons water
five-spice powder	1½ teaspoons grated fresh
1½ teaspoons cornstarch,	ginger root
divided	10 green onions, cut in ½″
4 teaspoons GF soy sauce,	pieces
divided	2 tablespoons salad oil

If the scallops are large, slice across to halve the thickness. Place in a bowl and sprinkle with a mixture of the five-spice powder plus 1 teaspoon of the cornstarch. Tumble gently to coat and place in refrigerator. Combine the remaining cornstarch and soy sauce with the sherry and water to make the sauce. Set aside.

Heat the wok or frypan over medium-high heat and add 1 tablespoon of oil. When hot, add the ginger root and onions. Stir-fry for about 1 minute. Remove from pan. Add remaining oil and stir-fry the scallops until they are firm and opaque (about 2 to 3 minutes). Return the ginger and onions to pan. Stir in sauce and cook until it bubbles and thickens. Serve immediately. *Makes 2 to 3 servings.*

Shrimp and Tofu in Lemon Sauce

Tofu has no flavor of its own, so it takes on the taste of shrimp and lemon in this dish. In season, substitute asparagus for the green onion for a delightful change. Serve this with quick-cooking bean threads (mai fun) or white rice and sliced fruit or a fruit salad.

¾ pound fresh or frozen uncooked shrimp in shell	2½ teaspoons cornstarch
	1 tablespoon vegetable oil
4 ounces firm tofu	2 teaspoons grated ginger root
½ cup chicken broth	1 clove garlic, minced
1 tablespoon GF soy sauce (optional)	6 to 8 green onions (or asparagus spears) cut to 1¼″
2 tablespoons lemon juice	

Peel and devein the shrimp. Set aside. Drain tofu and place between paper towels to squeeze out moisture. Cut into ¼″ cubes. Set aside.

Make sauce by combining the chicken broth, soy sauce (if used), lemon juice, and cornstarch. Set aside.

Heat the wok or frying pan and add the oil. When hot add the ginger root and garlic and stir-fry for about 30 seconds. Add the green onions and shrimp and cook until the shrimp is opaque (about 3 minutes). Add the sauce and cook, stirring until it thickens. Add the tofu and cook for about 2 minutes more. Serve immediately. *Makes 4 servings.*

Sweet and Sour Sauce

There are several sweet and sour sauces on the grocery shelves but, because they may contain gluten as one of the ingredients, I always make my own. This quickly made sauce is enough for 2 or 3 different dishes and will keep several weeks in the refrigerator. Use this in Sweet and Sour Chicken (page 345) or Sweet and Sour Pork (page 349).

¾ cup water
2 tablespoons cornstarch
2 tablespoons rice vinegar

3 tablespoons ketchup
⅔ cup sugar
1 teaspoon GF soy sauce (optional)

Place all the ingredients in a small saucepan and bring to a boil, stirring constantly. Remove from heat and use immediately or store, when cool, in a jar in the refrigerator. *Makes about 1¼ cups.*

Stir-Fry Sauce

There are stir-fry sauces on the market but they all contain soy sauce (probably made with wheat), so I discovered this way of saving time by making my own. You may use this in most of the stir-fry recipes in this book. Just replace the combined ingredients shown in the recipe with an approximate amount of this sauce.

1 cup GF soy sauce

⅓ cup dry sherry or mirin
   (rice wine)

4 teaspoons grated ginger root

2 teaspoons sugar

2 tablespoons cornstarch

Whisk together all ingredients and pour into a pint bottle or jar with lid. Refrigerate. This will keep up to 2 weeks and is enough for 3 meals of stir-fry. Be sure to shake well before using. *Makes 1½ cups.*

Citrus Stir-Fry Sauce

This sauce is especially good with chicken or pork stir-fries and for those who can't have soy sauce because of the salt. This keeps several weeks in the refrigerator and is good for 3 or 4 stir-fries.

1 cup orange juice

¾ cup chicken broth

1 tablespoon lime or lemon
   juice

1 tablespoon orange zest

¼ cup dry white wine

Pepper to taste

1 tablespoon grated ginger root

3 tablespoons cornstarch

Mix all together and place in bottle or jar. Keep refrigerated and shake well before using. *Makes 1 pint.*

Sauces, Relishes, and Condiments

Sauces

Cranberry Barbecue Sauce
Enchilada Sauce
Topping Sauce for Meatloaf
Hollandaise Sauce

Relishes

Cranberry Chutney
Pineapple and Orange Chutney
Chellie's Chutney
Pat's Sweet Pickle Relish
Pineapple Salsa

Mayonnaise and Dressings

Light Mayonnaise
Mock Blue Cheese Dressing
Low-Fat French Dressing
Coleslaw Dressing

Condiments

Low-Fat Mock Sour Cream
Sweetened Condensed Milk
Yogurt Cream Cheese
Confectioners' Sugar Substitute

We can buy most GF sauces and condiments if we are willing to search our neighborhood stores and read every label, remembering that a GF product might have changed formulas since our last purchase and now contain gluten. We must always be aware of any product marked "light," because to compensate for removing some cholesterol from eggs, some products contain a thickener of wheat flour.

If you'd rather stir up your own condiments, I've created three low-calorie, low-cholesterol salad dressings, a low-fat hollandaise, and yogurt cream cheese. I've added several relishes, a barbeque sauce, and an authentic enchilada sauce. I've even included a mock sour cream and a sweetened condensed milk you can make at home. But my very favorite is the Light Mayonnaise (page 366), which tastes better than any store-bought one and will hold up in all recipes.

You will find other sauces under the sections in which they are used. Two stir-fry sauces and a sweet and sour sauce are in the Stir-Fries chapter. In the Cakes chapter you'll find a raspberry cake filling (or jam) you can make any time of the year with unripened tomatoes.

Cranberry Barbecue Sauce

Use this sparkling new taste in barbecue sauces to spice up chicken, turkey, and pork, whether grilled outdoors or baked or broiled in your oven.

1 medium onion, chopped
2 tablespoons olive oil
2 cloves garlic, minced
2 tablespoons sugar
1 teaspoon salt

¼ teaspoon pepper
⅛ teaspoon cayenne pepper
One 15-ounce can tomato sauce
⅓ cup cranberry vinegar

In a 2-quart saucepan, sauté onion in the oil until translucent. Add the garlic, sugar, salt, and peppers. Stir in the tomato sauce and vinegar. Bring to a boil, reduce heat, and simmer 15 minutes. This will keep several weeks in the refrigerator. *Makes 2½ cups.*

Enchilada Sauce

If you're tired of insipid sauces from a package, try this authentically spicy one that takes only minutes to make, sent to me by a reader in New Mexico. I've used her measurements, but you can change the amount of chili powder and garlic salt to suit your taste. Originally this recipe was too spicy for my Northwest palate, so I diluted it with ½ cup tomato sauce (not authentic, but some testers liked it).

On pages 236–38 you'll find several suggestions for enchiladas and burritos. You can also use the sauce for seasoning pinto beans.

2 tablespoons chili powder
1½ teaspoons corn or
    vegetable oil
1 cup chicken broth or water

1 teaspoon garlic salt (or to
    taste)
1½ tablespoons cornstarch
1 cup water
½ cup tomato sauce (optional)

In a saucepan with a heavy bottom, brown the chili powder in the corn oil over medium heat, stirring to keep from scorching. Add the broth (or water) and bring to a boil.

Add the garlic salt and the cornstarch dissolved in the cup of water. Stir constantly to keep this from lumping (much like making gravy). At this point, taste and add more garlic salt, or dilute with tomato sauce if you desire. *Makes 2 cups, enough for 12 enchiladas.*

Topping Sauce for Meatloaf

I've been making this spicy, sweet sauce for meatloaf for more than forty years. When I served it recently, a guest asked if it was in one of my cookbooks. It wasn't because I thought it too simple. The onion garnish is optional.

¼ cup ketchup
2 teaspoons brown sugar (or to taste)

½ teaspoon prepared mustard
2 teaspoons thinly sliced green onions or chopped chives for garnish

Mix together the ketchup, brown sugar, and mustard. Spread over the meatloaf before cooking. Garnish immediately before serving with the onion or chives.

Hollandaise Sauce

(Low Fat)

Try this 3-minute microwave sauce that tastes amazingly like my old hollandaise with all the egg yolks. Use it to top plain vegetables and fish.

Note: Nondairy liquid (if used) should be either a low-fat product or a richer one, thinned.

5 teaspoons cornstarch or 4 teaspoons GF Flour Mix

½ teaspoon dry mustard

2½ tablespoons liquid egg substitute

⅔ cup low-fat milk or nondairy liquid (see note above)

2½ tablespoons lemon juice

2 teaspoons margarine (or butter)

Dash of salt (or to taste)

In a small microwave-safe bowl, combine the cornstarch (or GF flour mix) and mustard with a fork. Gradually add the milk (or nondairy liquid), blending well.

Microwave on High for 1 minute. Stir. Microwave for another 1½ minutes, stirring every 30 seconds, until thickened. Remove and add lemon juice, margarine, and salt. Whisk with the fork. Serve immediately or store and reheat to serve.

If storing, cover with plastic while cooling to avoid a skin on top. Then store, covered, in the refrigerator. *Makes 1 cup.*

Cranberry Chutney

Use this wonderfully spicy chutney as an accompaniment to poultry, pork, and all curries. This easy-to-make relish is one of the best I've tasted.

One 16-ounce can whole-berry cranberry sauce
¼ cup onion, finely chopped
½ cup golden raisins
¼ cup brown sugar

¼ cup fruit vinegar (cranberry, raspberry, or apple cider)
1 teaspoon pumpkin pie spice
1 teaspoon grated fresh ginger root

In a medium saucepan, combine all ingredients. Bring to a boil over medium heat, stirring often. Reduce heat to low and cook for 15 minutes, stirring occasionally. Remove from stove and allow to cool before pouring into a refrigerator bowl or into two 8-ounce glass jars.

This may be stored 3 weeks in the refrigerator or 3 months in the freezer. *Makes about 2 cups.*

Pineapple and Orange Chutney

Chutneys add spice, fruit, and fiber to a meal. Try this one with roast fowl, beef, or pork. Use it with curries and pastas.

1 small pineapple, peeled, cored, and chopped in a food processor
1 orange
1 small onion, finely chopped
1 tablespoon grated fresh ginger root

⅓ cup raisins
1 to 3 tablespoons sugar (to taste)
⅓ cup cider vinegar
⅓ cup orange or pineapple juice
½ teaspoon cinnamon
¼ teaspoon dry mustard

Prepare the pineapple. Grate the zest from the orange, then peel and cube the fruit. Chop in the food processor.

Place all ingredients in 2½-quart saucepan and bring to a boil. Cover and simmer for about 20 minutes, or until the fruit is soft. Cool before storing in refrigerator. Chutney is best if brought to room temperature before serving. *Makes about 3 cups.*

Chellie's Chutney

Chellie grew up in India, so eating at her house is always a culinary experience. At a recent dinner, she served this unusual chutney with her curry. It is wildly popular with my guests.

1 banana	1 tomato, diced
1 to 2 tablespoons lemon juice	¼ cup dried coconut
1 bunch green onion, sliced fine,	3 tablespoons sugar
or 1 cucumber, diced	

Dice the banana into small pieces in a small bowl and sprinkle on the lemon juice. Add the rest of the ingredients and tumble gently. Refrigerate until serving. *Makes approximately 1½ cups.*

Pat's Sweet Pickle Relish

When Pat sent me this recipe she wrote, "This recipe is for the cukes that got away from you and hid until they turned yellow. You'll be glad they did when you taste the relish." Use this tasty pickle relish mixed with tuna fish or salmon in sandwiches, add it to your potato and pasta salads, or use it to replace the sweet pickles and juice in Haitian Chicken (page 300, More from the Gluten-free Gourmet).

5 large ripe yellowed cucumbers	2 tablespoons mixed
5 large green cucumbers	pickling spice (in bag)
6 large onions	1 tablespoon celery seed
7 cups plus 5 tablespoons sugar	4 cups cider vinegar

Cover cucumbers with boiling water. Let cool. Drain.

Cover again with boiling water. Let cool. Drain. Split the cucumbers to remove and discard seeds.

Grind the cucumbers and onions through the coarse grinding wheel of a meat grinder or process lightly in a food processor, a little at a time. In a large kettle, bring to a boil the sugar, pickling spices, celery seed, and vinegar. Add the cucumbers and onions, bring to boil, and remove from the stove. Let stand 48 hours.

Wash 8 pint jars or 16 half-pints. Place them in a 220° oven to sterilize. Bring the relish to a boil again. Remove the spice bag and pack the relish in the prepared jars and seal at once. *Makes 7 to 8 pints.*

Pineapple Salsa

If you don't like your salsa hot, this light one uses pineapple instead of tomato and cilantro instead of jalapeño peppers. Try it with your recipes that call for salsa or picante sauce.

½ fresh pineapple, peeled, cored, and diced	3 green onions, sliced fine
	2 tablespoons chopped cilantro
1 small red bell pepper (seeds removed), chopped fine	1½ tablespoons fresh lime juice
	1½ teaspoons vegetable oil

Put all ingredients in bowl of food processor and pulse a few times to chop fine. Do not over-process; you want some shape and texture to the salsa. *Makes approximately 2 cups.*

Light Mayonnaise

(Cholesterol free)

A full-bodied mayonnaise for those who need to lower their cholesterol. This easy-to-make mayonnaise keeps in the refrigerator for about 1 month and can be used in all baking recipes. I like to use seasoned rice vinegar. Always check ingredient list to be sure your egg substitute is gluten free.

½ teaspoon sugar
1½ teaspoons salt
⅛ teaspoon paprika
½ teaspoon dry mustard
3 tablespoons rice vinegar

1 cup water
¼ cup GF Flour Mix (page 33)
¼ cup liquid egg substitute
1¼ cups vegetable oil

Place the sugar, salt, paprika, mustard, and vinegar in a deep 1½-quart mixing bowl. Set aside.

In a small saucepan, blend the water slowly into the flour mix, stirring to keep from lumping. Add the liquid egg substitute. Cook over medium-low heat, stirring constantly until the mixture simmers and becomes shiny and clear.

Remove from heat and turn into the bowl containing the seasonings. Beat with electric mixer while adding the oil in a slow stream until the mayonnaise is smooth, light, and thick. Store in a covered glass container in the refrigerator. *Makes about 3 cups.*

Mock Blue Cheese Dressing

This tastes like blue cheese and has the texture of blue cheese, but the fat has been cut and the Roquefort eliminated to avoid traces of gluten. Make this at least one day ahead for the flavor to permeate the whole and the cottage cheese to taste like bits of blue cheese. The addition of chives or onion will give it more zing.

4 ounces feta cheese	¼ teaspoon salt
½ cup soft tofu	¼ teaspoon black pepper
1 cup buttermilk	¼ cup farmer-style cottage cheese
1½ teaspoons lemon juice	Optional: chopped chives,
1 clove garlic, cut up	scallion, or red onion

Place all ingredients except the cottage cheese in a food processor or blender and blend until smooth. Stir in the cottage cheese and store in a capped jar in the refrigerator. *Makes about 1 pint.*

Low-Fat French Dressing

Need a French dressing that cuts the calories? Try this tasty and easy one.

1 cup nonfat yogurt	⅛ teaspoon dry mustard
½ cup ketchup	½ teaspoon paprika
½ cup unsweetened pineapple juice	⅛ teaspoon pepper
1 tablespoon apple cider vinegar	½ teaspoon sugar (optional)

Place all ingredients in blender and blend until smooth. Keeps well in refrigerator. *Makes about 1 cup.*

Coleslaw Dressing

This is another of my old favorites I've made for so long I never thought of adding it to a cookbook until, with my Light Mayonnaise, it was now healthier than any purchased slaw dressing. The milk may be increased slightly if you want the dressing thinner.

⅔ cup Light Mayonnaise (page 366)   1 teaspoon lime juice
⅓ cup milk or nondairy liquid   1¼ teaspoons sugar

Mix all ingredients with whisk and pour into a glass bottle or half-pint covered jar. Store in the refrigerator and shake well before using. Keeps for about 10 days. *Makes 1 cup dressing.*

Low-Fat Mock Sour Cream

Although there are some gluten-free nonfat sour creams on the market, we must always read labels. To be sure your sour cream is low fat and gluten free, why not make your own? This can be used in the Light Lemon Cheesecake (page 131) and any way you use sour cream. It will keep fresh-tasting for several weeks in the refrigerator.

¾ cup cottage cheese (uncreamed)
1 cup nonfat milk
2 to 4 teaspoons rice vinegar or
    apple juice concentrate

In blender or food processor, blend the cottage cheese and milk. If necessary, add more of either milk or cottage cheese to achieve the texture of sour cream.

For true sour-cream tang, add vinegar. For a sweet topping, use the apple juice. *Makes 2 cups.*

Sweetened Condensed Milk

No need now to run to the store for that can of sweetened condensed milk the recipe demands. Just stir up this quick substitute in the food processor or blender.

1 cup non-instant powdered milk
¾ cup sugar
⅓ cup boiling water

3 tablespoons melted butter
or margarine

Place ingredients in blender or small bowl of food processor and blend at low speed. Scrape sides and turn to High until the milk is smooth. *Makes 1 cup.*

Yogurt Cream Cheese

This low-fat cheese can be used as a substitute for its high-calorie cousin in cheesecakes, dips, sauces, and spreads. It's easy to make now that yogurt strainers are in most kitchen supply stores. I suggest purchasing two 16-ounce strainers and making up a whole quart of yogurt into two 1-cup packages.

One 32-ounce carton nonfat or low-fat plain yogurt (without gelatin)

Place the strainers over containers (2-cup measuring cups are ideal) so that they don't come in contact with the draining whey. Divide the yogurt evenly. Cover tightly with plastic wrap and place in the refrigerator.

Drain at 8-hour intervals. Leave 24 hours for a thick cream cheese or about 16 hours for spreads and dips. The cheese will keep up to 2 weeks in the refrigerator if wrapped in plastic wrap and sealed in foil or placed in 1-cup margarine tubs, covered with plastic wrap and plastic covers. *Makes two 8-ounce packages.*

Note: If this is to be used as a cream cheese spread, mix in ½ teaspoon maple syrup after the cheese is drained and before storing. This will cut the sharp tang of the yogurt but will not make it sweet.

If this is to be cooked, as in cheesecake or filling for the Sponge Roll (page 182), add 1 teaspoon cornstarch per cup so it won't break apart like scrambled eggs.

Confectioners' Sugar Substitute
(For Diabetics)

This easy-to-make sugar substitute works well in angel food cakes and frostings. Or use it to sprinkle on fruits and cereals. You will have to taste to decide on the quantity of sugar replacement; some brands will taste bitter if used in full amount.

> **2 cups nonfat dry milk powder or nondairy substitute**
> **2 cups cornstarch**
> **Replacement equivalent for 1 cup granulated sugar**

Measure all ingredients into a blender or food processor. Pulse for several seconds or until the texture resembles confectioners' sugar. *Makes 4 cups.*

The Gluten-free Diet

The gluten-free diet is a diet free of the toxic gluten protein found in wheat, rye, barley, and oats.

This list was compiled from information supplied to me by my physician, the Gluten Intolerance Group of North America, the Celiac Disease Foundation, and the Canadian Celiac Association. I followed the standards of the U.S. organizations.

Please note that food regulations vary from country to country. For example, in Canadian celiac organizations, whiskey is on the allowed list, as are condiments and pickles with distilled vinegar (not so in the United States). In Britain, wheat starch is allowed, but not in the United States or Canada.

Foods Allowed

Foods to Avoid

BEVERAGES

Coffee, tea, carbonated beverages, cocoa (Baker's, Hershey's, Nestlé), rum, tequila, vodka (if made from potatoes, grapes, or plums), wine.

Postum, Ovaltine, beer, ale, gin, vodka (if made from grain), whiskey, some flavored and instant coffees, some herbal teas.

Foods Allowed	Foods to Avoid

BREADS

Breads made with gluten-free flours only (rice, potato starch, soy, tapioca, corn, bean) baked at home or purchased from companies that produce GF products. Rice crackers or cakes, corn tortillas.

All breads made with wheat, oat, rye, and barley flours. All purchased crackers, croutons, bread crumbs, wafers, biscuits, and doughnuts containing any gluten flours. Graham, soda, or snack crackers, tortillas containing wheat.

CEREALS

Cornmeal, hot rice cereals, hominy grits, gluten-free cold rice and corn cereals (those without malt).

All cereals containing wheat, rye, oats, or barley (both grain and in flavoring, such as malt flavoring, malt syrup).

DAIRY PRODUCTS

Milk (fresh, dry, evaporated or condensed), buttermilk, cream, sour cream, butter, cheese (except those that contain oat gum), whipped cream, yogurt (plain and flavored if GF), ice cream (if GF), artificial cream (if GF).

Malted milk, artificial cream (if not GF), some chocolate milk drinks, some commercial ice creams, some processed cheese spreads, flavored yogurt (containing gluten), some light or fat-free dairy products (containing gluten).

DESSERTS

Any pie, cake, cookie, or other desserts made with GF flours and flavorings. Gelatins, custards, homemade puddings (rice, cornstarch, tapioca).

All pies, cakes, cookies, etc. that contain any wheat, oat, rye, or barley flour or flavoring. Most commercial pudding mixes, ice cream cones, prepared cake mixes.

Foods Allowed	Foods to Avoid

FATS

Margarine, vegetable oil, nuts, GF mayonnaise, shortening, lard, some salad dressings.	Some commercial salad dressings, some mayonnaise.

FLOURS

Rice flour (brown and white), soy flour, potato starch flour, potato flour, tapioca flour, corn flour, cornmeal, cornstarch, rice bran, rice polish, arrowroot, nut or legume flours.	All flours or baking mixes containing wheat, rye, barley, or oats.

FRUITS AND JUICES

All fruit, fresh, frozen, canned (if GF), and dried (if not dusted with flour to prevent sticking).	Any commercially canned fruit with gluten thickening.

MEAT, FISH, POULTRY, AND EGGS

Any eggs (plain or in cooking), all fresh meats, fish, poultry, other seafood; fish canned in oil, vegetable broth, or brine. GF prepared meats such as luncheon meats, tofu, GF imitation seafood.	Eggs in gluten-based sauce, imitation seafood containing gluten flour, prepared meats that contain gluten, some fish canned in HVP, self-basting turkeys injected with HVP. Imitation seafood containing wheat flour.

PASTAS

GF homemade noodles, spaghetti, or other pastas, oriental rice noodles, bean threads, purchased GF pasta made with corn, rice, tapioca, and potato flours.	Noodles, spaghetti, macaroni, or other pastas made with gluten flours. Any canned pasta product.

Foods Allowed	Foods to Avoid

SOUPS AND CHOWDERS

Homemade broth and soups made with GF ingredients, some canned soups, some powdered soup bases, some GF dehydrated soups.	Most canned soups, most dehydrated soup mixes, bouillon and bouillon cubes containing HVP.

VEGETABLES

All plain fresh, frozen, or canned vegetables; dried peas, beans, and lentils.	All creamed, breaded, and scalloped vegetables. Some canned baked beans, some prepared salad mixes.

SWEETS

Jellies, jams, honey, sugar, molasses, corn syrup, syrup, some commercial candies.	Some commercial candies, some cake decorations. Note: Icing sugar in Canada may contain wheat.

CONDIMENTS

Salt, pepper, herbs, food coloring, pure spices; rice, cider, and wine vinegars; yeast, GF soy sauce, GF curry powder, baking powder, baking soda.	Some curry powder, some mixed spices, distilled vinegar,* some ketchup, some prepared mustards, most soy sauces. Some pepper with wheat flour added (often found outside the United States).

This is just a general list for your information. Always remember to read the full ingredient list when purchasing any product that might contain any form of gluten.

* These are vinegars distilled from grains toxic to celiacs. Corn distilled vinegar is acceptable.

Where to Find
Gluten-free Products

When I was diagnosed with celiac disease twenty years ago, I was handed a wrinkled, almost unreadable list of foods I could eat, and, opposite them, a much longer list of ones I couldn't. It was absolutely daunting, for I had no clue to where I could find those acceptable items.

I bought a can of vegetable soup thinking it was safe and later poured it down the disposal because it contained barley. I don't remember seeing rice cakes, which were just then making their appearance. I know that I craved baked goods and had to satisfy my craving with some potato starch muffins so crumbly I licked them out of my hand. I hungered for the smell of fresh bread so much that I cheated—with dire consequences.

Today there is still a dearth of safe baked goods in grocery stores, but we have some products in the specialty food shops and more in health food stores and Asian markets. But by far the largest source of our products has come to be suppliers who are cooking, mixing, or grinding—all gluten free for those intolerant to wheat or gluten.

The list has grown from a few in my first book to the thirty-four that follow here. They can supply anything from the basic flours in any quantities to baked products fresh from the oven. Many of them supply mixes so you can, with the addition of a few simple fresh ingredients, make your own delicious home-baked gluten-free goodies.

Many of the suppliers also have an in-house retail store for the convenience of those living in the area. Most of these companies accept orders by phone, fax, or mail, and you can use your credit card when you call.

Note: Canada allows several flours that have not been cleared as gluten free in the United States: teff, amaranth, and quinoa. Check for them in baked products, mixes, and cereals when ordering from Canadian companies.

Alpineaire Foods (freeze-dried foods for camping with complete ingredient list available): P.O. Box 926, Nevada City, CA 95959; phone (916) 272-1971. Accepts orders by mail or phone. Write or call for a free catalog. Some products can be found in specialty sporting goods stores and health food stores.

Arrowhead Mills, Inc. (GF flours, rice, beans, cereals, and pancake mixes): P.O. Box 2059, Hereford, TX 79045; phone (806) 364-0730. Accepts orders by mail and phone. Most products can be found in health food, gourmet, and grocery stores.

Authentic Foods (light bean flour, GF baking mixes, pasta mix, bean burger and falafel mixes, xanthan gum, maple sugar, vanilla powder): 1850 West 169th St., Suite B, Gardena, CA 90247; phone (310) 366-7612, fax (310) 366-6938. Accepts orders by phone, mail, or fax. Write for complete product list. Some products can be found in health food stores.

The Bean Bag Mail Order Co. (bean flours, beans, bean soup, and chili mixes; gourmet rices, puddings, and cereals): 818 Jefferson St., Oakland, CA 94607; phone (510) 839-8988. Accepts orders by mail or phone. Write for a catalog for $1.00, refundable on first order. Products can be found in retail store at above address.

Bickford Flavors (gluten-free flavorings): 19007 St. Clair Ave., Cleveland, OH 44117; phone (216) 531-6006, fax (216) 531-2006. Accepts orders by mail, phone, or fax. Visa and MasterCard accepted. Products can also be found in health food and specialty food stores.

Bob's Red Mill Natural Foods (xanthan and guar gum, gluten-free flours including legume flours, baking mixes, cereals, rices, pastas, legumes, soup mixes, yeast, gluten-free cookbooks): 5209 S.E. International Way, Milwaukie, OR 97222; phone (503) 654-3215, fax (503) 653-1339. Accepts orders by mail, phone, or fax. Write for an order form. Some products can be found under "Bob's Red Mill" label in health food stores and in health sections of grocery stores.

Celia Cooks (gluten-free condiments, convenience foods, snacks, and desserts): P.O. Box 2698, Darien, CT 06820; phone (800) 717-0005, fax (203) 656-4400. Accepts orders by mail or phone.

Cybros, Inc. (GF flours, breads, rolls, nuggets, and cookies): P.O. Box 851, Waukesha, WI 53187-0851; phone (800) 876-2253. Accepts orders by mail or phone. Products can also be found in health food stores.

DE-RO-MA (Food Intolerance Centre) (gluten-free flours, baking mixes, baked products, pastas, and cereals): 910 Jarry Blvd., Laval, Quebec H7W 2W6, Canada; phone (514) 687-2289 or (800) 363-DIET. Call or write for their full catalog.

Dietary Specialties, Inc. (xanthan and guar gum, gluten-free pastas, cookies, crackers, mixes for breads and cakes, etc., flavorings, condiments, and pickles; gluten-free cookbooks): P.O. Box 227, Rochester, NY 14601; phone (800) 544-0099. Accepts orders by phone or mail. Write or phone for complete, long list.

El Peto Products (bean, rice, and other GF flours; pastas, baking mixes, soups, fresh-baked products, cookbooks, snacks, and crackers; GF flours milled specially for them by The Mill Stone); 2-41 Shoemaker St., Kitchener, Ontario N2E 3G9, Canada; phone (800) 387-4064, fax (519) 748-5279. Order by phone, fax, or mail. Some products can be found in specialty markets and health food stores.

Ener-G-Foods, Inc. (xanthan gum, methocel; popcorn, bean, rice, and other gluten-free flours; Bette Hagman's GF Gourmet Flour Mix, Egg

Replacer, Lacto-Free, baked breads, cookies, pizza shells, and other baked products; mixes, cereals, pasta, soup mixes, gluten-free cookbooks, etc.): P.O. Box 24723, Seattle, WA 98124-0723; phone (800) 331-5222. Accepts orders by phone or mail. Phone for a catalog of their long list. Products can be found in some health food stores and specialty markets.

Food for Life Baking Co. Inc. (gluten-free breads, muffins, pasta): P.O. Box 1434, Corona, CA 91718; phone (800) 797-5090, fax (909) 279-1784. Accepts orders by mail or phone. Products can also be found in natural food stores and some groceries under the "Food for Life" label.

The Gluten Free Cookie Jar (cookies, cakes, breads, pretzels, and other baked goods): P.O. Box 52, Trevose, PA 19053; phone (215) 355-9403. Accepts orders by phone or mail. Write or phone for complete list. Products can also be found in local health food stores.

The Gluten Free Pantry, Inc. (gourmet baking mixes for bagels, pizza, pancakes, Irish soda bread, breads, cookies and cakes; xanthan gum, guar gum, pasta, and cookbooks): P.O. Box 840, Glastonbury, CT 06033; phone (800) 291-8386 or (860) 633-3826, fax (860) 633-6853. Write or phone for their free catalog. Accepts orders by phone, mail, or fax.

Grain Process Enterprises, Ltd. (dark bean flour and other gluten-free flours, baking mixes, cookies, cereals, pasta, seeds): 39 Golden Gate Court, Scarborough, Ontario M1P 3A4, Canada; phone (416) 291-3226, fax (416) 291-2159. Write or phone for their list. Takes orders by mail, phone, or fax. Some products can be found in health food stores.

King Arthur Flour (GF baking mixes, tapioca flour, white rice flour, potato starch flour, xanthan gum): P.O. Box 876, Norwich, VT 05055; phone (800) 827-6836. Accepts orders by phone or mail. Please request King Arthur Flour Baker's Catalog.

Kinnikinnick Foods (GF baked products, baking supplies and flours, prepared mixes, pastas, cereals, soup bases, and nut butters): 9857 76th Avenue,

Edmonton, Alberta T6E 1K6, Canada; phone (800) 663-9551 (local 433-4023), fax (403) 432-7634. Phone or write for their list. Accepts orders by mail, phone, or fax.

Legumes Plus, Inc. (lentil soups, chili, casserole and salad mixes; snack bar): P.O. Box 383, Fairfield, WA 99012; phone (800) 845-1349, fax (509) 283-2314. Accepts orders by phone, mail, or fax. Some products can be found in health food and gourmet stores and specialty super-markets.

Life Source Natural Food Ltd. (brown and white rice pasta, spinach rice pasta, organic rice pasta): 1773 Bayly St., Pickering, Ontario L1W 2Y7, Canada; phone (905) 831-5433, fax (905) 831-4333. Sold through health food and grocery stores. Call to inquire where products are distributed in your area.

Lundberg Family Farms (brown rice and rice blends, aromatic rices and rice blends, rice cakes, hot rice cereal): P.O. Box 369, Richvale, CA 95974-0369; phone (916) 882-4551, fax (916) 882-4500. Accepts orders by mail, phone, or fax. Write for their order form. Products can be found in health food stores and natural food sections of grocery stores.

Thomas N. Mace & Associates (bean flour, brown rice flour, xanthan gum, maple sugar, baking mixes for breads, cakes, etc., mixes for pasta and falafel): P.O. Box 1498, Monument, CO 80132-1498; phone (800) 692-7323, fax (719) 488-8189. Accepts orders by phone and mail. Products can be found in some health food stores.

Mrs. Leeper's Pasta (gluten-free corn and rice pastas and sauces): 12455 Kerran St. #200, Poway, CA 92064; phone (619) 486-1101, fax (619) 486-5115. Sold through health food stores and some gourmet sections in large grocery stores under the label Mrs. Leeper's Pasta or Michelle's Nat-ural Sauces. Write or phone to inquire where distributed in your area. Mail orders will be filled for those living too far from stores handling these products.

Natural Feast Corporation (fresh frozen fruit pies, pastries, pizza crust): 435 Coggeshall Street, New Bedford, MA 02746; phone (508) 984-4230, fax (508) 984-1496. Accepts orders by mail and phone. Write or call for their order form.

Pamela's (gluten-free biscotti, cookies, and baking mixes): 364 Littlefield Avenue So., San Francisco, CA 94080; phone (415) 952-4546. Accepts orders only by mail but phone for a catalog. Products can be found in health food stores nationwide under the "Pamela's" label.

Pastariso Products Inc. (a large variety of shapes of rice pasta, spinach rice pasta, tomato rice pasta): 55 Ironside Crescent, Units 6 & 7, Scarborough, Ontario M1X IN3, Canada; phone (416) 321-9090. Sold through health food stores nationally at present, soon in grocery stores also. Call to inquire where products are distributed in your area.

The Really Great Food Co. (GF baking mixes for cornbread, pancakes, muffins, pizza crust; cereals, rice flour mix): P.O. Box 319, Malverne, NY 11565; phone (800) 593-5377, fax (516) 593-5587. Accepts orders by mail, phone, or fax. Call or write for a full product list.

Red Mill Farms, Inc. (gluten-free cakes and macaroons): Gluten-free Products Division, 290 So. Fifth St., Brooklyn, NY 11211; phone (718) 384-2150. Mail order only. Write for product list. Also sold in health food stores as "Jennies of Red Mill Farms."

Miss Roben's (gluten-free mixes for breads, cakes, muffins, pizza, etc.; flours, xanthan and guar gum, cookbooks, pasta): P.O. Box 1434, Frederick, MD 21702; phone (800) 891-0083. Accepts orders by mail or phone. Call or write for brochure.

Schiffy III Catering (gluten-free baking, stuffing, pie and pizza crust mixes; rice mix and seasoning): 9 Underhill Avenue, Hicksville, NY 11801; phone (516) 681-0895. Accepts orders by mail or phone. Call or write for complete product list.

Son's Milling (dark bean flour and other GF flours, baking mixes, cookies, cereals, pasta, seeds): Unit #11, 130 Dallas Road, Victoria, BC V8V 1A3, Canada; phone (604) 389-6743, fax (604) 389-6719. Accepts orders by phone, mail, or fax. Write or call for complete list. Some products may be found in health food stores.

Specialty Food Shop (gluten-free bread, cookies, baking mixes, granola bars, rusks, crackers, ladyfingers, dry pasta, canned pasta, fruitcake, and more): Radio Centre Plaza, Upper Level, 875 Main Street West, Hamilton, Ontario L8S 4P9, Canada; phone (800) SFS-7976 or (905) 528-4707, fax (905) 528-5625. Accepts orders by phone, mail, or fax. Write for product list. Also has retail stores in Hamilton and Toronto.

Sterk's Bakery (guar gum, gluten-free flours; baked breads, rolls, cakes, pizza crust; baking mixes, etc.): 3866 23rd Street, Vineland, Ontario L0R 2C0, Canada; or 1402 Pine Ave., Niagara Falls, NY 14301; phone (800) 608-4501, local/fax (905) 562-3086. Accepts orders by mail or phone. Accepts Visa and MasterCard. Write for list of products made with guar gum.

Tad Enterprises (xanthan and guar gums, gluten-free flours, bread mix, baked products, cereals, pasta, baking powder): 9356 Pleasant, Tinley Park, IL 60477; phone (708) 429-2101, fax (708) 429-3954. Accepts orders by mail, phone, or fax. Write for order form for complete list of products.

Tamarind Tree (Indian style freeze-dried gluten-free full meals and breads): 1037 State Street, Perth Amboy, NJ 08861-2001; phone (800) 432-8733, fax (732) 293-1500. Accepts orders by mail, phone, or fax. Write for complete list.

This list, offered for the reader's convenience, was updated at the time of publication of this book. I regret I cannot be responsible for later changes in names, addresses, or phone numbers or for a company's removing some products from its line.

Index